Is Satire Saving Our Nation?

Is Satire Saving Our Nation?

Mockery and American Politics

Sophia A. McClennen and Remy M. Maisel

First published in 2014 by PALGRAVE MACMILLAN® in the United States—a division of St. Martin's Press LLC, 175 Fifth Avenue, New York, NY 10010.

Where this book is distributed in the UK, Europe and the rest of the world, this is by Palgrave Macmillan, a division of Macmillan Publishers Limited, registered in England, company number 785998, of Houndmills, Basingstoke, Hampshire RG21 6XS.

Palgrave Macmillan is the global academic imprint of the above companies and has companies and representatives throughout the world.

Palgrave® and Macmillan® are registered trademarks in the United States, the United Kingdom, Europe and other countries.

ISBN 978-1-137-42796-0   ISBN 978-1-137-40521-0 (eBook)
DOI 10.1057/9781137405210

Library of Congress Cataloging-in-Publication Data

McClennen, Sophia A.
  Is satire saving our nation? : mockery and American politics / Sophia A. McClennen and Remy M. Maisel.
      pages   cm
  Includes bibliographical references and index.

  1. Mass media—Political aspects—United States.
  2. Political satire, American.   3. Political culture—United States.   4. United States—Politics and government—Humor.   5. American wit and humor—History and criticism.   I. Maisel, Remy M., 1993–   II. Title.
  P95.82.U6M383 2014
  302.23'0973—dc23   2014019336

A catalogue record of the book is available from the British Library.

Design by SPi Global.

First edition: October 2014

10 9 8 7 6 5 4 3 2 1

For my brother, my first accomplice in comedy.
                                              −SM

To Russia, with love.
                      −RM

Contents

List of Figures

List of Tables

Preface and Acknowledgments

This book is making history. And we're not just referring to its groundbreaking analysis and paradigm-shifting critique. This book is making history because a Full Professor at a research-intensive university decided to pair up with an undergraduate student to write a book—as peers. As far as we know, this sort of collaboration has *never* happened at Penn State; and it seems it has almost never, if ever, happened anywhere in the United States.

So it won't surprise you to learn that at least one of us (the professor) had a lot of people suggest to her that she was foolish for taking such a chance since it seemed impossible that a student could produce the sort of work required. And it won't surprise you to also hear that another one of us (the student) also got a series of blank stares and puzzled looks when she announced the project. How could a student find the time? Wasn't the professor just using the student as a research donkey? Didn't this just mean that the professor would have to rewrite everything the student did? Why do that when it would be easier to just write the book alone? How is this supposed to work anyway? The questions were endless, but the message was clear: this was a crazy idea.

Well it also won't surprise anyone who has actually met us that the sort of skepticism we encountered was just the fire we needed to prove all the naysayers wrong. (The idea of making history was also especially appealing.) It is true that the professor likely had a better idea of how hard this would get at times, and it is true that her previous experience would mean she would have moments when she would have to guide the project more directly—but isn't that what any sort of collaboration ultimately is? Don't we collaborate precisely because the person we work with has skills and insights we don't? We believe that our success in pulling this off should serve as a model for future potential collaborations between faculty and students. In our case it made sense to pair a scholar and a millennial—we both had unique talents we could bring to the project.

Now we don't want to encourage every professor out there to just go find a student and start a book: there were lots of ways in which our collaboration was unique. First, before we ever met, both of us had a history of blogging on satire for *Huffington Post*. In fact, it was when Remy noticed that she had a professor in her own backyard who also blogged on Stephen Colbert that we first met. After that we began collaborating on her Penn State Colbert-inspired Super PAC and we started blogging together. We quickly realized that we worked well together and that we had an easy flow to writing collaboratively.

Then Sophia did an interview with *Washington Post* reporter Paul Farhi. Farhi contacted her saying he wanted to cover her new book on Colbert because he was excited to see this sort of work happening in academia. He then published an entirely different sort of piece: "Truthinessology: The Stephen Colbert Effect Becomes an Obsession in Academia."[1] It should be pretty clear from the title that Farhi took a different angle than what he pitched. Needless to say, the article went viral and was picked up by almost every major news outlet in the nation. Also needless to say, we had to respond. The answer was one of our favorite co-written blogs: "Is it Stupid to Study Colbert?"[2] After that it became clear that we had to do more.

Remy had the idea that we should do a college course together and we even met with faculty to talk about the idea—but the system didn't seem nimble enough for us to pull something off before Remy graduated. A book, however, we could do on our own time. It would be a lot of hard work, squeezed into our existing overloaded schedules. But it was a book on a topic we love so we decided to take the plunge and go for it. There were late nights (for Remy), there was hand-wringing (for Sophia), and there was lots of collaborative fun. The rest, as they say, is history. Seriously!

Sophia's Acknowledgments

This book wouldn't have been possible without Facebook. It turns out I have a really amazing set of friends on Facebook, some of whom I have never met, but all of whom helped keep me up to date on satire and social media. It is easy to bash Facebook (as we discuss in the chapters to come), but the simple truth is that almost every day a Facebook post led me to read an article, watch a video, or take in a status update that helped me write this book. Thanks to Facebook I saw tweets, memes, BuzzFeeds, and UpWorthy videos that gave me much-needed comic relief and valuable material you will read more about in the pages to come. And, more importantly, I get to now consider Facebook time as "research," so my Facebook procrastinating days are officially over.

I am also especially grateful to the Colbert News Hub, particularly Katt Downey, and to other fellow travelers in the world of satire and Internet media such as Leah Wescott of Cronk News. Making connections with them helped inspire much of what you will read here. I also had the benefit of thinking about this book while doing lots of media interviews related to *Colbert's America*. Among them I truly enjoyed connecting with Peter Bart, Angel Clark, Patrick Gavin, Kris Kitto, John Rash, Fern Siegel, Gail Shister, and Alex Strachan. Those interviews helped me sort out some of the key ideas that we further developed here. And I hope that Remy and I get a chance to talk to each of you again.

I continue to feel that none of my work would be possible without the intellectual mentoring of Henry Giroux. So much of what I think in relation to media, democracy, radical hope, and political possibility comes from his insights and sharp critique. Since he happily moved away to Canada I have seen much less of him, but his presence in my intellectual life is just as vigorous and engaging as ever.

It was the series he edits with Susan Searls Giroux that gave my book on Colbert a home and laid the groundwork for the book you are reading today. I can't thank him enough.

Peter Hitchcock has become one of my closest intellectual comrades and, even though I only see him a couple of times a year, I am always grateful for his sharp wit and keen observations. He is one of those few friends who will push you to be better rather than coddle you and he never hesitates to ask the tough question when you most need to hear it. Best part is that we always find a way to decompress with friends and good cheer after the work is done.

Joey Slaughter deserves special thanks. From giving me tips on a question to ask when attending a live taping of *The Colbert Report* to always finding time to catch up and connect, his friendship and intellectual support are so valuable to me. I always appreciate how he makes time to help me sort out tough questions and I greatly value our camaraderie.

I also want to send special thanks to Jeffrey Di Leo, who has become an important interlocutor and ongoing source of support. He has been especially patient with me as I juggle too many things and has graciously included me in a number of projects that have kept me engaged with key issues facing the humanities, higher education, critical theory, and public intellectuals. His invitation to join the Society for Critical Exchange's Winter Theory Institute has been a very valued part of my recent intellectual life.

Last, but certainly not least, I have to give special thanks to José (Pepe) Alvarez, who modeled the exact sort of friendship and intellectual collaboration that I have also developed with Remy. We first met when he was an undergraduate in Peru. He then came to get his PhD at Penn State, and over time our mentoring relationship developed into the critical collaboration of peers and the mutual support of dear friends. My daily life has been much smaller since he moved on to his first job, but my best consolation is knowing that his career is just taking off and that, thanks to Facebook, we can still stay connected.

I have been thankful for the connections I have made with a number of other scholars who work on satire, media, and contemporary politics. I have been inspired by the work of Amarnath Amarasingam, Geoffrey Baym, Jeffrey Jones, and Geoffrey Nunberg—and grateful for our Facebook virtual friendships as well.

A number of other colleagues and good friends lent a ear, provided important dialogue, and offered insights to me while I was working on this book. Jon Abel, Liz Anker, Idelber Avelar, Marc Bousquet, Chris Breu, Deb Cohn, Angela Dadak, Greg Dawes, James Dawes, David Downing, John Gastil, Susan Searls Giroux, Robin Truth Goodman, Debbie Hawhee, Kerry Hegerty, Jeffrey Middents, Matt Jordan, Luz Kirschner, Lisa McLaughlin, Leerom Medovoi, Adam Miyashiro, Bill Mullen, Laurie Mulvey, Brantley Nicholson, Jessica O'Hara, John Protevi, Jennifer Reimer, Matthew Restall, Sam Richards, John Riofrio, Ken Saltman, Claudia Sadowski-Smith, Ali Schultheis-Moore, Hoda Shakry, Cindy Simmons, Amara Solari, Jeffrey Williams, Santiago Vaquera, Hap Veeser, Zahi Zalloua and many others have been valued sources of engaged critique and friendship.

Shortly after publishing *Colbert's America* I had the good fortune to shift the core of my academic position to Penn State's School of International Affairs (SIA).

It is a welcome relief to work with colleagues who understand and value academic work in the public sphere. And it is a real benefit to work with colleagues that have such extensive experience working with media appearances, blogs, and major public lectures. Special thanks to Larry Backer, Richard Butler, William Butler, Beth Farmer, Johannes Fedderke, Scott Gartner, Amy Gaudion, Dennis Jett, John Kelmelis, Flynt Leverett, and Catherine Rogers for being such inspiring and supportive colleagues. I am extremely grateful to Jim Houck and Tiya Maluwa for their leadership and encouragement. And I give extra thanks to Nick Jones, our new provost, for being immediately supportive when he heard about this project and realized its significance as a research initiative at Penn State.

This book would not be what it is without the support and hard work of a number of research assistants who tracked down research materials, found websites and other resources, and helped with the citations and editing of the manuscript. Special thanks to Caroline Egan who helped steer this book into our editor's hands. I am very grateful for Matthew Hoffman's hard work, sharp wit, and eye for detail. He was always a source of inspiration. I also had very valuable support by Molly Appel, Laura Ariza, and Marcela Velez. Thanks also to my students who offered me opportunities to share my work and get their feedback, especially Antonio Angotti, Andres Amerikaner, Yiyang Cao, Zack Goncz, Casey Hilland, Said Maloof, Sara Marzioli, Garrett Redfield, Leisa Rothlisberger, Billy Saas, and Fawad Sultani.

Special mention must go to the staff with which I have had the good fortune to work this past year. Thanks to Meg Abplanalp who was a literal lifesaver when she joined the team at SIA. Thanks also to Maggie White, Sarah Lyall-Combs, and Cortnie Showers for all of the various ways that they have offered me support. Thanks to Ellen Foreman and to Ankitha Rajendaran for their media and publicity support at PSU. Also to Tess Woods and Bud Parr for their promotion efforts. I am grateful for the work of Brian O'Connor and the staff at Palgrave who helped steer this book to press.

Shortly before I began writing this I had my 25th reunion at Harvard, an event that helped me reconnect face to face with a lot of friends I hadn't seen in years. One of the amazing things that happens in those moments is that you get to return to a version of your former self and think about the person you have become. I am pretty sure none of my friends from that time expected me to become a professor— but I am guessing that few of them would be surprised to see me working on satire. It was great to reconnect with Kathe Pate, Stephanie Connaughton, and Diana Hurwitz, also to make new connections to Karen Bergreen and Ellen Jovin. I remain forever grateful for my *Harvard Lampoon* friends—Bob Neer, Steve Young, Bill Oakley, Ned Hodgman Steve Pomper, and Steve Tompkins, they helped me learn so much about satire and parody and started my commitment to combining work and fun.

Here at home there have been many friends who have helped create a warm and supportive environment to live and work and raise a family. I am so appreciative of Dave Skipper for his warmth, wit, and musical talent. Friends like Jim and Gretl Collins, Steve Christensen, Liz Grove, Olivia Jones, Jonathan Matthews, Judd and Lynn Mantz, Keith Nelson, Denise Solomon, Regan Takac, and many more also made the experience of writing this book much more enjoyable. Thanks to Nancy Chiswick for all the many ways she supports me. Also thanks to Bradley Ennis and Sean Holt for helping to keep me on the go. I have to thank two of my favorite millennials—Bryn and Devyn Spielvogel. They are great models of the hope of their generation.

I have been fortunate to have the support of a wonderful network of family and close friends, who remind me to—and sometimes just make me—be more than the scholarly geek who teaches, lectures, and writes. I've dedicated this book to my brother, Peter, since his sense of humor and playful personality are still a very important part of what makes my life full. I am also grateful for the support of his wife, Michelene. I look forward to seeing the generation that my nephew Ryan will forge. I can only hope it is even more exciting than the millennials. Every summer I get the benefit of reconnecting with Jamie, Stephania, Mim, Susu, Edgar, Doug, Amy, Andrew, Michelle, Krystyana, James, Peter, and Kathy and I am most grateful for that. I send special thanks to my BFF LeAnn, who still has my back when I need it most. Every day I parent I become ever more appreciative of my mom, who made it all look a lot easier than it seems to be. She is so extremely generous and supportive and I always know I can count on her. My growing-up-fast children, Isabel and Sebastian, are funnier and more insightful every day. They ground me and they let me cut loose. They never let me take myself too seriously and they remind me that I am seriously valued. And, even though I often feel torn between wanting to write and wanting to be with them, they remind me that life isn't carved up into separate pieces. They show me that when you love your work, it is easier to love those you hold dear.

I close with thanks to Eric. Our life together this last year has often seemed full of exactly the sort of not-funny mockery Remy and I analyze in this book. We have felt like characters on reality TV, replete with backstabbing family members, clandestine meetings, public shaming, backroom deceptions, disingenuous exes, and constant double speak. It hasn't been easy. We have strived for authenticity, honesty, and a positive outlook. And we haven't always succeeded in cutting out the noise and achieving it. Despite all that, we have still never lost the ability to glow when we smile at each other, to find stolen moments and precious getaways, to take refuge in each other's arms and joy in each other's love.

Remy's Acknowledgments

Two incredible forces of nature came together to make my role in creating this book possible: one of those forces is the great cosmic coincidence that Arianna Huffington should come speak at Penn State during my freshman year, leading to my becoming a blogger for the *Huffington Post*. The other is Sophia McClennen.

The very fact that we are making history by writing this book proves how utterly unique the opportunity Sophia offered me is. There is no question that this venture was a risky one, and that without any precedents to consult, there was no guarantee that it would work. Sophia lent me her credibility, expertise, and indefatigable support, yet treated me as a peer worthy of both giving and receiving honest critique. Still, that is not what I most want to thank Sophia for. While providing me with an unparalleled academic and creative opportunity, Sophia and Eric, Sebastian and Isabel also gave me a true home away from home. It is not enough to say that I could not have written this book without you. I would never even have tried.

I'd also like to thank all of my professors at Penn State, as well as those I have never had class with, but whom I have been fortunate enough to get to know. I am enormously grateful for the range of intelligent, enthusiastic, and kind people I have met here. Special thanks to Dr. Robin Schulze, who told me I can really write, to Dr. Lisa O'Hara, for helping me see what I really love doing, to Dr. Jessica O'Hara, for her insight, to Dr. Mike Schmierbach for pointing me toward some very helpful research. Thanks also to Dr. John Sanchez, for his tremendous support, and to Dr. John Betlyon for igniting a passion for Religious Studies that led to my minor. I'd also like to thank President Rodney Erickson, Dean Christian Brady, Melissa Doberstein, Lisa Breon, Ed and Helen Hintz, and the rest of the Presidential Leadership Academy for the opportunities and support. When you are the first to do something, there are naturally some road bumps, and I would especially like to thank everyone who helped me manage my courseload so that this project was possible.

Without my teachers at Clarkstown North High School, I would not have had the necessary foundation to benefit from the opportunity Sophia offered. You are the gold standard in teachers, and the proof that there's hope for public education. I owe you all a great debt, especially my English teachers. Thank you to Mr. Pete Rodrigues, who once lent me an entire bookshelf. To Mrs. Karen Czajkowski, who gave me my first opportunity to teach writing to others. To Mr. Anthony Celini, who gave me a reason to take English senior year. And to Ms. Susan Phalen, whose unit on satire introduced me to its formal study—every page I have written in this book has something of you all in it. I also want to thank Mr. Jordan Turner, who was the first person to ask my opinion about politics, who taught me everything about campaign finance law that I had to unlearn when I started a Super PAC, and who told me when I was 16 that he knew he'd read one of my books someday. (Sorry I rolled my eyes at you when you did.)

Not all learning takes place in the classroom, and I would like to thank my parents both for teaching me that and for enriching my life in other ways. Thank you to my dad, Louis, who taught me to love NPR and how to be an achiever. Thank you to my mom, Grace, who taught me to love spinach and how to be happy. Thank you both for not being surprised when I told you I had a book contract. Also, thank you both for taking it in stride when I changed my major from Animal Science to Media Studies. Thank you Zoe, Skye, and Willow, who taught me about sisterhood, and who have my back (and the shirt off my back).

Thank you to my dearest friends, Monica Osher, Sarah Price, and Rebecca Giglio, who taught me that a shared horror of the mealworms in 7th grade Earth Science is the foundation for a lasting bond. To paraphrase from one of many shows we've watched together: I am a ridiculous person, redeemed only by the warmth and constancy of your friendship. As we near a decade of friendship, I grow increasingly aware of how lucky I am to have found you. Our friendship transcends time, distance, and mid-2000s girls' fashion. I am not concerned with chronicling our memories of many happy Friday night dinners together, because instead, I'm focused on the plans for our next one. You girls mean everything to me, and I owe who I am today to you.

Thank you to my friends who shared my enthusiasm for fake news, and to those who waited hours with me to see Jon Stewart and Stephen Colbert live. Dylan Reid Miller, Victoria Maher, and Sharilyn Johnson—you made those nights truly memorable and fun, and are a big part of the reason I have the level of appreciation for and interest in fake news that was necessary for me to write this book. A special thank you to Sharilyn for letting me write about Colbert's 1,000th episode with her on her blog, Third Beat, and for introducing me to writing about comedy. You took me under your wing and gave me invaluable advice.

Thank you to my friend Jess Cody, who was the first person to say hello to me at Penn State, and who crocheted me a hat. And to Yaayaa Hunt, who was the second, and remains my friend even after living with me. I also want to acknowledge how much I appreciate my friends at Penn State for allowing me to continue a tradition of many years—cooking Shabbat dinner—and Sophia, for letting me use her kitchen. Thank you to Sophia and Eric, and regulars Rose Velázquez, Kyle Tresnan, Laurel Petrulionis, Lauren Lewis, Louis van der Elst, Fabulous Flores, and all of our occasional guests. You breathed new life into an old comfort and gave me something regular to look forward to at the end of a long, hard week.

I'd also like to thank a wise friend who came with me to Penn State. My partner, my teacher, my pride and joy: my horse, Alibi. Together with my trainer, Debbie Morano, you taught me so much. You taught me about dedication and responsibility, perseverance and frustration, about hard work in harder weather. You taught me about anatomy, training, and technique. You taught me about mouthfuls of sand, bruised noses, scraped knees, and getting back on the horse. You taught me about the elation of the "Aha!" moment, about courage, and about flying. Thank you, Debbie, for bringing us together. And thank you to my trainer in Pennsylvania, Stephanie Dobiss, for helping us blaze new trails together and reminding me to breathe. And speaking of getting back on the horse—I would like to thank Jill Brighton, Christie Val, and the girls at Central Pennsylvania Dance Workshop for providing an excellent reprieve from my workload, and for their indulgence and support of me achieving my childhood dream of performing *en pointe* after several years away from ballet. I also thank my horse's English Setter mini-me, Gladstone, for teaching me to run far.

When you're running toward a big hill, from the bottom, it looks insurmountable. There were times, at the beginning of this process, when I doubted I could do it at all. But the unwavering faith and support of my family, friends, and teachers kept me going. I owe this book to all of you.

A Note on Citations

To facilitate reader ease we are using a modified version of MLA citation standards. All print books and articles use a format where authors are referenced (in text or in parentheses) and page numbers are indicated parenthetically with the full citation in the works cited. For online citations, we have included the URL in an endnote to the chapter. For references to clips from sources like *The Daily Show* and *The Colbert Report* we have included their URL as well.

The Politics of Seriously Joking

If you were watching the news during September of 2013, it might have seemed like our nation's democracy was coming to an end. In what was portrayed in the media as an epic battle between Republicans and Democrats, US citizens watched as politics came to an impassioned impasse and the US government headed toward a shutdown. Bill O'Reilly told viewers, "it is absolute chaos in Washington, DC as both parties fight over Obamacare."[1] CNN ran a countdown clock to the shutdown as though it signaled the end of time or, as Jon Stewart pointed out, the birth of Christ.[2] Then Rep. Todd Rokita (Republican, Tennessee) told Fox News: "We just want to help the American people get through one of the most insidious laws created by man, that is Obamacare."[3] At the heart of the crisis was a standstill in the Republican-controlled Congress over the budget and the debt ceiling. A group of dominant Republican congressmen affiliated with the extremist Tea Party wanted to use the budget vote as a way to defund the Affordable Care Act, unaffectionately termed Obamacare, which they considered as yet another example of Democratic big government. The idea was that they could leverage the vote on the budget as a way to push through their interest in delaying and defunding universal health care. On the other side of the fence, the Democrats and Obama's administration refused to allow the Republicans in Congress to hold the nation hostage, claiming that the Affordable Care Act had already been passed and scrutinized by our democratic process. As both sides battled, the country entered into a sixteen-day shutdown on September 30, 2013.

We begin this book by pointing to the 2013 shutdown since it signals a key moment in our democracy when satire, especially citizen-satire, played a historic role in bringing public attention to the core issues at stake in American politics. And it shows the wide range of reasons why satire has emerged as a dominant political voice since the government shutdowns of 1995–96 when Bill Clinton battled over similar budget/health care conflicts with Newt Gingrich. It also points to important ways that political deliberation, media coverage of politics, and citizen participation have changed over the last two decades. When Clinton and Gingrich were going head-to-head there was no Twitter, no Facebook, and very little citizen-journalism on the internet. Craig Kilborn still hosted *The Daily Show* and Stephen Colbert's pundit persona had yet to be developed. While satirists certainly engaged with the absurdity of the political impasse back in the

1990s, their fans were not able to share clips of them on their Facebook pages, retweet their favorite lines, or launch their own satirical Twitter hashtags like "#NoBudgetNoPants," which was used over 3,600 times in twelve hours.

Thus one of the key differences between the two most recent shutdowns in US history is that in 2013 citizens truly had other sources of information to use in order to help process the political implications of the shutdown and they were able to share that information while also producing some of their own critical media sources. And that was a good thing since, if you watched mainstream media during the fall of 2013, it might have been difficult to wade through the competing talking heads who seemed to repeatedly miss the core of the crisis. As *ThinkProgress* pointed out on the second day of the shutdown, most mainstream media ran stories that insisted on "pushing the false equivalence that 'both sides are to blame.'"[4] Media coverage constantly overshadowed the central facts of the story, substituting them with hysteria, spectacle, and misinformation. The reality was that Republicans wanted to use the budget vote as a way to meddle with a law that had already been passed and that had already undergone scrutiny by the Supreme Court. It was not a question of whether Democrats and Republicans could compromise, nor was it a case of Democrats being intransigent; rather it was yet another example of Republican politicking based on fear, hype, and faulty logic. While shutdown-instigator Republican representative Ted Cruz began his budget filibuster saying, "I intend to speak in support of defunding Obamacare until I am no longer able to stand," Democrat Mike Doyle would later counter his vitriolic rhetoric by reading a tweet by *ThinkProgress* editor Judd Legum on the House floor (see Figure 1.1).

Legum's tweet is smart, funny, and insightful, and it symbolizes a pervasive way in which citizen-satirists (a term that plays on the idea of the citizen-journalist) are processing and responding to the political events of our time. Most important, it was not only retweeted over 22,000 times and favorited over 9,000 times; it made its way into the *Congressional Record*, thereby showing that these sorts of satirical interventions aren't just commenting on politics, they are shaping it.

What perhaps signaled the greatest threat to our democracy during this period was the fact that there were two completely different versions of the shutdown offered to the public. Republicans and the media supporting them suggested that (1) the shutdown was good since it would lead to a smaller government, showed the power of the Republicans, and was based on their commitment to not compromise; and that (2) it was bad and all Obama's fault since the Republicans were willing to talk but the Democrats were not. Fox News was one of the main voices for this schizophrenic view, glibly referring to the shutdown as the "slimdown" and alternating between blaming Obama for the impasse and claiming that the shutdown was really not that big a deal. Fox News commentators like Sean Hannity worried about the tragedy of closed National Parks one minute and chortled that they "didn't feel" any effect from the shutdown the next. In a similar vein right-wing radio pundit Laura Ingraham told her audience that she was "beginning to enjoy" the shutdown, only to then switch gears and tweet her worry that the closure of a parking lot on federal land meant that "ppl risk their lives pulling off the GW Pkwy."[5]

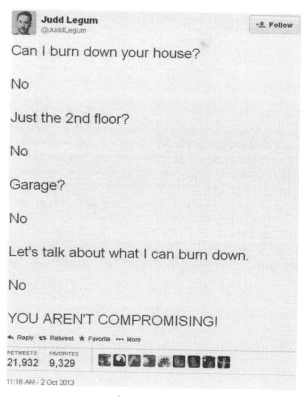

Judd Legum
@JuddLegum

Can I burn down your house?

No

Just the 2nd floor?

No

Garage?

No

Let's talk about what I can burn down.

No

YOU AREN'T COMPROMISING!

↩ Reply ⇄ Retweet ★ Favorite ••• More

RETWEETS   FAVORITES
21,932   9,329

11:18 AM - 2 Oct 2013

Figure 1.1   Judd Legum tweet is read on the House floor[6]

In contrast, those critical of the shutdown attempted to point to the very real ways that it signaled a deep threat to the health of our democracy. While Secretary of State John Kerry strangely called the shutdown "an example, really, of the robustness of our democracy,"[7] Obama pointed out that a central cause of the crisis was the increasing corporate control of the democratic process that had begun when the Supreme Court's 2010 Citizens United decision allowed for corporations to give unlimited funds to influence politics. Shortly after the shutdown ended, President Obama blamed the gridlock and brinksmanship on the influence of big money: "I've continued to believe that Citizens United contributed to some of the problems we're having in Washington right now." He went on to explain, "You have some ideological extremist who has a big bankroll, and they can entirely skew our politics."[8]

Thus the 2013 shutdown reveals a number of issues that are influencing the current state of our democracy. It exposes an ever-increasing political standoff between Democrats and Republicans, with the Republican Party turning more and more often to what might be termed "hostage-taking" tactics rather than democratic deliberation and political compromise. It also exposes a critical moment in our democracy when corporations increasingly have more power over politics than citizens and where the dominant media offers more disinformation and hype than valuable information. This would all signal a very dire moment for our nation's democracy, but luckily there is more to the story. For the first time in US history, the narrative of the shutdown was not controlled by either politicians or by big media. Instead, alongside the tired rhetoric, there was an ongoing buzz of satire, mockery, and entertaining critique produced by professional satirists and by the public. In this way the 2013 shutdown reveals an increasing ability of satire, citizen-journalism, and internet media to offer the public alternative avenues of information and critical engagement.

Arguably, a government shutdown is one of the most severe examples of a democracy in crisis. Our two main political parties were unable to reach an agreement and that inability led to thousands of US government employees losing valuable work time, millions of citizens being denied fundamental services, and exorbitant federal costs on an already stressed economy. At a basic level, politics was at a standstill. To make it worse, the mainstream media—the public's main source of information about its government—chose to cover the shutdown with hysteria and hype rather than practical information and reasoned logic. To fill in the gap, satirical sources like *The Onion*, *The Daily Show*, and *The Colbert Report*, exposed the core issues involved and, unlike the mainstream media's dumbing down of politics, they presented the public with information that was fun, intelligent, and committed to encouraging critical thinking.

In one example, *The Onion* ran a piece entitled "Psychiatrists Deeply Concerned For 5% Of Americans Who Approve Of Congress." Satirizing the idea that any US citizen, regardless of political affiliation, could approve of using a shutdown to advance a political agenda, they wrote: "We're not entirely sure who these people are or where they come from—perhaps they are psych ward patients, or unstable recluses living in remote huts on the outskirts of society—but what we do know is that they are extremely disconnected from reality and in need of immediate attention if they are not already receiving it. We need to find these people and get them the help they need before their illnesses get worse."[9] In another example, Jon Stewart repeatedly refused to allow the Republicans to claim the shutdown was not their responsibility. On his October 8, 2013 show, right in the middle of the shutdown, Stewart rolled a clip of Speaker John Boehner admitting that he had made a deal with Harry Reid that he then broke: "Look, you think Obamacare's a big enough threat to this country that you need to shut down the government over it, fine. Own it. Don't fart and point at the dog."[10] Stephen Colbert chimed in by repeatedly bashing the false logic offered by the Republicans and pundits as well. In one clip from October 8, 2013 he played "Not a Game: The Government Shutdown Home Game" with a little boy to illustrate that the shutdown was neither a game nor a joke (see Figure 1.2).

Explaining the rules, he tells the boy, "This timer right here represents the fast-approaching debt ceiling. So you set that, then ignore it." Then he went on to frustrate the child with rules like, "I go first and I refuse to take my turn." Colbert explained he would only agree to take his turn if his opponent would concede the whole thing, leading the boy to exclaim: "That's not fair, why even play the game?"[11]

Figure 1.2   Colbert plays the "NOT a Game" game[12]

In one short example Colbert was able to expose the false rhetoric of compromise and collaboration coming from the Republicans.

The chorus of engaged professional satire was already a major difference from the public critique of the shutdowns from the 1990s. For the first time in US history a government impasse was satirized in the media, reaching millions of citizens who were then able to tweet, share, and "like" satire in ways that added to public debate. But that's not all, since citizen-satirists did more than share media produced by professionals: they also created their own. The shutdown led to a series of viral memes, hashtags, and other forms of social-activist media that allowed US citizens to express their frustration over the shutdown while having a laugh. Hashtags like #Govtshutdownpickuplines and #NoBudgetNoPants blended the satirical with the cynical. And Twitter was not the only venue for citizen-satire activism; users engaged with Tumblr, BuzzFeed, Upworthy, and a host of other internet venues to share their outrage and create a community of dissent.

One of the noteworthy features of these internet interventions is that many of them were started by members of the millennial generation—those born from the early 1980s to the early 2000s. Millennials are an increasingly important part of the political picture. As we will explain, they are more politically active than previous generations and they vote at the highest percentage of their generational demographic. They volunteer and they pay attention to politics. And, what really interests us is that satire is a constant and ongoing feature of how they understand and engage with political issues. For them, joking about politics can have serious consequences, and the standard line between serious politics and frivolous entertainment is blurred. For example, millennial Matt Binder created the Tumblr page "Public Shaming" where he posted hypocritical tweets from users that showed their positions on the shutdown as idiotic. As he explains, "I discovered that as I would retweet these, my followers would start @replying these people and let them know they were idiots. They would then delete their offending Tweet. Well, I couldn't let that happen. So, I screenshot away."[13] Binder went on to repost tweets calling for Obama's assassination, indicating, "p.s. The Secret Service is not furloughed" and that the tweeters should all be expecting a knock on their doors soon. Binder, who says he does "comedy, politics, tech + web stuff," has 11,000 followers on Twitter, and his Tumblr post about the assassination tweets was liked by over 1,000 users. Binder shows us how social critique of politics by citizens is able to reach more of us than ever before, and his mix of comedy, techie skills, and social critique is a sign of a new generation that blends citizen engagement with entertaining comedy.

Is Satire Saving our Nation? Mockery and American Politics looks at satirical comedy produced by professionals like Stewart and Colbert, as well as by citizen-satirists like Binder, in order to show that one of the strongest supports for our democracy today comes from those of us who are seriously joking. At a moment in US history when both politics and mainstream media seem dangerously distant from reality, the voice of reason and the defense of democracy increasingly come from satirists. This book will show you how we got to this place and why satire may be the only way we can save our democracy and strengthen our nation. Most importantly we'll explain that, even though these new developments may have sprung from crisis, they signal a promising era for American politics.

How Our Democracy Became a Demockracy

While we opened with examples from the 2013 shutdown, the primary historical framework for this book is the period from 9/11/2001 to 2014. The attacks of 9/11 set in motion a series of challenges to our democracy as the public was lied to, misinformed, and manipulated by an administration that began a never-ending war on terror, took us to war in Iraq on false information, and bailed out banks rather than citizens. Not only was it a low point in terms of the integrity of our government, it was also a low point in media coverage of politics as news increasingly turned toward spectacle and hype over information and critical thought. To make matters worse, this era saw the increased control of politics by corporations and big money alongside a rise in fundamentalist thinking that made debate, compromise, and rapport-building virtually impossible. And that's not all. After 9/11, any critique of government was considered treason and democratic dissent was demonized. Journalists, intellectuals, and other public figures who dared to offer alternative views to those provided by the government and mainstream media were persecuted, fired, and publicly shamed. In that context, satire emerged as one of the strongest voices of critical thought and democratic deliberation. With its witty mix of humor, critical thinking, and speaking truth to power, satire transformed our withering democracy into a robust *demockracy*.

Thus we begin our study by observing that, since 9/11, satire has played a major role in shaping public debate of national issues that are often ignored or misrepresented by the mainstream media. Post-9/11 satire has aimed at critiquing structures of power and the media outlets that fail to thoroughly report on them. Contemporary satire blossomed during an especially dire time for dissent, public debate, and critical engagement with US politics. But even well after 9/11, it continues to flourish and grow, a sign that satire has become a larger part of public media than ever before in our nation's history. The ongoing power of satire means that it is not just a response to the crises of 9/11; it also reflects a much broader series of social changes that are connected to shifts in the media, in voting demographics, and in public perceptions of the role of entertainment in political behavior. It does more than serve a court jester's function of poking fun at an authoritarian system; it actually invigorates active citizenship and engaged debate of social issues. Thus the thesis of our book is that contemporary satire has played a central role in shaping public debates and in fostering productive engagement with democracy.

In order to make our case, this book draws on a range of critical issues that intersect and overlap with our thesis. We reference scholarship on the state of our democracy and our media, while also studying the critical potential of satire and the satirists most influential in our nation today. Added to that is research on the millennial generation and their impact on a redefined notion of engaged citizenship and activism. We also study whether satire strengthens or weakens public perceptions of politics. Drawing on the insights of these various fields 3 *claims*. of research our book rests on three verifiable claims: (1) Contemporary satire has undergone significant change over previous eras in US history; (2) Today's satire exercises tremendous influence on public opinion; and (3) Post-9/11 satire is shaping a new version of US democracy. Our goal is to analyze these three developments in order to answer the key question our book poses: Is satire saving our nation?

Before giving an overview of the chapters to come, let's explore the three connected concepts that frame our book:

Today's Satire has Undergone Significant Change.

Satire is a unique form of comedy and it depends on creating a cognitive space for the audience that allows them to recognize that things they have taken for granted need to be questioned. As Ralph Rosen explains, satire's guiding premise is "that something is not 'as it should be,' and it takes a satirist to set the world straight" (17). Central to satire, then, is a link between entertainment — *news* — and critical thought. That link is no different today; but what has changed is the fact that the object of much satirical mockery—the news media—has become increasingly disconnected from information, so much so that satire has become a *source* of information rather than just a critic of it. Even though satire has always been a form of comedy that asks the audience to be critical, today it is often the source of serious news, and regularly it is the only source audiences consult due to frustration with and distrust of the mainstream news media. In the past, satire mocked news sources the public had already consumed. Today, satire is often the *only* source of news the public consumes. And it is often a more trusted source of the news than the mainstream news outlets. That shift is extremely significant.

In a 2007 study done by the Pew Research Center for the People & the Press, Jon Stewart ranked higher than Peter Jennings and Wolf Blitzer as the "most admired news figure" (see Table 1.1).[14] This was the first time in US history that a satirical comedian had been considered on par with a journalist as an admired source of news. The study points out that in 1987 Dan Rather was admired by 11% of the public, but twenty years later "no individual news person is named by more than 5% of the public." Perhaps even more importantly, 44% of those surveyed gave no answer to the question of which news figure they admired most.

As we will explain in more detail in later chapters, mainstream news media has become the object of corporate and political influence in ways that have led to major public distrust. As Jeffrey Jones points out, "television news media have been implicated in two of the most egregious public failings of the new millennium—the fabricated reasons for conducting the Iraq War and the American banking and financial sector crisis in 2008–2009" (*Entertaining* 117). The failures of the news media to inform the citizenry has a major impact on the health of our democracy since, as Angelique Haugerud explains, "Citizens constitute themselves and imagine their nation partly through media consumption" (13). Thus when the news media failed to ask tough questions of the Bush administration after 9/11, Stephen Colbert stood before the president during his speech at the White House Correspondents' Association's annual dinner in 2006 and used satire to voice the concerns of the US public. Marking the reluctance of the news media to

Table 1.1   Most Admired News Figures

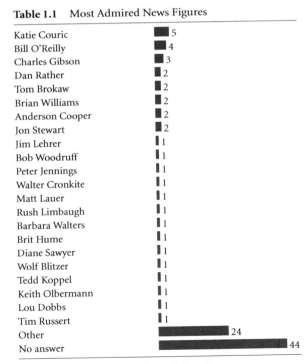

Katie Couric	5
Bill O'Reilly	4
Charles Gibson	3
Dan Rather	2
Tom Brokaw	2
Brian Williams	2
Anderson Cooper	2
Jon Stewart	2
Jim Lehrer	1
Bob Woodruff	1
Peter Jennings	1
Walter Cronkite	1
Matt Lauer	1
Rush Limbaugh	1
Barbara Walters	1
Brit Hume	1
Diane Sawyer	1
Wolf Blitzer	1
Tedd Koppel	1
Keith Olbermann	1
Lou Dobbs	1
Tim Russert	1
Other	24
No answer	44

Source: Pew Research Center for the People & the Press

do its job and report difficult information after 9/11, Colbert satirically intoned, "Over the last five years you people were so good—over tax cuts, WMD intelligence, the effect of global warming. We Americans didn't want to know, and you had the courtesy not to try to find out."[15] But Colbert didn't stop there; he went on to blast the news media on its lack of integrity during a moment when the nation desperately needed accurate information and critical reflection. Mockingly suggesting that he admired the news media for passive acceptance of Bush administration rhetoric he tells his audience:

> Here's how it works: the president makes decisions. He's the Decider. The press secretary announces those decisions, and you people of the press type those decisions down. Make, announce, type. Just put 'em through a spell check and go home. Get to know your family again. Make love to your wife. Write that novel you got kicking around in your head. You know, the one about the intrepid Washington reporter with the courage to stand up to the administration. You know—fiction![16]

Colbert's performance that evening and its unprecedented viral circulation on the internet is a prime example of how satire professionals had begun to do the work of the news media. As the politicians and journalists were losing public confidence, the satirists were getting all of the attention and all of the respect. As Amber Day explains in *Satire and Dissent*: "While voter apathy may be a perpetual problem, interest in traditional news coverage may be on the wane, and professional political dialogue may be merely a repetition of partisan talking points, there is nevertheless a renaissance taking place in the realm of political satire" (1).

That renaissance also includes satire activism like that of the Yes Men and Billionaires for Bush. Unlike comedians such as Colbert and Stewart, satire-activists like the Yes Men have performed publicity stunts that have exposed the failings of the news media while publicly shaming the corporations they increasingly protect. In April 2011, when the public learned that many major US corporations paid no federal taxes and that some even received tax credits, Billionaires for Bush cofounder Andrew Boyd teamed up with the Yes Men to create a media hoax that claimed that the General Electric Corporation would "donate [its] entire $3.2 billion tax refund to help offset cuts and save American jobs."[17] As Haugerud explains, the collaboration between the Billionaires and the Yes Men did the work of the news media, and "during the half hour or so when the public believed the hoax, GE's stock plunged" (27). Satirical interventions like these demonstrate that satire has morphed into a direct form of information and a primary source of political debate. As Day points out, "Whether or not satire has become verifiably more popular, satiric media texts have become a part of (and preoccupation of) mainstream political coverage, thereby making satirists legitimate players in serious political dialogue" (1).

Alongside the increase in the social significance of satire, a chorus of critics worried that its rise signaled dangerous times for democracy. We will dig in to those concerns in a chapter to come, but for now we want to point out a couple of crucial problems with the worries over satire. First, satire can't be blamed for the retreat of news media from its role as a source of information to the public.

So, if satire moved in to fill that gap, it makes little sense to criticize the one form of media that actually is informing the public, even if that role is distinct from its earlier versions. And second, those who fret over satire's power in shaping public perception don't understand satire today. If satire were just negative mockery, then those worries would make sense. But satire today is connected with significant "fan-activism." As Day, Jones, Russell Peterson, and a host of other critics point out, satire is different from cynicism and mockery. Its goal is not to denigrate but to spark active thinking. Most importantly, such worries miss the fact that engaged citizenship during the era of social media, political performance, and citizen-journalism is increasingly marked by a refusal to separate entertainment and politics. Jones explains the dated view that entertainment and politics can be logically separated in *Entertaining Politics* where he argues against "the rigid binary construction of 'entertainment' and 'information,'" claiming "that such a dichotomy obscures the array of interactions that citizens have with political programming forms, engagements that cannot be captured by such limited categorization. Political communication and popular culture are now thoroughly integrated and intertwined, and at times, mutually constituting" (13). According to Jones, while "changes in the media-politics landscape can still be derided and dismissed by claims that entertainment culture has polluted the important business of democracy," such a position fails to understand the changes that have taken place in contemporary political culture (13).

One of the significant changes in audience consumption of political media is the increasing presence of the internet and social media as the prime sources of citizens' information. In the Pew study cited above, comparison of viewer attention to the stock market crises of 1997 and 2007 revealed that the internet grew its share of the media market ten times while sources like television dropped significantly (see Table 1.2). "One-in-five Americans who were paying at least some attention to the stock market news say they first heard about the drop in stocks by going online. After a major market tumble in 1997 only 2% of those following the news story said they first heard about it online."[18] This shift from television to the internet is even more marked among the millennial generation as evidenced by the effective mobilization of that generation by the Obama campaign in 2008. Morley Winograd and Michael Hais explain that, "Barack Obama's remarkable showing among millennials was a direct byproduct of his campaign's ability to couple the promise of change with the tools of social media. Using e-mail, texting, and a rudimentary version of Facebook, the campaign built a small army of people who were willing to turn their online enthusiasm for the campaign into offline grassroots action, especially voter registration and turnout efforts" (91).

The millennial generation is not only consuming more internet media than television, they also trust Jon Stewart as a source of news even more than older generations. Pew reported "Jon Stewart, host of *The Daily Show* on Comedy Central, is popular mainly with young people. Among those under age 30, 6% say Stewart is their favorite journalist, making him along with O'Reilly the top pick among this age group. This compares with less than 1% of those over age 30, who admire Stewart most."[19] Thus the changes in satire relate to other changes in

Table 1.2   Stock Market News: Internet Surges

First learned about stock turndown...	November 1997	March 2007
TV	59%	43%
Online	2	20
Radio	19	19
Newspaper	7	9
Conversation	12	8
Other/didn't hear	1	1
Don't know	–	–

Based on those following the story very/fairly/not too closely

Source: Pew Research Center for the People & the Press

the media and in public trust of politics; they relate to generational shifts; and they reflect new understandings of the definitions of information, politics, and entertainment that are not necessarily mutually exclusive.

Satire Exercises Tremendous Influence on Public Opinion.
Directly connected to the changes in contemporary satire is its increased influence on public perception. Satire's ability to shape public opinion is a consequence of (1) heightened distrust of mainstream news media, (2) pervasive public exposure to professional satirical commentary, (3) the interaction between professional and citizen-satire, and (4) satire's role in shaping the "entertained" citizen. Today satire is a key part of the attitudes and understanding of the "entertained" citizen. Moreover, satire is an increasing presence in the ways that political issues are framed.

As Jones explains, "audiences are receptive to, if not also hungry for, political programming that is meaningful and engaging to them—programming that connects with their interests and concerns, provides new ways of thinking about politics, criticizes that which needs scrutiny, and speaks to them through accessible and pleasurable means" (*Entertaining* 15). This means that any sort of traditional distinction between serious news and entertaining comedy no longer applies. What is fascinating, though, is that satire is both entertaining *and* informative, while most mainstream news is neither. It has been satire's ability to both educate and amuse its audience that has led to its tremendous role as a source of media power.

Most worries over satire are connected to the notion that it leads to apathy—or worse—to distrust of the value of political action, but such worries miss the true nature of political satire today. The first flaw to this thinking is the notion that politics has to be serious and that any mix of entertainment means the "dumbing down" of political engagement. And yet, as Liesbet van Zoonen explains, such notions are nostalgic for an era of politics long gone (3). She proves that the presence and relevance of entertainment in politics has only intensified over time, and that the consequence is greater engagement in politics by the population. What she explains is that entertainment is a central part of politics today, but it is not equally useful for encouraging productive democratic participation. The sort of political participation encouraged by the entertaining spectacle of satire is related to fan activism and to the encouragement of critical thinking in relation to specific issues relevant to the present moment. For instance, Marcus Schulzke studied fan action and political participation of viewers of *The Colbert Report* and found that there was a direct link between fandom and political activity: "In addition to challenging fans to interpret the show's political satire and empowering them to take part in traditional forms of political activity such as voting, petitioning, and direct action, *The Colbert Report* promotes the expansion of the concept of citizenship to the contestation of information. The show encourages critical appraisal of sources of information, especially information from the experts who have traditionally drawn the line between fact and fiction, and directs fans to take part in determining what information is politically relevant" (6.1).

Thus one of the key ways that satire is exercising influence over the public sphere is in its direct participation in the reconstruction of what it means to be politically active. Satire, whether in the form of Colbert's satire TV or the Yes Men's satire activism, is increasingly attracting citizens to find ways to develop and act on political ideas while enjoying themselves. But won't such redefinitions lead to sloppy knowledge? If there are jokes mixed with political information, won't that necessarily lead to confusion? And how can one measure the impact of satire on public knowledge anyway? For those looking for specific data on the actual presence of satire in the production of political knowledge, we have bad news: it is almost impossible to trace public consumption of satire. Colbert and Stewart regularly log over one million viewers a night, but their programs are then watched online, in Facebook-posted clips, and through other forms of digital media. While we can't give specific data on the actual presence of satire in the consumption patterns of US citizens, we can point to a range of studies that showed that viewers of *The Daily Show* and *The Colbert Report* were more informed than those of mainstream news sources. To briefly summarize data we will study in more detail in a later chapter, there are a few surveys that have revealed consumers of satire to have greater knowledge of public affairs than viewers of Fox News. In 2004, the National Annenberg Election Survey conducted by the Annenberg Public Policy Center at the University of Pennsylvania found viewers of *The Daily Show* were among the best-informed news consumers in the country.[20] Comedy Central, relying on data from Nielsen Media Research, also found that Stewart's audience not only knew more about current events, but were far better educated than Bill O'Reilly's audience. Meanwhile the Program on International Policy Attitudes found Fox News viewers among the most confused in the public, with 67% of Fox viewers believing that Saddam Hussein had close ties to al-Qaeda in 2003.[21] In 2007, the Pew Research Center published a report showing that viewers of *The Daily Show* and *The Colbert Report* have the highest knowledge of national and international affairs, while Fox News viewers rank nearly dead last (see Table 1.3).[22] The only category that ranked lower than Fox News was the Morning News shows. What perhaps is most remarkable about the Pew study was the fact that they simply referred to *The Daily Show* and *The Colbert Report* as cable sources,

Table 1.3   Knowledge Levels by News Source

Nationwide	Knowledge Level		
	High %	Medium %	Low %
	35	31	34=100
Among the regular audiences of…			
Daily Show/Colbert Report	54	25	21=100
Major newspaper websites	54	26	20=100
NewsHour with Jim Lehrer	53	19	28=100
O'Reilly Factor	51	32	17=100
National Public Radio	51	27	22=100
Rush Limbaugh's radio show	50	29	21=100
News magazines	48	27	25=100
TV news websites	44	33	23=100
Daily newspaper	43	31	26=100
CNN	41	30	29=100
News from Google, Yahoo, etc.	41	35	24=100
Network evening news	38	33	29=100
Online news discussion blogs	37	26	37=100
Local TV news	35	33	32=100
Fox News Channel	35	30	35=100
Network morning shows	34	36	30=100

How to read this table:

Nationwide, 35% of Americans score in the high knowledge category (answering at least 15 of 23 questions correctly.) Among regular viewers of the Daily Show and Colbert Report, 54% scored in the high knowledge category.

Source: Pew Research Center for the People & the Press

considering them in the same category as *The O'Reilly Factor*. As we think back on some of the most historic satirical media interventions in recent history, programs like *The Smothers Brothers* or certain trends on *Saturday Night Live*, we can recall that there was never a moment in the life of those programs where they polled alongside media journalists as sources of public knowledge.

Added to their influence on public knowledge, satirical comedians are having a direct effect on law and politics. One of the most noteworthy of these is the "Colbert bump," which, according to Colbert's character, refers to "the curious phenomenon whereby anyone who appears on this program gets a huge boost in popularity." Mike Huckabee was one of the most well-profiled cases of the "Colbert bump" since he gained greater campaign support directly following his appearance on Colbert's show:

Another lucky recipient of the Colbert Bump is former Arkansas Governor Mike Huckabee. Before he came on the Report, his presidential campaign was polling at 1%. After his appearance, he soared to 3%. That's a 300% increase after a two-and-a-half-minute interview. If he keeps up that pace between now and the election, he'll be the first candidate ever to get elected with 88,128,000% of the vote.[23]

James Fowler states that, for the size of Colbert's audience, he "appears to exercise disproportionate real world influence" (534). He also found that all Democratic candidates who appeared on his show received 40% more in contributions for the thirty days following their appearance.

John Edwards announced his run for president on *The Daily Show* in 2003, and Stewart would host almost all of the major candidates that year. While appearances of politicians on late-night television are not new—even John F. Kennedy went on Jack Parr's *The Tonight Show* in 1960 and Richard Nixon appeared on *Laugh-In* in 1968—by the 2004 election, most candidates recognized that appearing on satire TV had real value for their campaigns. By 2012, satire had thoroughly influenced the discourse and strategy of political campaigning. It has become completely commonplace for politicians and for the mainstream news to cite what happened the night before on satire TV shows. In one almost absurd example, during his 2012 run to be Republican nominee, Herman Cain referred to himself as the candidate who would bring humor to the White House, as though such a quality was something the American public would want in their president. And that's not even dipping into the story of Colbert's own runs for president in 2008 and 2012.

As if hosting appearances by politicians and then influencing public opinion afterwards were not enough, satire comedians have engaged in direct political action in unprecedented ways as well. The Occupy Wall Street Movement was decentralized and claimed no clear leader, but it traces its origins to the anti-consumerism magazine *Adbusters* published out of Vancouver. While many might dispute the long-term effects of the protests, one thing is clear: the slogan "The 99%" is a common part of the US public lexicon and it has played a major role in pointing to the ever-widening income inequality plaguing the nation. Similar interventions by the Yes Men and by Billionaires for Bush have helped to directly influence the ways that the public understands issues like corporate tax law, bank bailouts, and more. These satire activists follow the legacy of other similar satirical public intellectuals like Michael Moore, who balances satire with social critique in fun, accessible media. In his most recent film, *Capitalism: A Love Story*, which studies the financial crisis of the early 2000s, Moore raises public awareness of how government protections of big business are damaging the nation's citizenry. Addressing a press conference at its release, Moore said, "Democracy is not a spectator sport, it's a participatory event. If we don't participate in it, it ceases to be a democracy. So Obama will rise or fall based not so much on what he does but on what we do to support him."[24] Moore's point, and one echoed by his fellow satirists, is that his goal is to remind the audience of their role in ensuring the health of our democracy. The satirist pulls back the curtain to expose the truth behind the mask, but if the public does not act, then nothing will change.

Satire Is Shaping a New Version of Democracy.

There is little question that our democracy is in crisis and transition. Whether that crisis will be definitive, or whether it will result in positive and progressive change remains to be seen, but certainly the 2013 government shutdown gives cause for concern. Many of the challenges to our democracy that we face today were set into motion shortly after 9/11 when conservatives strove not only to redefine American democracy, but also to control it. As Megan Boler explains, during "the Bush administration, 'democracy,' while a term comfortably familiar to all Americans, increasingly became part of the conservative foreign policy lexicon" (167). She explains that democracy was one of the chief rhetorical weapons employed by the administration in the aftermath of 9/11, citing Bush's repeated reference to "democracy" in public speeches. For instance, she highlights the use of the words "freedom" and "democracy" in President Bush's speech at George Washington University in Washington, DC in 2006: "The war on terror is a struggle between freedom and tyranny, and . . . the path to lasting security is to defeat the hateful vision the terrorists are spreading with the hope of freedom and democracy" (168).

Not only did 9/11 lead to the exporting of democracy abroad, it also led to the association of Bush and his supporters with democracy, patriotism, and support for the core values of this nation. Geoffrey Nunberg explains that the right has spent years attempting to claim that the core values of this nation are uniquely connected to the Republican Party, even though many of the core values of the Democratic Party are equally, if not more so, tied to the American tradition. While after 9/11 Republicans were slightly more likely than Democrats to say that they were "extremely proud" of their nation, there is little question that US patriotism remains high regardless of party affiliation. But, if you tune into right-wing talk radio or watch Fox News, that isn't the view of patriotism and pro-American support you will get. Instead you will hear that the only patriots in this nation are Republicans, and that Democrats are not only unpatriotic, they hate their country and are trying to destroy it. Nunberg explains that Republicans have effectively cornered the market on patriotism, professing loudly and aggressively that they and only they know what it means to be an "American." The effect of this is that even the concept of a liberal patriot feels like an oxymoron. Nunberg notes that on the web the phrase "patriotic liberal" is outnumbered 40:1 by the phrase "patriotic conservative" (189). And that doesn't even count what has happened since the advent of the Tea Party.

When the Tea Party was launched in 2009, the country was already deeply divided on the future course of our nation. Decades of free market fundamentalism had combined with reactionary conservatism to shape the trajectory of Republican beliefs. The culture of fear generated by the War on Terror had combined with a retrenchment in conservative values across religion, economics, and the role of government. And the pundit world of most mainstream news media had reduced reasoned debate and discussion to vitriolic attacks and spectacular spin. Beginning shortly after 9/11, anyone who did not agree with the positions of the conservative right was simply labeled a traitor to the nation. But it would be the rise of politicians like Sarah Palin, Ted Cruz, and Michele Bachman, and the bankrolling of the Koch brothers, that would take these oppositions to a new level. Despite the fact that these politicians ensconce their party rhetoric in labels meant to reflect core American values, their policies have been directly aimed at weakening the functions of democracy. In addition to ongoing struggles over the budget where Republicans, often affiliated with the Tea Party, stagnated and stalled the functioning of government, major shifts have taken place to limit the functioning of our democracy, most notably:

1. The 2010 Supreme Court Citizens United decision that gave corporations and wealthy individuals the ability to make unlimited campaign donations,
2. The push to redistrict congressional seats to create districts where it is virtually impossible for the Republican candidate to lose, and
3. The 2013 Supreme Court decision overturning the Voter Rights Act of 1965, which had been passed to ensure that all American citizens had an equal right to vote regardless of race.

To signal the severity of these shifts David Wasserman pointed out in the middle of the 2013 shutdown that congressmen supporting the shutdown had little reason to compromise. Comparing the make-up of Congress in 2013 to that of the shutdowns of 1995–96 under Clinton, he explained: "Back in '95 and '96 when Republicans had 236 seats during that shutdown, there were 79 out of those 236 seats that were carried by Bill Clinton in 1992. That was many more than the 17 districts that Republicans represent that were won by Barack Obama in the 2012 election. So you're talking about going from 79 districts where there was some incentive to compromise to 17."[25] The point is that the Republicans "own" almost all of these districts today since there is virtually no chance they can be challenged by a Democrat due to demographics. As Wasserman puts it, these "Republicans are living in a completely alternate universe from the rest of the country."[26] And in that world the mantras are "You're on your own," "Why should anybody else have what I do not have?" "The market can solve all problems," and "Why should I help pay for someone else's health care, education, or unemployment benefits?"

It turns out, though, that when your nation's politics are being controlled by those living in an "alternate universe," your best strategy to defend democracy may well be satire. One of the most refreshing ways that satire has emerged as an antidote to the alternative universe is its own vision of what our nation can and should be. In her research on the Billionaires for Bush, Haugerud emphasizes the way that their satire encourages hope, optimism, and a spark for political change: "it is helpful to keep in mind not just their rhetorical positions on wealth, lobbyists, taxes, and corporate accountability but also matters more ineffable: a spirit of hope, a moral sensibility. There is space in the study of social movements or political activism for those who are attracted to definitive strategies and results, verifiable connections between intentions and outcomes, as well as those interested in the poetics of politics and those who approach agency as other than 'a simple projection toward the future'" (15). Haugerud goes on to explain that her research shows that the "more sustained subversions of the status quo require humor as well as earnestness" (21). Such positive rhetoric combats the language of insult, anger, and intolerance that has come to characterize the discourse of the right.

In addition to the blurred lines between pleasure and politics that both Jones and van Zoonen note in the development of contemporary citizenship, we find that many of the key terms used to define the pillars of democracy need to be recast. Fan activism merges with citizen activism: as noted by followers of Colbert, information is not opposite to spectacle as seen in the staged protests of the Billionaires for Bush, and civic participation is not the dry, boring seriousness associated with the postwar period. For instance, Van Zoonen argues that "fan groups are structurally equivalent to political constituencies," in which fandom is linked to political citizenship through "affective identification" (58).

All of these changes have converged to reframe the definition of the citizen and to herald the most hopeful part of the political landscape we are studying in this book. In an atmosphere where too few of us are voting and where very real material shifts are making it increasingly difficult for the people of the nation to be heard over the din of big business and their acolytes, there is another side to the story. In that story two younger generations are working together to reshape the definitions of citizenship and democracy. Russell Dalton traces these changes in his work on "The Good Citizen," where he suggests that we are now in a moment that compares duty-based citizenship (associated with baby boomer mentalities) and the engaged citizenship of gen Xers and millennials: "The engaged citizen is less trustful of politicians when compared to those who stress citizenship as a duty, but engaged citizens are also more supportive of democratic principles and democratic values. This suggests that changing citizenship norms are pressuring democracy to meet its ideals—and challenging politicians and institutions that fall short of these ideals" (18). This means that the strength of our democracy can't only be measured by voting patterns, but must also include measures like inclusive worldview, civic commitment, and volunteering, all of which are at high levels with gen Xers and the millennials. Not sure where you fit? Try Dalton's easy quiz:

> If you own an iPod, know who Bono is, cross streets on the red if there is no traffic, don't vote but are a civic volunteer, and worry as much about the fate of the world as the fate of your city, then you probably lean toward norms of engaged citizenship. Neither description is completely accurate nor exclusive, but they tap into the essence of these two different faces of citizenship. The "crisis of democracy" literature misdiagnoses the current situation because it focuses on the negative consequences of the shifting balance of these two norms, without paying sufficient attention to the full process of change. (162)

Where satire plays an essential role in all of this is in its ability to bridge the entertained citizen with the engaged citizen. In complete contrast to cynicism and other forms of negative humor, satire is a form of comedy that inspires the audience to ask questions, resist the status quo, and be engaged. US satirists from famous gen Xer Stewart to millennial Matt Binder share a common commitment to helping their audiences make better decisions while also enjoying their lives. This new momentum promises to reinvigorate left-leaning politics away from the dour, sour, and heavy left politics of earlier eras. As Stephen Duncombe explains, "truth and power belong to those that tell the better stories" (8). Thus for Duncombe one of the most exciting things about satire today is that it has the ability to combine passion with politics. Rather than shy away from the irrational, this new left politics remembers that any fight for the future must include a heavy dose of dreaming and desire. Satirists bring their audiences together by creating a shared community that "gets" the joke and cares about the reality behind the joke. As Duncombe explains, this new vision for left politics does not contrast the real with spectacle; it understands that spectacle can play a central role in amplifying the real (155). In this way, satirists and other leftist public intellectuals can work together to create what he calls "ethical spectacles" that contrast the unethical charades that characterize so much of the information circulating in the public sphere (154). When the Billionaires for Bush dress up and parade around Central Park, they draw attention to the actual spectacle that is never acknowledged as such. Thus, they use ethical spectacle to remind their audience of the real. In this way, satire serves a unique function not only in defending our democracy, but also in redefining it.

Chapter Breakdown

In order to dig more deeply into the issues we have outlined here we have divided this book into eight chapters that analyze these developments and provide essential background. Chapter 2, "Comedy U: Lessons Learned Where You Least Expect It," explores the civics lessons satire has offered the US public in recent years. How has satire in the contemporary moment served as a source of knowledge about how our political process works and why has it seemed to overtake other traditional venues for public education? Is it dangerous that more students know how our elections work from the comedy of Stephen Colbert than from lectures from college professors? Focusing on Colbert's launch of his own Super PAC and his ongoing effort to educate his fans on election financing, this chapter studies how satire has become a prime venue of public political education.

The era of post-cable television has brought with it dramatic changes in news media. From increased graphics, sidebars, and moving news tickers, to online clips with opportunities for viewers to comment, news media today has radically changed its aesthetic and public interface. In addition, corporate and government-sponsored news items combine with mundane and often downright silly news to offer viewers less and less of the crucial material they need to be informed citizens. Chapter 3, "Some of the News That's Fit to Print: Satire and the Changing News Cycle," studies these changes and analyzes their impact on contemporary satire.

No study of contemporary satire would be complete without significant attention to the work of Jon Stewart and Stephen Colbert. In fact, it is fair to say that while their public influence is due to a range of social shifts, there is little doubt that their vision for the social role of satire has played a large role in shaping the satire we live with today. Chapter 4, "The Dynamic Duo: Jon Stewart and Stephen Colbert Redefine Political Satire," tracks the rise in these satire icons and analyzes the complementary, yet distinct, ways that their satire has played a direct role in bolstering civic debate and public knowledge of political issues. As an example, we study, among other things, their rally on Washington during the mid-term elections of 2010. "The Rally to Restore Sanity and/or Fear" was a hallmark of their collaboration and their influence.

Our study then moves to pay specific attention to the exact ways that satire promotes critical reflection. Chapter 5, "When I Mock You, I Make You Better: How Satire Works," explains the difference between satire, cynicism, mockery, and frivolous comedy. In a moment when the US public is increasingly barraged by logical fallacies, false debates, and pundits posing as experts, satire has emerged as one of the few ongoing sources of support for the sort of critical thinking essential for democratic deliberation. Understanding how it differs from other less-engaged forms of comedy and explaining its link to types of thought that underpin civic engagement helps explain why today's satire is a vital part of our democratic tradition.

Chapter 6, "Mesmerized Millennials and BYTE-ing Satire: Or How Today's Young Generation Thinks," explores the rise of the millennial generation and its effect on the political landscape. Voting at a higher demographic than preceding generations, this generation holds the key to understanding the future of our nation. This is a group of citizens that volunteers more than any other and that spends more time online. And in that online world, this generation is a regular consumer and producer of satire. What is it about the quick, nimble form of tweets, Facebook posts, and Tumblr feeds that has turned these media into active sites of millennial satire activism? Is this all a sign that we are witnessing a self-absorbed generation that is more interested in the latest iPhone app than the most current political scandal? Or is it a mistake to dismiss this generation since they show signs of being one of the most vigorous political generations of the last fifty years?

In order to have a better sense of the role that satire has played in our nation's history, Chapter 7, "Savin' Franklin: Satire Defends Our National Values," studies our national history in order to claim that (1) satire is very much an American form of political engagement, and that (2) recent satirists like Stewart and Colbert have tried to remind the public of this long history in the face of a rise in political pundit books that suggest that the only citizens that care about our country are associated with the political right. Riffing on the murder-themed series of books published by Bill O'Reilly—*Killing Lincoln, Killing Kennedy*, and more recently, *Killing Jesus*—"Savin' Franklin" analyzes the centrality of satire for American political discourse and studies the way that a number of today's left-leaning satirists have fought over the idea that only the right cares about the core values of our nation.

By now it should be clear that we are firmly on the side that satire provides an important support role to democratic deliberation and political engagement. We would be remiss, however, if we did not take seriously the criticisms and concerns of those that suggest that satire has a neutral or negative role in contemporary politics. Chapter 8, "Laughing So Hard I Could Cry: Analyzing the Satire Scare," dives into the research and data on audience response to satire and explores the anti-satire hype. We evaluate the conflicting studies on satire's effects and demonstrate that one of the key problems with this research is the way that political engagement is understood and defined. One of the central dilemmas one faces when attempting to quantify the effects of satire is that satire is never consumed in a bubble. Audiences consume information in complex ways, making their knowledge of issues always informed by more than one source. Who concludes that satire has a negative effect on audiences and why? And, if there are studies that denigrate the role of satire, should we worry about what that means for the future of our nation?

Taking up the other side of this challenge, the last chapter, "I'm Not Laughing at You, I'm Laughing With You: How to Stop Worrying and Love the Laughter," explains that the goal of satire is not a demoralizing, cynical attack on democracy, but rather an insightful, witty invigoration of it. While satire attempts to get the audience to distance itself from those in power and question the status quo, that does not translate into a weakened democracy, but rather a stronger one with a more informed, more active citizenry. Our concluding chapter argues that satire is a unique form of comedy that is not about mockery, but rather about critique and dialogue. It is not a form of humor meant to distance the subject from democracy—even if it distances the audience from those in power. Of course not all of the funny jokes about our society are that sort of satire. But once that distinction is made clear, it is then possible to see that our democracy depends on satire. Moreover, in satire the audience is part of the joke: it has to "get it." That form of community is an essential component of a healthy democracy. Today's satire makes citizenship fun and puts the future of our nation back in the hands of the people it is meant to serve.

2

Comedy U: Lessons Learned Where You Least Expect It

Since 9/11, a number of research studies have traced the ability of mainstream news media to educate the citizenry of this nation. And most of the information on the accuracy of the news has been bad. In study after study the US public has been informed that they are not that well informed. For example, two years after the attacks of 9/11, The Program on International Policy Attitudes (PIPA) at the University of Maryland found that:

- Viewers of Fox (67%), CBS (56%), NBC (49%), CNN (48%), ABC (45%), and NPR/PBS (16%) believed that the "U.S. has found clear evidence in Iraq that Saddam Hussein was working closely with the al Qaeda terrorist organization."
- Many viewers still believed that "The U.S. has found Weapons of Mass Destruction in Iraq"—Fox (33%), CBS (23%), ABC (19%), NBC (20%), CNN (20%), and NPR/PBS (11%).
- Viewers believed that "the majority of people in the world favor the US having gone to war" with Iraq—Fox (35%), CBS (28%), ABC (27%), CNN (24%), NBC (20%), and NPR/PBS (5%).[1]

While these numbers clearly skew toward more misinformation among Fox News viewers than those of the other mainstream sources, the fact that *anyone* who watched the news in this nation could hold any of these falsehoods as true was a disturbing development for our democracy. That would have been bad news enough, but we can now point to a series of studies on the knowledge of facts by mainstream news viewers, all of which confirm that the trend of an uninformed populace is on the rise.

It would not be fair, though, to blame the media as the only source of misinformation. During the eight years of the Bush Jr. administration, "truthiness" replaced truth. "Truthiness"—Stephen Colbert's term for determining the truth of things by your gut rather than facts—was launched on his opening show on October 17, 2005.

Subsequently he explained out-of-character that for him the term was meant to get at the heart of a crisis that was tearing the nation apart:

> It used to be, everyone was entitled to their own opinion, but not their own facts. But that's not the case anymore. Facts matter not at all. Perception is everything. It's certainty. People love the President because he's certain of his choices as a leader, even if the facts that back him up don't seem to exist. It's the fact that he's certain that is very appealing to a certain section of the country. I really feel a dichotomy in the American populace. What is important? What you want to be true, or what is true?
>
> Truthiness is "What I say is right, and [nothing] anyone else says could possibly be true." It's not only that I *feel* it to be true, but that *I* feel it to be true. There's not only an emotional quality, but there's a selfish quality.[2]

Truthiness in politics was exemplified by politicians and their representatives consistently lying to the US public so much so that for some members of the administration lying was the norm. One study done by the Center for Public Integrity and its affiliated group, the Fund for Independence in Journalism in 2008, claimed that the Bush administration lied 935 times in the lead-up to the Iraq War.[3] They found that Bush himself lied to the public 260 times.

So if the media—one of the main sources of information about our nation—has become increasingly inaccurate, and if politicians have played a major role in feeding inaccuracies to the media, how can we have a healthy democracy where public debate over meaningful social issues is grounded in facts, reason, and democratic dialogue? If we are being constantly lied to and manipulated, how are we to navigate those lies, discover the truth, and develop informed opinions about it? Training for exactly that sort of democratic deliberation is supposed to take place in our schools, especially in our nation's colleges and universities, where students are trained to think critically, weigh evidence, and debate complex issues. Schooling is the primary way in which citizens are taught to be part of a larger society, to be committed to the public good, and to be dedicated to fostering the health and vision of our democracy. From taking turns in kindergarten to the playground drama of fourth grade to the group projects of high school and college, education teaches us how to think and how to interact with our peers. So while the media and the politicians after 9/11 were not helping restore the health of our democracy, what was happening in schools? Was there hope for our nation there?

The simple answer, as this chapter will show, is not really. In the post-9/11 era schools have undergone a radical transformation. The influence of fundamentalist free market ideologies, often called neoliberalism, has led to the increasing corporatization of schools. Selling out school space to vendors and corporations in order to replace much-needed public funds has meant that schools have transformed students into consumers. College campus dining halls now look like the food court at the local mall, and more and more primary schools are following the trend. Textbooks and in-class newsfeeds are more about big business than the advancement of knowledge. But it's even worse. Students are not only rendered consumers rather than citizens-in-training; they are also stripped of their ability to critically think by the culture of "teaching to the test." Students today spend more time in standardized testing than at any other time in US history, creating a boom for the testing industry and an all-out assault on thinking outside of the box—or bubble, to be more precise.

Most of these trends can be attributed to the rise of neoliberal market mentalities, the culture of war and fear after 9/11, and the demonization of our nation's youth as either "stoned slackers" or criminals. At precisely the moment when our nation needed a strong public sphere for engaged deliberation on core democratic issues, we witnessed a culture of lying and an educational system that was ill equipped to train the young to help shape the future of our nation. As Henry Giroux explains in *Youth in a Suspect Society,* one of the most distressing features of post-9/11 society is the way it has converted the nation's young from promise and potential to suspect and commodity. In today's context of militarized schools and zero tolerance, youth become subject to a whole host of punitive measures "governing them through a logic of punishment, surveillance, and control" that fail to imagine the young as worthy of redemption (xii). Giroux charts the direct link between the decline of democratic values required by free-market ideologies that favor the market over citizens and the increase in the criminalization and commodification of youth. He shows how rising malnutrition, declining health care, burgeoning juvenile prison populations, and militarized schools link to a media culture that tends to present youth as either stupid or dangerous. Giroux offers example after example of representations of young people in the media that depict them as "dangerous, unstable, or simply without merit" (15). He explains that these depictions have led to the removal of youth from "the register of public concern, civic commitment, and ethical responsibility;" they are now considered a "bad social investment," lingering only in the public imagination as "dim-witted, if not dangerous, ingrates unworthy of compassion and so justifiably relegated to the civic rubbish pile" (16).

Despite the fact that the members of the millennial generation vote at a higher percentage of their demographic than any previous generation and despite the fact that they are surpassing previous generations in their volunteering and community service, young people are perceived as having attention spans that last only slightly longer than a nanosecond. They are perceived as selfish and unfocused. If they write, it is a narcissistic post on Facebook. If they read, it is a short, frivolous blog. The media doesn't only portray youth as stupid and lazy and threatening and worthless, but the growth in reality TV and the rise in television programs that highlight the basest human qualities only serve to further depict a society incapable of civic commitment and democratic action. But there is another side to the story of contemporary youth culture, and it is evident in the realm of satire.

Satire has become one of the major sources—if not *the* major source—of social critique in the United States. While it is true that satire is a form of comedy meant to educate the public, it has never played as significant a role in shaping public perceptions about major social issues as it does today. How did this trend start? And why? This chapter focuses on how satire comedy has offered audiences civics lessons since 9/11. It begins by describing a series of changes that have affected US education, especially higher education. Examining the rise in neoliberalism as a force for transforming education from a site of public good to one of market mentalities, it traces how the public commitment to educating its citizenry is in real jeopardy. Despite these very real challenges to the health of democratic deliberation in our nation, the news is not all bad. Into the void left by schools, the media, and our politicians, satire has stepped in to help create a vibrant space for teaching the public about major social issues and encouraging citizens to engage in debate. Thus this chapter gives an overview of some major examples of satire serving as a civics lesson. The paradigmatic case we cover is Stephen Colbert's mission to educate the public about campaign finance law through establishing his own Super Political Action Committee (PAC) and then asking viewers to open their own as well.

Post-9/11 Education and the Crisis in the Public Sphere

When our nation was attacked on September 11, 2001 we entered an era when our commitment to democratic values was severely tested. But it is important to note that the atmosphere before the attacks had already primed our nation for struggles over our values and our future goals. While marking this shift is tricky, it would be fair to say that many of the issues confronting the health of our democracy began during the Reagan presidency, when the administration began to adopt and implement extreme free market economic policies that moved resources away from social welfare while investing heavily in militarization. As Douglas Kellner explains in *Media Culture*, after the liberal-democratic period of the Kennedy presidency of the 1960s, "intense struggles between liberals and conservatives broke out, capped by the victory of Ronald Reagan in 1980, which established over a decade of conservative hegemony" (59). Kellner underscores the way that Reagan ushered in a new "common sense" for the nation, one that had an enormous impact on how we understand our commitment to our fellow citizens. According to Kellner, the "common sense" of Reagan (that was carried over into the Clinton era) was that "government must be limited and taxes reduced; business must be strengthened to create jobs and national wealth; government 'red tape' (and thus regulatory policies) must be eliminated; individual entrepreneurialism is the best road to success and producing a strong society, therefore government should do everything possible to encourage such business enterprise; life is tough and only the fittest survive and prosper" (59).

The attitude that one has to provide for oneself would have extreme consequences on our schools, since the idea that schools would serve to help ameliorate social privilege by offering extra support for disadvantaged kids would vanish into a logic of competition and assessment. The free-market fundamentalism—often referred to as neoliberalism—that began in the Reagan years was based on the notion that economies function best when they are deregulated and governed solely by the force of the market. Wherever possible, the "public" is eliminated in favor of private competition and market forces. Thus an example of a neoliberal policy would be the argument that we should not have public schools, but that we should have consumer choice, a move that has been implemented through the charter school system, vouchers, homeschooling, and other options that bypass a common public school. The idea is that schooling would improve if schools had to compete for students. The problem, though, is that such logic turns schools into businesses that must vie to attract students, since there is now a marketplace for the students that bring resources into the school. While the idea of parents as consumers choosing a school for their children, rather than sending them to the local school, may seem positive, the downside is that when there is no community commitment to schools, the relationship between the community and the school becomes fractured and replaced by one defined by service and the market. School competition is less likely to encourage the sort of foundational principles necessary for a public education linked to democratic ideals, such as a commitment to serve all groups evenly, to assist and aid students from disadvantaged backgrounds, to foster principles of democracy and civic education, and so on.

Instead of working together to make our schools a site for educating our nation's citizens-in-training, we now have a system dominated by privatization and profit. Federal money (through policies such as No Child Left Behind and Race to the Top) is geared to test scores—a practice that diminishes interest in teaching critical thinking and moves toward teaching to the test. These changes have also brought on the era of schooling as big business and corporations have increasingly sought ways to tap into the $600 billion industry. The business nature of education is evidenced by the multi-billion dollar textbook industry, for-profit management of schools, and educational services such as contracting and tutoring (Di Leo, Giroux, McClennen, and Saltman 5). And lest it seem like these policies were limited to Republican presidents, it is important to note that most of these policies have simply gotten worse under Obama and his selection of Secretary of Education, Arne Duncan. As Giroux explains, "In Arne Duncan's world, the language of educational reform is defined primarily through the modalities of competition, measurement, and quantification."[4]

The neoliberal attacks on higher education did more than dissolve the bond between community and public school; they also challenged the public commitment to education as a common good. In one stark example we have seen college tuition rise at an unprecedented rate as state and federal funding for higher education has come under attack. As Brian Kapitulik, Hilton Kelly, and Dan Clawson write in *Critical Experiential Pedagogy: Sociology and the Crisis in Higher Education*, tuition at state universities has been increasing as their budgets have been cut, and there has been a reduction in available federal funding for students with financial need. More of the burden of paying for higher education has shifted onto the students and their families, effectively excluding many of the working-class students who would traditionally have been attracted to public colleges and universities (135). For example, in Massachusetts, between 2001 and 2004, the state appropriation for higher education was reduced by 32.6%—more than any other state in the country. Half of that cut was made up for with substantial increases in tuition and fees, and unionized employees were not paid the salary increases they had been promised in their contracts. Tuition has gone up, salaries for teachers have gone down, and class sizes have increased (138–39). More classes are taught by adjunct and non-tenured faculty that get paid piecemeal for teaching ad hoc classes, while more time is spent on assessment than ever (135).

But that's not all. After the election of Obama, resources for higher education were often cut with no other explanation than the economic crisis. The 2011 cuts to federal funding for higher education were the most extensive in decades.[5] Federal resources for international studies (Title VI grants) saw a decrease in total funding from $125.9 million in FY 2010 to $75.7 million in FY 2011, a reduction of approximately 40%. Title VI Domestic Programs would receive $66.7 million in FY 2011 as opposed to $108.4 million in FY 2010. The Fulbright-Hays program was cut from $15.6 million in FY 2010 to $7.5 million in FY 2011. In addition, the Javits Fellowship program that awards graduate students in the social sciences, humanities, and arts saw its funding of $9.7 million reduced by $1.6 million or 16.5%. The department simply eliminated the Thurgood Marshall Legal Scholarships, a $3 million program to help underrepresented minorities prepare for law school. As the Consortium of Social Science Associations notes, "Other programs eliminated are some of the small programs that previous administrations have sought unsuccessfully to end many times. These include: Women's Educational Equity ($2.4 million); Close-Up Fellowships ($.19 million); Academies for American History and Civics ($1.8 million); Javits Gifted and Talented ($7.5 million); and Civic Education-We the People ($21.6 million), the rest of Civic Education was reduced by $12.2 million or over 91%."[6] It is worth noting that many programs focused on training students in civics were cut from the budget by an administration that had to be fully aware of the real civic crisis we faced as a nation. Three programs with these goals were eliminated entirely. As a contrast to these cuts, the Obama administration under Duncan increased Race to the Top funding by $699 million. Henry Giroux and Kenneth Saltman have called Race to the Top funding "the market-based and penal model of pedagogy."[7]

Replacing public funds for higher education we now have corporate-sponsored professorships and research funds. In one case, Dr. Jerome D. Williams, a leading expert in the area of multicultural advertising, accepted the Anheuser Busch/John E. Jacob Endowed Chair in Marketing at Howard University. But after receiving the offer, the position was rescinded because Williams had written articles critical of minority-targeted alcohol marketing.[8] Corporations sponsor professorships and invest in research with the expectation that they can influence the research of the professor, an obvious and direct assault on their academic freedom. In one high-profile case, BP teamed up with UC Berkeley offering $500 million over ten years to establish an Energy Biosciences Institute in 2007. While some of the faculty members receiving the support have claimed that the corporate influence from BP is minimal, others suggest that "[i]t creates an apartheid within the university between the haves and have-nots."[9] The tensions got worse, though, after the 2010 BP oil spill in the Gulf of Mexico, when many Berkeley faculty members urged the administration to cease the partnership. How can independent research essential for the growth of our nation take place under the purse strings of corporations? The conflict between profit and public good is an intense struggle when the resources are attached to big business. "Our bottom line is the public good, and their bottom line is profit," said Ignacio Chapela, a UC Berkeley professor of environmental science, speaking after the oil spill: "There comes a point where those positions are irreconcilable, and I think that point is now."[10]

All of these changes were in place well before 9/11, but the attacks that day set in motion another key set of limits to the value of education as a force for teaching civic responsibility. Ideologically the nation had come under attack from the neoliberal notion that there was no common good and that everyone had the unique responsibility to make their own way, regardless of the circumstances into which they had been born. Connected to that was the idea that the nation's job was not to help citizens thrive, but rather to make sure that the market could thrive. Many have considered those ideas as market fundamentalism, where the market is infallible and unquestionable and the citizens must make their own way. But even though those ideas had been affecting our nation, 9/11 brought a whole new level of assault to our core values. The sense of alarm and insecurity that emerged that day led to an environment of militarization and a constant state of fear. In order to defend our freedom and democracy, we weakened our democracy and freedom and our nation quickly went from a country that had a long tradition of advancing the ideals of civil rights to one where illegal surveillance (wiretapping), torture, secret prisons, and extraordinary rendition were not only practiced, but were publicly accepted. Too much changed that day to detail all of it here, but there are a number of key consequences to the events of 9/11 that directly influenced the possibilities for a democratic society. As Henry Giroux describes it in *Hearts of Darkness*:

> With democracy in retreat in a post 9/11 world saturated by a culture of fear and uncertainty, public life was more and more militarized, shredding all vestiges of civil liberties, civic agency, and compassion for those that deviated from normative expectations by religion, race, class, age, and ethnicity; meanwhile dissent was increasingly treated as un-American. Under the Bush administration, a seeping, sometimes galloping, authoritarianism began to reach into every corner of culture, giving free reign to those antidemocratic forces in which religious, market, military, and political fundamentalism thrived, casting an ominous shadow over the face of democracy. (4)

Schools would be one of the obvious places where the culture of fear and the policies of punishment would first become most visible. In moves reminiscent of the McCarthy era, teachers and professors quickly came under attack for anti-Americanism and many lost their jobs. As Hugh Gusterson explains, "it is no coincidence that the right targeted dissent on campus after September 11" (84). There was a real worry that the critical thinking and questioning inherent in university settings would threaten to influence public perceptions of the legitimacy of the War on Terror. Rather than imagine that sort of thinking as helpful to our democracy, critical thinking was characterized in an "us versus them" logic that suggested that anyone asking questions was not sufficiently loyal. Groups like The American Council of Trustees and Alumni (ACTA) characterized the university after 9/11 as "the weak link" (Martin and Neal 1). Lynne Cheney, co-founder of ACTA and wife of Dick Cheney, argued that there was no room for students to question the meaning and values of America. In 1995, she wrote: "As American students learn more about the faults of this country and the virtues of other nations, they will be less and less likely to think the country deserves their special support. They will not respond to calls to use American force . . ." (quoted in Giroux and Giroux 29). In addition, groups like Campus Watch, which monitor the alleged bias in teaching about the Middle East, claimed that "many U.S. scholars of the Middle East lack any appreciation of their country's national interests and often use their positions of authority to disparage these interests."[11] So 9/11 not only advanced the neoliberal corporatization of education in this nation, it also led to an assault on the critical thinking essential to a vibrant democracy with an engaged and active citizenship.

Education and Democratic Deliberation

The intersection between neoliberalism and the post-9/11 culture of fear, militarization, and insecurity led to a devastating assault on the notion of the public good—a concept central for any democracy's sense of its future, its dreams, and its ideals. The events of 9/11 would solidify a rise in oppositional, adversarial thinking that has come to characterize our nation. You know how most mainstream election news coverage portrays the nation as red or blue states? Well you may not realize it, but that practice is relatively recent. It began during a broadcast of the *Today* show in October of 2000 and is credited to NBC's Tim Russert.[12] Since that first time, the phrases "red state" and "blue state" have come to stand in for Democrat and Republican communities. But the key takeaway here is that the visual graphic and the terminology describe completely oppositional political views. They don't signal dialogue or debate or compromise. They present differing political views in stark terms, where states, like the people that live in them, are labeled in ways that are static and discrete. The visual trick—as innocuous as it may seem—suggests to the public the idea that we are at irreconcilable odds.

Nevertheless, the catch was that after 9/11 the nation was supposed to be united as one behind a common commitment to fighting our enemies. Generally, though, given our public's retreat from dialogue, that notion simply meant that right-wing, conservative views were the only views one should hold since it was so often the Right that vociferously espoused that they were the guardians of true American values—a notion many of the our nation's satirists felt compelled to ridicule. Democratic deliberation gave way to certainty—and that certainty was not based on facts, but rather on belief. As Lauren Berlant notes: "*Nuance* quickly became a moral buzzword of the George W. Bush administration: even to pursue nuanced thought was deemed a performance of antipatriotism" (46). She cites Bush stating: "look, my job isn't to try to nuance. My job is to tell people what I think. And when I think there's an axis of evil, I say it. I think moral clarity is important, if you believe in freedom" (46). She explains that during the Bush era, any call for nuance was characterized by the administration as "pedantic nuisance" or "genuine treason" (46). This meant that on the heels of blue versus red states we now had leaders who refused to consider complex solutions to complex problems. For them it was "my way or the highway." Everything had to be black and white, good or evil, us versus them, blue versus red. Again and again the right way was the Right way. And there was absolutely no space for debate or compromise.

The party standoff and the authoritarian rhetoric of the Bush administration were exacerbated, though, by the already existing tensions in our nation between religious fundamentalists and secularists. All silliness about the "war on Christmas" aside, the nation had long been battling its own holy war. So in addition to free market fundamentalists who had no room for debate about the responsibilities of our government toward its citizens, we also had a very active group of Christian fundamentalists making up the Christian Right. As Markos Moulitsas explains, these groups are "filled with a moral certitude born of religious conviction" (6). For them, "freedom means being free to submit to their god" (6). He cites Gary Potter, president for Catholics for Christian Political Action, saying: "After the Christian majority takes control, pluralism will be seen as immoral and evil and the state will not permit anybody the right to practice evil" (6). And thankfully the satirists have tried to draw our attention to the ways that these ideas are completely closed off and intolerant of dialogue or discussion. You might recall Colbert's riff on Bush's claims that everyone is free to find their own path to Jesus during his roast at the White House Correspondents' Association dinner. And *The Daily Show* regularly airs critiques of religious fundamentalism, most notoriously in Colbert's pre-*Colbert Report* segment "This Week in God." But in the mainstream news we have Fox News commentators who actually continue to advance the idea that Obama is too pro-Islamic.[13] The point is that the rise in religious fundamentalist thinking has not been good for democracy and critical thinking.

And, as we will explain more below, the satirists are doing much-needed work, since schools have also increasingly become spaces ill-equipped to teach and model democratic deliberation and productive dialogue, caught as they are in the cross-fire of ideologically driven conflict. One clear sign of the ways religious fundamentalists are trying to affect public schools is in the ongoing debates over creationism. As hard as it may be to believe in the 21st century, our nation is still in the midst of a battle over whether evolution should be taught in science classrooms. As *Alternet* reports, "Thanks to constant pressure from the Religious Right, many public schools are battlegrounds in a culture war that does great damage to our nation's scientific credibility as creationists work overtime to slip their ideas into the curriculum."[14] Despite all of the weight of scientific evidence, the question of evolution in a science classroom (and creationism at church) remains a hot button debate: "There are states that teach the criticisms of evolution, such as Ohio. And others who teach Creationism along with evolution, including Kentucky. Colorado and New York are two states that do teach evolution, but it is up to the schools, teachers, and counties on how this subject is taught and portrayed to the students."[15] All this in the face of a vast amount of scientific evidence. And we haven't even started talking about issues related to climate change, which have somehow—again—managed to dislodge scientific data in favor of partisan/religious spin.

The ideological debates over the material taught in our schools were not just limited to religious bias against science; they also spilled out in partisan terms, especially after 9/11, when teachers and professors throughout the system came under fire for not being sufficiently patriotic, for defending Islamic culture, and for teaching liberal values over conservative ones. David Horowitz led the attacks at the college level with his group, Students for Academic Freedom, "whose goal is to end the political abuse of the university and to restore integrity to the academic mission as a disinterested pursuit of knowledge."[16] That all seems fine, except that their mantra of teaching all sides to a topic can mean teaching that the Holocaust did not happen, that the use of fossil fuels is not doing damage to the planet, and that automatic weapons are not a public health risk. And when they feel professors are not teaching "all sides" they are labeled as dangerous and submitted to witch-hunt practices that often jeopardize their jobs as well as their academic freedom.

The most serious realm where these battles were waged, though, was over the very idea of American values and the meaning of democracy. Too often it seemed that the right had monopolized what it meant to be an American citizen, claiming that those on the left were un-American when they asked questions and worried over lost rights and damaged ideals. The "good versus evil" and "with us or against us" logic that has ruled public discourse since 9/11 signals an absolute breakdown in democratic possibility. Rather, the nation becomes a place where two opposing groups vie for control, having lost any sense of ways to mediate differing ideas. Such posturing leads to the entrenchment of ideas over dialogue and it cultivates loyalty as the primary function of the citizen. Speaking on loyalty in reference to an earlier moment in US history, Edward Said noted that: "Loyalty and patriotism should be based on a critical sense of what the facts are, and what, as residents of this shrinking and depleted planet, Americans owe their neighbors and the rest of mankind. Uncritical solidarity with the policy of the moment, especially when it is so unimaginably costly, cannot be allowed to rule" (351). Giroux similarly notes that "within the rhetoric and culture of shared fears, patriotism becomes synonymous with an uncritical acceptance of governmental authority" (*Youth* 3). Giroux has suggested in a number of recent books that the current culture of fear depends on minimizing the possibilities of critical citizenship, which has led directly to an assault on our nation's youth, on schooling as a site of civic engagement, and on critical pedagogy.

Intersecting all of these issues was what role schooling would play in preparing citizens to participate actively in a public sphere. Many believe that democracy can't function without a vibrant and open public sphere that allows all stakeholders to engage in meaningful debate. The concept of the public sphere was developed by Jürgen Habermas in his well-known work: *The Structural Transformation of the Public Sphere*, originally published in German in 1962 and appearing in English in 1989. Habermas explains that the public sphere is the place between individuals and the government where people come together and debate important social issues. The public sphere in this nation, as explained above, has been radically threatened by the rise in corporate power and the cult of the market. Gerard Hauser worried over the worsening state of public debate in 1998: "In an era when special interests and the state have reduced politics to mass media spectacle, and 'audience' has become an economic variable of spectators expected to applaud and purchase, current deliberations over the public sphere advance a critical antidote" (20–21). But after 9/11 those corporate interests bundled together with radical oppositional, adversarial thinking, blue versus red state logic, making the idea that we would be able to debate and discuss issues of common concern and find a compromise solution increasingly alien. If our schools had turned into places for profit and for ideological opposition what chance did we have that they would help advance the types of critical thinking central to democratic deliberation?

Satire Civics Lessons

So into the void left behind by an educational system under attack by neoliberalism and fundamentalist thinking and a public sphere weakened by attacks on democratic process, satire has stepped in to play a larger and larger role as a prime source of civics lessons for the public. As McClennen explains in her book on Colbert, satire today is a major form of "public pedagogy." It literally teaches the public about vital issues central to the health of our democracy. We've explained how the educational system came under attack after 9/11 to limit its abilities to work as a force for "public" education—by this we mean the public was simply lacking education on how democracy can and should work. Meanwhile, though, there was an emerging educational force gaining greater and greater visibility as a central site for important democratic education: that force was satire.

Increasingly, political humor is fulfilling a role traditionally held by hard news programming and we will outline those shifts in greater detail in the next chapter. Here we want to discuss how political humor is helping teach us how to think about political issues and how it is helping us understand our role as citizens. What we find especially noteworthy is the fact that satire isn't just taking on the role of the news media; it is also playing a role as an educational force. While the conditions after 9/11 led to a greater role for satire as a form of public education, it is important to note that humor and satirical humor can play a role as a source of teaching material even when nations are not in crisis.

As Marilee Kuhrik, Nancy Kuhrik, and Paula Berry argue in their article "Facilitating Learning with Humor," laughter creates a freer atmosphere in which creative deviation from the linear thinking process can occur, and humorous examples can aid comprehension and retention of new material, because relaying and explaining jokes allows people to reciprocate knowledge and create associations between information and a memorable joke. This means that, contrary to some assumptions, humor is an extremely effective teaching tool. But humor is useful as an educational force not only because it is memorable. And when it is combined with satire, it has the ability to teach students about activism and engagement. Craig Stark argues in his article "'What, Me Worry?' Teaching Media Literacy through Satire and *Mad* Magazine" that consuming satire can lead to social activism later in life. According to Stark, after satire increases awareness among students, it can help them take the next step to becoming informed and engaged citizens, critical of the media and information they consume:

> Satire can potentially help a student see the world in a different way and even spur the student to work for change. The link between the concepts of awareness and power should be obvious: satire is useful in helping students gain not only further knowledge, but also the potential to do something with that knowledge in the world at large. (306)

Figure 2.1   Jon Stewart talks with 9/11 First Responders about the health care bill[17]

Stark demonstrates that the process of understanding the joke creates a highly productive critical experience for students and creatively helps them connect with key information central to their role as citizens. What is of interest is the idea that a combination of entertaining and fun humor has a higher chance of leading to student engagement. This idea runs counter to those skeptics that claim that humor leads to apathy.

Indeed, both *The Daily Show* and *The Colbert Report* provide examples of satire that educates viewers and inspires activism. One of *The Daily Show*'s most influential moments was when Jon Stewart dedicated an episode to the plight of the 9/11 First Responders, whose financial and medical futures lay in the hands of the 111th Congress (see Figure 2.1). First Responders were lobbying for better health care, but the issue was not getting the public attention it needed and it looked as though the bill might not pass. Stewart decided to take up the cause, educating the public about the key issues, allowing the First Responders to appear on his show, and mobilizing his considerable fan base to pressure government to pass legislation. The founder of the New York City Firefighter Brotherhood Foundation, Kenny Specht, credited Stewart with the passage of the health care bill that had been threatened by Republican filibuster, as did then-Mayor Michael Bloomberg. Stewart's success led Professor Robert J. Thompson of Syracuse to place him alongside Ed Murrow and Walter Cronkite as television advocates who had been able to quickly and decisively alter policy by focusing on an issue. Thompson attributed the impact of Stewart's activism to its pithiness, stating that "once the argument was made, it was really hard to do anything else [but pass the bill]."[18]

Stewart was able to use his satire to get legislation passed, but his colleague Colbert has made civic education a key part of his show. It often seems that *The Colbert Report* has decided that it has a central charge to educate the public on key civic issues. One of the best examples of this effort is the recurring segment

"Better Know a District," which profiles congressmen from across the nation. In a nation where many people do not even know the name of their congressman,[19] Colbert is able to draw attention to the political role played by the House of Representatives. And in fact, as Geoffrey Baym writes in "Representation and the Politics of Play," every one of the 27 members of Congress who appeared on "Better Know a District" won in the 2006 midterm elections, as did one challenger Colbert had profiled. Baym contends that it is remarkable enough that a late-night show would devote time to the House of Representatives since mainstream national news tends to focus on the executive branch, but it is even more impressive that this attention to these politicians has had a clear influence on elections. Stepping into the gap after 9/11 when the US public was increasingly uninformed about the internal working of government, satirists like Colbert offered viewers important information on one of the main branches of government.

These satirical interventions in civic education join a number of other satirical forms of political humor, including parodic activism, mockumentaries, and parodic political campaigns. Satiric mockumentaries are perhaps the most obvious place to look for educational satire because of the documentary's established role as a film form dedicated to raising viewer knowledge on issues. Some of the most influential mockumentary makers are Michael Moore, Morgan Spurlock, and Bill Maher, who inject their satiric personalities into their films. Films like *Super Size Me, Fahrenheit 9/11,* and *Religulous* were able to raise public attention to key social issues. *Fahrenheit 9/11* created immediate scandal for the way that it portrayed the Bush administration's response to the events of that day and many accused the film of inaccuracies.

But it would be the screening of Moore's film in college classrooms that would really enrage the right. For instance, *Gun Owners of America* attacked the idea of using the film in a classroom to discuss political issues: "[Moore's] latest 'documentary,' *Fahrenheit 9/11,* is his latest attempt to demonize America and skewer conservative politicians. His movies have gained traction among leftist educators, and in at least one case, a Michael Moore movie has been required viewing in a UCLA classroom."[20] They go on to claim that most teachers are a threat to national values: "even if most educators would not be so crass as to force feed Moore's bilge on their students, the sad truth is that American students are still being forced to swallow leftist propaganda in their government classes."[21] Robert L. Dahlgren explains that the reaction to the use of the film in college classroom is a telling sign of the way the right has attacked academic freedom and the use of the classroom as a space of civic engagement and critical questioning. He argues that "the concerted campaign against the use of the film by teachers reveals the activities of a complex network of parents, advocacy groups, and right-wing media pundits that has been organized specifically to challenge the curricular choices made by classroom practitioners" (26). One of the main goals of these groups, according to Dahlgren is to "get politics out of schools" (26).

And that of course is the key irony. After 9/11 even teaching civics became ideologically divisive and many classrooms avoided the topic. This meant that films like Moore's became one of the few places one could go to learn about and debate these issues. It is no surprise, then, that Moore explicitly envisioned the film to be a pedagogical tool for teachers, and the DVD release of the film was accompanied by a "Teacher's Guide" posted on Moore's website that included critical thinking questions teachers could use to spark classroom debate and discussion. According to the site: "The lessons and activities in this GUIDE are designed to help students develop a critical analytical ability, historical perspective, and applied math skills that will open their minds beyond the current issues covered in *Fahrenheit 9/11*."[22] The mere idea of using the film as a way to discuss key national issues incited Moore's critics, who saw the film as purely propagandistic. Dahlgren reports that there was a storm of protest after the National Education Association (NEA) decided to screen the film at its annual conference in 2004, and he refers to a number of instances where commentators expressed outrage that students were "forced" to view the film (29–30). Dahlgren explains that the debate over the use of the film in classrooms is a clear indication of post-9/11 McCarthyism and he suggests that it signals the notion that the mere idea of teaching critical thinking is often considered treasonous by those on the right. What is of great interest to us is the way that the film not only attempted to teach students key civics lessons, but that the debates over the film itself served a pedagogical public role at a time when discussion of these issues was often silenced.

Another key way that satire has emerged as a public source of education is through the work of parodic activists and culture jammers, who employ satire to make their actions interesting, engaging, and media-friendly. Satirists like The Yes Men, Billionaires for Bush, and other performers have gained widespread public attention for their staged events, hoaxes, and stunts. Such satirical activism is perhaps the most democratic form of satire of all, because one does not need to be a media personality to get an audience. In fact, The Yes Men started off as unknown professors who created a fake website and were later contacted to be speakers at a conference in Austria. The question, then, is why satirical activism, and why now? And is it effective? According to David Tewksbury and Jason Rittenberg:

> The 20th century is the period that put information at the core of citizens' political activity. It also saw the rise of political activity built around the establishment and protection of citizens' rights in the political system. The role of the news in each of these periods is tied to the needs of the citizen for political information. In all times, information matters. But the need for citizens to follow a range of events, issues, and people in public affairs certainly depends on the dominant model of citizenship at any one time. (7)

In our post-9/11 world, satire has had a particularly strong impact in the public sphere; it has been able to draw people together at a time when society is increasingly fragmented. More importantly, satire activism offers the public access to different models of citizenship. What is noteworthy is the way that two reasonably disaffected citizens like Andy Bichlbaum and Mike Bonnano, who make up The Yes Men, were able to gain major international attention through their hoaxes. The Yes Men self-describe as "two guys who couldn't hold down a job until they became representatives of Exxon, Halliburton, Dow Chemical, and the U.S. federal government." Their stated goal is to "use humor, truth and lunacy to bring media attention to the crimes of their unwilling employers."[23] Even more, they operate the Yes Lab, which teaches others how to emulate their public satire activism. They explain that it is extremely entertaining to play the role of the exact sort of person that you would like to take down:

> [O]ne fun exercise when you're taking on some evildoer is to really pretend to be them, and actually defend their (insane) cause as they might have to if they were just a little more conscious of and up-front about their insanity. A lot of jokes will automatically come out.[24]

The Yes Men encourage their fans to be like them and to exercise their satirical citizenship by joining them. Breaking down the boundaries between the celebrity performer and the average citizen, The Yes Men create a civic community that holds the hope of invigorating our democracy while allowing citizens to enjoy themselves.

Running for political office is another way for a satirical persona to insert themselves into the real world of politics and highlight the flaws of the system. Pat Paulsen famously ran for president in 1968 on the Straight Talking American Government ticket, parodying real American politicians on *The Smothers Brothers Comedy Hour*.[25] Paulsen was responding to Vietnam-era social division and national crisis, and his campaigns were able to draw attention to fundamental ways that many politicians were disconnected from their constituencies. Paulsen's equivalent in the post-9/11 era is Colbert, who has run for president twice (see Figure 2.2). In 2008, Colbert launched his first mock-campaign for president

Figure 2.2   Colbert announces his first run for president[26]

of the United States, going on NBC's *Meet The Press* to explain the reasons behind his choice to run for office:

> MR. COLBERT: I'm doing it, Tim, because I think our country is facing unprecedented challenges in the future. And I think that the junctures that we face are both critical and unforeseen, and the real challenge is how we will respond to these junctures, be they unprecedented or unforeseen, or, God help us, critical.
>
> MR. RUSSERT: You've thought this through.
>
> MR. COLBERT: That's a generous estimation. Thank you.
>
> MR. RUSSERT: The press reaction to your announcement has been mixed. Here's one headline.
>
> MR. COLBERT: OK.
>
> MR. RUSSERT: This was on Thursday. "Electile Dysfunction: Colbert Running For President."
>
> MR. COLBERT: That's good work. That's good work.
>
> MR. RUSSERT: Are they, are they questioning, shall we say, your stamina?
>
> MR. COLBERT: I don't know. I think a lot of people are asking whether—they say is this, is this real, you know? And to which I would say to everybody, this is not a dream, OK? You're not going to wake up from this, OK? I'm, I'm, I'm far realer than Sam Brownback, let me put it that way.
>
> MR. RUSSERT: Authenticity's important to the voter.
>
> MR. COLBERT: Absolutely. You got to, you got to convey to them that you mean what you say, and that you've put some thought into what you do.[27]

That Colbert claims that authenticity is important to the voter is darkly hilarious on many levels, not the least of which being the irony of such a sentence coming from the mouth of someone who is playing a satirical persona. What made this funny, though, was that Colbert's empty rhetoric was not that far off from the things actual candidates said at the time. So he might have been inauthentic in character—but in reality his words rang pretty true. The campaign also allowed him to discuss his positions on various social issues, as any other candidate would, and satirize them as well. When Colbert announced that he was again exploring a presidential run in 2012, he had a specific issue on his agenda. This time, the civics lesson was on campaign finance laws and especially on Super PACs, which have money to invest in campaigns but supposedly are not tied to a specific candidate. Having established his own Super PAC—a remarkable piece of educational satire we will explore later in this chapter—his discussion of a run for office allowed him to reveal the rules (or lack thereof) for the relationship between candidates and Super PACs, which he called "100% legal and at least 10% ethical."[28] Colbert had to step down as head of the Super PAC in order to run for office, so he passed on the reins to Stewart in a move that brilliantly illustrated the fake ways that Super PACs don't "coordinate" with candidates. In Stewart's coverage of the issue, he included clips from both Gingrich and Romney explaining that they could not "coordinate" with the Super PACs that supported them—a concept that makes almost no sense since, as Gingrich explains, "he can call on them as a citizen, he just can't coordinate with them." In a parody of "non-coordination" Colbert then comes on the show to help explain to Stewart how they can avoid being "stymied

Figure 2.3   Colbert warns Stewart they can't coordinate, but they can exploit the small loop-chasm[29]

by the impossibly strict federal regulations concerning federal elections." Colbert then explains the "small loop-chasm" that allows Colbert to speak to Stewart by simply saying things in public he wants Stewart to hear (see Figure 2.3). The bit allowed Stewart to not only emphasize that he had unlimited funds to use any way he wanted, but it also allowed Colbert and Stewart to mock the ridiculous lack of regulation over these funds.

Colbert's run for president also pointed to the process it takes to appear on ballots, educating the public about the steep fees that candidates are required to pay, and illustrating the real ways that our democratic process depends on exorbitant campaign funding. Viewers of his show learned, for instance, of the vast difference between the fees charged by Democrats ($2,500) and Republicans ($35,000) to get on the South Carolina ballot. And they also learned that the party could simply block you from appearing on the ballot.[30] This information showed voters how closed our so-called open system of democracy really is. But most of all, Colbert taught his audience about these civic realities while they also had fun. That connection meant that more people learned about these details of our democracy than would typically happen if they were dryly taught in a civics education class in college. The debate about the effects of satire is ongoing, with supporters arguing that satire brings attention to subjects that many would not otherwise know anything about by making them smart and entertaining, and detractors arguing that it neither truly educates its consumers nor stimulates any real action. But, as you will see in our next section, the example of the Colbert Super PAC is evidence that satire can not only be informative and engaging, but that it is sometimes the only way the public can learn about the democratic process.

Citizens for a Better Tomorrow, Tomorrow

In January 2010, the Supreme Court ruled 5–4 in the case of *Citizens United v. Federal Election Commission* that the government may not bar corporations from donating to political campaigns. According to the majority, the ruling was in keeping with the First Amendment principle that the government cannot regulate political speech, and that political expenditures constitute speech. The minority, however, predicted that an influx of corporate money would flood the political sphere, creating corruption and worsening cronyism in government. According to the *New York Times*, this decision overturned precedents, including *McConnell v. Federal Election Commission* in 2003 that upheld parts of the 2002 Bipartisan Campaign Reform Act (commonly referred to as McCain-Feingold), which restricted corporate campaign distributions.[31] This now meant that corporations and organizations could use their funds to directly advocate, endorse, or call to vote against specific candidates without limit. President Obama sharply criticized the ruling, saying that it "gives the special interests and their lobbyists even more power in Washington—while undermining the influence of average Americans who make small contributions to support their preferred candidates."[32]

Then, in July 2010, a new kind of Political Action Committee (PAC) was born out of the result of *SpeechNow.org v. Federal Election Commission*. Independent expenditure-only committees, known as Super PACs, like traditional PACs, are not allowed to donate money directly to political candidates. But Super PACs *can* raise unlimited sums of money from anyone—corporation, union, or individual—and overtly advocate for or against political candidates. Super PACs have to report their donors to the Federal Election Commission (FEC) on either a monthly or quarterly basis, chosen by the Super PAC.[33] In practice, however, this reporting either takes place long after the information becomes irrelevant to the election, or the money is funnelled through non-profit "social welfare" groups called 501(c)(4) organizations, which are allowed to participate in politics, but must spend less than 50% of their money that way. This type of organization, unlike a Super PAC, does not need to disclose its donors—so a donor could influence a campaign anonymously through a 501(c)(4).[34] What all of this means is that beginning in 2010 a series of court decisions made it legal for political donations to become more secretive and more rampantly controlled by corporations and the wealthy. Thus the stage was set for a catastrophically expensive and corrupt election in 2012.

And most of that would have gone unnoticed—bogged down in the tedious details of campaign finance and covered dryly in the news media were it not for Stephen Colbert. In 2011, Colbert founded a Super PAC, "Americans for a Better Tomorrow, Tomorrow," colloquially known as Colbert Super PAC, to highlight the fact that as a result of the Citizens United Supreme Court decision, American campaign finance lost all semblances of regulation and oversight. Hiring former Commissioner and Chairman of the Federal Election Committee Trevor Potter to oversee his actions and ensure their legality, Colbert began to draw attention to an issue that hadn't received media attention commensurate with its importance. The lack of attention was the inevitable result of a combination of factors, including the fact that there is a conflict of interest that arises when the media we rely on to report on something receives direct financial benefits from it. Don't forget that most of that campaign finance money goes directly to media outlets that run their ads. So it is not surprising that the media largely avoided covering the momentous changes that had taken place. But once Colbert stepped into the mix, they could no longer ignore the story.

The Super PAC, according to Colbert, was born out of an email from Viacom referencing an allusion to ColbertPAC.com at the end of a parody of a Tim Pawlenty ad that appeared on *The Colbert Report*. The fake Pawlenty ad, which *Slate*'s Dave Weigel called "fast-cutting, hyper-dramatic,"[35] was the first one to receive tribute from Colbert, but it was certainly not the last. Colbert decided to produce a series of mock ads that would help viewers recognize the flaws in the use of advertising for campaigns—since in today's electoral process it takes extraordinary resources to produce ads that often do nothing more than attack opposing candidates or offer up ridiculously empty campaign slogans. In one case, Colbert ran ads up to the Ames Straw Poll, asking voters to write in "Rick Parry . . . that's Rick Parry, with an 'a' . . . for 'America'" (see Figure 2.4).[36]

Mocking both the style and content of the real Super PAC ads, as well as the fact that multiple Super PACs were fighting to be known as Republican primary candidate Rick Perry's number one Super PAC, Colbert said that the Colbert Super PAC—"not affiliated with this show"[37]—was asking Iowans to vote for Rick Parry, who he sold as "not *their* Rick Perry—*our* Rick *Parry*."[38] Colbert said that the purpose of the ad was to show that Colbert Super PAC was "the only Super PAC Rick Perry really needs," allowing the ad to ridicule the idea of having multiple 'independent' groups fighting to lay claim to a candidate and make ads in his name. The silly game of misspelling Perry's name allowed viewers to think more deeply about how these ads attempt to build brand recognitions for their candidates.

Figure 2.4   Colbert Super PAC urges people to vote for Rick Parry[39]

Figure 2.5   Colbert's ad calls Mitt Romney a serial killer[40]

Another notable ad the Super PAC ran nominally targeted Mitt Romney, while actually satirizing the exaggerated nature of the Super PAC ads. Calling Mitt Romney "Mitt the Ripper" because his work at Bain Capital involved "carving up" corporations, the ad was called "Attack in B Minor for Strings" and featured the same fast cuts and extreme drama Weigel noted in the first Colbert parody ad (see Figure 2.5). Since corporations are people, Colbert argues in a brilliant satirical twist on logic, Mitt Romney is a serial killer.

The ad ends with "He's Mitt the Ripper. . . . If you believe corporations are people, do your duty and protect them. On Saturday, January 21st, stop Mitt the Ripper before he kills again."[41] Here, Colbert manages to get in a dig about Mitt Romney's previous work in the private sector while satirizing the Citizens United decision that made the campaign finance system what it is today. Since these ads were comedy, though, they received lots of critical attention. Some worried he was mocking the system, while others saw that if Colbert was able to create a Super PAC and launch satirical ads that exposed weaknesses in our electoral process, then he was teaching citizens that those outside of the system had a voice too.

A parodic ad or two might have been as close as Colbert ever got to the under- belly of the campaign finance world. After all, "ColbertPAC.com" only appeared in the original mock Pawlenty ad because it was a direct parody of an existing ad and needed to look as authentic as possible. But Colbert would go on to make a fake URL for his Super PAC after realizing that a satirical Super PAC had the potential to be an incredibly powerful tool for comedic mischief. Foreseeing the potential for "trouble," he told NPR, Comedy Central emailed Colbert after the original ad aired to ask if he really intended to start a Super PAC. The initial question was how far could he go, and eventually, in searching for the answer to that question,

Colbert unearthed the answer to how far *anyone* could go on this new campaign finance frontier. The email led him to realize that that the ramifications of Citizens United was "what this whole year is about," and that if, in fact, having a Super PAC would be trouble, then the laws that allow it were trouble, as well.[42] Colbert couldn't resist testing Viacom and the system and decided to respond to the email by pursuing his own Super PAC. The key, though, would be to do all of this on his show, in full satirical splendor, as a way to draw public interest in the issue.

So Trevor Potter visited the show on March 30 to fill out the paperwork to register a Super PAC with the FEC. That move immediately led to complications from Colbert's coverage of the potential Super PAC on the show, since there was a question about whether the show's airtime would have to count as a donation to the Super PAC. To address this issue Colbert visited the FEC in Washington to ask for a media exemption allowing him to continue and several hundred fans showed up to hear Colbert speak outside the FEC's offices.[43] Colbert won and was granted permission to form the Super PAC on June 30, 2011.[44]

The establishment of the Super PAC seemed to go well beyond traditional satirical performance entering dangerously close into real political action. As if that were not enough, Colbert took it to the next level when Potter helped Colbert form a 501(c)(4) shell corporation called Colbert Super Pac SHH Institute, although he filed for non-profit tax-exempt status under the name "The Making America a Better Place Tea Party Patriot 9–12 Place to Constitution America Tea Party Nominally Social Welfare Conservative Political Action Tea Party Secret Money Liberty I Dare You to Deny This Application of America Tea Party."[45] Colbert was now able to accept Super PAC donations through the shell corporation, of which Colbert was the Director, President, Secretary, Treasurer, and sole board member, without disclosing the identities of the original donors.[46] In a beautiful example of life mimicking art mimicking life, Stephen Colbert's PAC treasurer Salvatore Purpura left to work for a Republican nominee, Rick Perry, prompting Austin columnist Sarah Rufca to note that, in addition to Purpura, "Rick Perry and Stephen Colbert have so much in common it's hard to tell them apart sometimes. Both love to espouse provocatively conservative talking points on camera (though Colbert hasn't come out for Texas secession quite yet) and both have gorgeous heads of man-hair."[47]

The most important element of the Peabody Award-winning series about Super PACs, for the purposes of this chapter, is undoubtedly the interactive element of the stunt. Colbert engaged with our population of interest—millennials, and specifically college students—by inviting them not only to witness, but also to participate in his lampooning of the campaign finance regulatory system. Beyond attempting to teach his audience about campaign finance, Colbert decided to try to get his audience to be social actors in the process, not just by contributing money to his Super PAC, but also by creating their own Super PACs. Inspired by an email from University of Texas, Austin student Howie Benefiel, Colbert invited college students across the nation to participate in a hands-on experiment: founding their own Super PACs, so that he could "extend 'the reach of my political tentacles across the college campuses of America.'"[48]

Colbert sold a starter kit, valued at $99, called the Colbert Super PAC Super Fun Pack. According to the newsletter sent to members and available on the PAC website, the Super Fun Pack:

> is a limited edition, genuine corrugated cardboard box containing everything you need to start that Super PAC. You'll get the F.E.C. paperwork, a detailed instruction manual, and of course, an allen wrench. Before you know it, you'll be receiving and spending unlimited corporate, union, and individual donations like a pro![49]

One thousand Super Fun Packs were sold, and students did indeed register their own PACs with the FEC. These officially registered PACs were bound by the same rules—or lack thereof—that bound the Super PACs funding the 2012 election (see Table 2.1).

It is not surprising that skeptics worried that Colbert was making a mockery of our system. But it is hard to accuse Colbert of mockery when all he did was follow the legal process of campaign fundraising. The name of his Super PAC might seem condescending, but it is worth remembering that Romney's Super PAC was called "Restore our Future"—which Buzzfeed pointed out "makes no sense at all." They reported, "It's an actual contradiction, an inscrutable zen koan for this election cycle. It is, concedes a top Romney supporter, 'a head-scratcher.' The Democratic consultant Paul Begala, who heads Obama's counterpart group Priorities USA, goes one step further. 'It drives me fucking crazy,' Begala said. 'It just doesn't make any sense. It's like saying, 'I'm out in the garage restoring my 2020 Ford car.'"[50] Surely, then, it cannot be Colbert who can be blamed for making a mockery of our democracy. The question is not "Is Colbert seriously joking about this?!" but rather "Is Colbert joking seriously about this?" and the answer is a resounding yes. Colbert single-handedly managed to draw public attention to the ways that campaign finance had become corrupted and unregulated, he got his young audience to get directly involved, and he helped offer our nation a valuable civics lesson. Cynthia Bauerly, an FEC commissioner who chaired the commission when it approved Colbert's PAC explained, "Through his humor, there's education actually happening."[51]

ABC News noted that "The Stephen Colbert Super PAC is run by a comedian, but the Political Action Committee's bank account is no joke, based on federal

Table 2.1   A Sample List of Super PACs for a Better Tomorrow, Tomorrow

Raising Awareness of H_2O/Better Tomorrow, Tomorrow
San Diegans for a Better Tomorrow, Tomorrow
Utes for a Better Tomorrow, Tomorrow
Rauhmel Fox is for a Better Tomorrow, Tomorrow
Students for a Better Tomorrow, Tomorrow
Cats For A Better Tomorrow, Tomorrow
Herschal & Moley for a Better Tomorrow, Tomorrow
Penn Staters for a Better Tomorrow, Tomorrow
My Cat Xavier for a Better Tomorrow, Tomorrow

Source: OpenSecrets.org

reports filed today."[52] Politico noted that what they called a stunt "could have real—and potentially broad—implications in the world of campaign finance . . . If nothing else, it could help the cause of campaign finance advocates by highlighting the ability of corporations to spend unlimited amounts to support or oppose candidates."[53] Potter—a former FEC Chairman—characterized the campaign finance rules as nonsensical and said that Colbert's show did a good job of representing problems with the system. He also noted that "It is fair to say that no one ever stopped me on the street before and said, 'Aren't you John McCain's general counsel?'" but that he does get stopped by Colbert viewers to talk campaign finance law.[54]

The point is that Colbert mustered public attention to the issue in ways that no one else had been able to do. A satirical civics lesson of this kind may, in fact, be entirely without precedent. It is certainly noteworthy that Colbert was able to raise well over $1 million in his satirical stunt. As Colbert explained to Ted Koppel, "We raised it on my show, and used it to materially influence the elections—in full accordance with the law. It's the way our founding fathers would have wanted it, if they had founded corporations instead of just a country."[55] Colbert was able to use satire to teach a civics lesson—while also reminding us how far our nation has come from the ideals on which it was founded.

So, did the audience know they were being educated about something serious in the process of joking, or did they take the whole thing lightly? Was Colbert able to teach college-aged viewers of the significance of these campaign finance laws? The fact that Colbert-influenced Super PACs represented 2.5% of all of the nation's established Super PACs certainly seems noteworthy.[56] But what if these baby PACs were just silly exercises in satirical copycatting? What if their founders were just having too much fun to think about the politics behind the stunt? One of the best sources is the range of interviews done with millennials that followed Colbert's lead and started their own Super PACs. Here are just a few samples of their comments.

The Hill interviews Stefani Jones, founder of "Americans for a Better Tomorrow, Yesterday":

> "With great power comes great responsibility and in the United States, money is power," Jones said.[57]

Huffington Post interviews Joshua Mines, founder of "Utes for a Better Tomorrow, Tomorrow":

> "If he can continue to raise awareness on a national level, and I can raise awareness on a local level," Mines said, "then I think our super PACs will have accomplished something really great."[58]

Politico interviews David Jensen, founder of "Cats for a Better Tomorrow, Tomorrow":

> "Super PACs are a joke in and of themselves, so why not do this?" he said.[59]

Uproxx Interviews Tyler Bobik founder of "San Diegans for a Better Tomorrow, Tomorrow":

> "I formed a super PAC to help show how super PACs are undermining the political process."[60]

From *USA Today*:

> Among those heeding the call: Jon Rachowicz, 23, who started "America's Super PAC for the Permanent Elimination of America's Super PACs." Rachowicz, who is studying for a master's degree in mathematics at Purdue University-Calumet, said his initial goal is to raise $1,000 to publicize the super PAC in the hope of raising enough money to run television ads criticizing super PACs. "It really is a problem in our elections right now," he said. "The more super PACs that are started to make people more aware of what the problem is, the better."[61]

CNN Money interviews Danny Ben-David, founder of "Why Not ZoidPAC?":

> "I was just sitting in my dorm room one night and said "oh hell, why not?" It was almost frustratingly easy," Ben-David said. "It cost no more than a 44 cent stamp and 5 pieces of paper," said Ben-David, who according to FEC documents is the president and grand poobah of the super PAC. "Although I did call the FEC to make sure the question mark was okay," he added.[62]

What it boils down to, and what it took Stephen Colbert to show us, is "that if Stephen Colbert can do it, a group of college students can do it too."[63] This message is the constant among the college students the media interviewed about Colbert Super PAC. The main lesson, in addition to all we learned about campaign finance law, was that anyone can jump in and see how things work first-hand. Colbert didn't just educate the public; he got us involved and showed us how easy it was to be involved. *Huffington Post*, writing about our own super PAC, Penn Staters for a Better Tomorrow, Tomorrow, quoted us sharing the same sentiment:

> "Without the Colbert Report, I don't ever think I would have had the idea to do it," said Remy Maisel, a Penn State freshman studying animal science, who now has 175 students on her nonpartisan Penn Staters for a Better Tomorrow, Tomorrow mailing list. "I want to use this to raise awareness of campaign finance law—money is the single-most corrupting influence in politics today."[64]

HuffPost also examined social media discussions of the super PACs, linking to PAC Facebook pages and embedding tweets about them, including our own (see Figure 2.6).

Blending social media with direct political participation, having fun with satire while taking aim at political corruption, the Colbert Super PAC experience went well beyond a publicity stunt promoting the antics of an entertainer. Viewers were not just educated about a major civics issue that was being ignored in the media; they actually managed to get involved and bring that involvement to public attention.

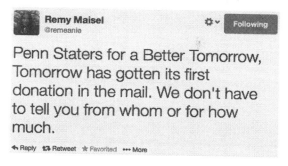

Figure 2.6   Is this tweet ironic or just true?[65]

We think it's clear that not only did students learn from this process, but that they did so willingly, because it was a fun, entertaining experience. The Super PAC story illustrates how education and humor are not mutually exclusive. Humorous satire may have been the main vehicle for the lesson, but it was the viewers that processed the lesson and then turned that knowledge into direct political action. The one component of the joke that did not serve any obvious educational purpose was the inclusion of a treasure hunt in Colbert's Super Fun Pack. Generally unrelated to the Super PAC exercise, the treasure hunt consisted of a quite difficult treasure map and clues, and even a decoder ring, with the puzzle's solver promised a visit from Stephen Colbert himself to their university. Even coverage of the University of Pittsburgh students "impressive" locating of the hidden treasure—a 101-year-old sterling silver turtle bell—in Reagan's hometown of Dixon, Illinois noted that "the praise here should go to the Colbert camp, giving college students a real opportunity to use their (monetary) voice to influence the 2012 presidential election."[66] The treasure hunt proved two things: that Colbert was still in the business of having fun and that even when he tried to distract his viewers with silliness, they never lost sight of the bigger picture.

Thus, whether the silliness was a distraction or the main draw, this award-winning running joke was an interactive, memorable civics lesson on campaign finance law, the likes of which you would be hard-pressed to find in the classroom, or indeed, as we will later discuss, in the "hard news" media. Politico called the whole thing a "gag" up until the very end. But it is unlikely that the gifts of "$125,000 each to the Hurricane Sandy relief efforts of charities DonorsChoose. org, Team Rubicon and Habitat for Humanity, plus another $125,000 to Yellow Ribbon Fund, which supports injured military members"[67] that Colbert made with the remaining Super PAC funds were taken anything but seriously. The newly-registered Super PACs—many of which bear a similar name to Colbert's Americans for a Better Tomorrow, Tomorrow were both parody and reality. Most importantly, the implications of every one of Colbert's stunts, as they were called, were not limited to the potential for getting a laugh.

3

Some of the News That's Fit to Print: Satire and the Changing News Cycle

Take a quick scan of satirical coverage of the mainstream news and it won't be long before you'll see the Fox News Channel as the butt of the joke. From Stephen Colbert's Twitter hashtags poking fun at Fox News to Jon Stewart's media appearances with Fox News figures like Chris Wallace and Bill O'Reilly, there seems to be an ongoing connection between the news channel and satirical comedians. Unquestionably Fox News is more often the center of satire fun than CNN or MSNBC. Is Fox News just being unfairly picked on by satirists or is there more to the link between Fox News and today's satire? Well, to trope on Fox News's own tagline, we'll report; you decide. One thing is clear though: in order to fully understand how satire is shaping news today, we have to start by telling you the story of Fox News. Without Fox News (and friends) it is unlikely that satire would be playing such a major role in shaping the way that the public perceives news. In many ways it has been the presence of Fox News that has provided the backdrop for much of our satirical alternatives. As we will explain in detail in this chapter, there are a number of shifts that have taken place across all forms of news media that have changed the way that we receive information about the world, but Fox News deserves special attention.

The Fox News Channel was launched in 1996 by media mogul Rupert Murdoch. The goal of the channel was to compete with the news programming of CBS, NBC, and ABC, and with the two other 24/7 news stations, CNN and MSNBC. Some suggest that Fox News was launched when Murdoch's bid for CNN failed; others claim that the channel emerged from Murdoch's belief that the public needed an alternative news source to cover Bill Clinton's administration. Either way, we do know that Murdoch explicitly intended for the channel to help people "understand" the news. As he explained when he announced plans for the station: "The appetite for news—particularly news that explains to people how it affects them—is expanding enormously."[1] Thus from the start the station signaled that it would be radically changing the way that the US public received its news. The channel launched with a series of political pundit shows that were meant to offer opinions on the news and that were largely representative of conservative politics. Its programming was almost 50% opinion and the brand became quickly associated with opinion programming, especially that of Bill O'Reilly and Sean Hannity. From day one the channel's pundits were almost entirely right-leaning, if not overtly associated with the Republican Party, a fact made most obvious by the channel's own CEO Roger Ailes, who had formerly been a political and campaign adviser to Presidents Nixon, Reagan, and Bush before taking over leadership of the network. Ailes clearly stated that the goal of Fox News was to build a channel to cater to conservatives. Ed Rollins, a political strategist for the GOP, explained: "He knew there were a couple million conservatives who were a potential audience, and he built Fox to reach them."[2] As David Brock and Ari Rabin-Havt of Media Matters explain in their book, *The Fox Effect: How Roger Ailes Turned a Network into a Propaganda Machine*, there is little doubt that Ailes has specifically used Fox News to support Republican Party politics. While channels like MSNBC are now associated with a progressive political platform, it's worth remembering that MSNBC originally launched with a show hosted by conservative pundits Laura Ingraham and Ann Coulter. That sort of ideological balance was never present on Fox News, despite original shows like *Hannity and Colmes* that ostensibly presented two opposing political views on current topics.

Fox News personalities have expressed contrasting views on whether their channel has an overt political agenda or not. Fox News host Chris Wallace admitted to Jon Stewart that there is a political slant to the channel: "I think we are the counter-weight [to MSNBC News] . . . they have a liberal agenda, and we tell the other side of the story" (see Figure 3.1).[3] What Wallace might have forgotten was that MSNBC's programming became increasingly more left-center in response to the perceived bias of Fox News. Certainly Fox News has never had the progressive ideological equivalent of Ann Coulter hosting a show in its history. But we should credit Wallace with at least openly expressing the pro-Republican Party nature of Fox's news programming. Other Fox News personalities have been less forthcoming. In one especially noteworthy example, Sean Hannity claimed Fox News is the "only media organization on this planet that has delivered fair and balanced coverage" of President Obama.[4] This statement was uttered by a man who proudly owns a painting of President Obama burning the constitution.[5] We won't even go into detail on the numerous examples of Fox News misrepresenting or blatantly lying about left-leaning politicians like Obama. Besides being perceived as the most ideologically slanted news channel, Fox News boasts a viewership that is 94% Republican.[6] Added to that we have reports from a former Fox News insider that reveal that Fox News routinely reports false information to "prop up Republicans and knock down Democrats," confirming that in many cases Fox News reports things that are "just made up."[7] That seems telling, but you decide.

What made Fox News a news media game changer was not simply its ideological slant; it was that viewers received at least as much opinion about news as news itself—a fact that greatly impedes a viewer's ability to draw conclusions and generate personal opinions. Even Bill O'Reilly has admitted that a more accurate tagline might be "We report. We decide."[8] And, as we will discuss further, if those opinions

Figure 3.1   Jon Stewart expresses shock that Chris Wallace would admit to Fox News's ideological slant[9]

are ideologically skewed, that further hinders the ability of the viewer to generate an informed decision. But it was not just the slant and the heightened presence of opinion that marked Fox News's transformation of news media; it also innovated the visual presentation of the news. You know that scrolling ticker tape news bar that is at the bottom of almost every channel on television news, weather, and sports? Well, that innovation is thanks to Fox News's coverage of the events of 9/11. In order to provide as much information that day as possible, Fox News began using a ticker on the bottom of the screen to run continuous updates (CNN and MSNBC followed with their own tickers shortly after).[10] After 9/11, it became permanent on the channel, and is now ubiquitous on most news and sports stations. Now many are quick to critique the information blast that happens when various sources of news come at viewers. But that's not our point. We operate in a world where we regularly read, watch videos, and MSM at the same time. We never have less than four screens open on our computers and we don't think Fox News should be blamed for that—assuming that such a state of affairs requires blame. What Fox News has done successfully is transform the way that news appears on-screen away from the dryness of a talking head; viewers now have two to three sources of information—a flow that most channels emulate today. Like it or not, Fox News gets credit for adding more visual graphics and information sources to the screens we watch.

In addition to using tickers on the bottom of the screen, Fox News began the practice of offering bullet points to viewers of the exact same information that the newscasters were voicing. This practice, which Stephen Colbert parodies in his "The Wørd" segment, creates a graphics-heavy visual field for news—one that is radically different from the television news of earlier eras. And one of the ways that this information blast works is through the use of slogans. Before Fox News, all channels had their slogans, but now most significant news stories also have slogans, and almost all satire of these news stories has its own slogans too. Think of Stewart's coverage of "Mess O'potamia." While CNN had begun that practice prior to the launch of Fox News, it would take on a whole new level under the leadership of Ailes. Ailes took his political slogan experience and turned it to the news world. He launched the channel with two main slogans: "Fair and Balanced" and "We report. You decide." Both slogans almost immediately came under fire for inaccuracy, leading to lawsuits in both the United States and Great Britain, both of which failed to get the news media station to change its branding. There are two important takeaways from the use of these two main slogans: (1) They are not true. Research has proven that the station is neither fair nor balanced. And it has further shown that both the pundit programming and the so-called straight news do not allow viewers to form their own opinions. And (2) they are a great way to get publicity for the channel. Since the channel first launched, "fair and balanced" has come under constant criticism. If Fox News had debuted with a slogan that was less provocative, it would not have generated nearly as much news media for the station itself. Like it or not, Ailes' branding of the station was genius. In a certain sense, the birth of Fox News was like opening a Pandora's box. After it was unleashed, nothing would ever be the same again.

Now if you read the alternative internet news, you will find quotes by most major news figures (except those on Fox News) complaining about the lack of "fair and balanced" reporting on Fox News. Media critics also mainly agree. But their critiques are often found in blogs or print pieces in venues like Media Matters or Alternet. So, if you are looking for criticism of the "fair and balanced" reporting of Fox News on television, your best bet is the satirists. As we will explain in the chapter we dedicate to Stephen Colbert and Jon Stewart, both comedians have engaged on numerous occasions with Fox News reporters and pundits—most especially with Bill O'Reilly. And they have also modeled their programs on some of the trademark Fox News formatting. But they are not alone. *Saturday Night Live* (*SNL*) has dedicated segments to parodies of Fox News, most notably the roast of Fox News's morning show *Fox & Friends*—a roast that suggested that the real parody was the actual original show itself since in the bit actual comments made by host Steve Doocy were simply attributed to his co-host, Gretchen Carlson.[11] Comedian Bill Maher has also spoken out about Fox News on numerous occasions, including on a segment with CNN's Piers Morgan: "Facts never get in the way of their talking points. And so for people who only listen to Fox News, they can wake up with Matt Drudge and have lunch with Rush Limbaugh and go to bed with Bill O'Reilly," Maher explained in his brutally frank style. "All they're going to know is what they hear there. And very often these people do not care what the truth is."[12]

But perhaps one of the best examples is the fact that Fox News has a history of using satirical pieces and passing them off as truth, as was the case when they picked up a story posted by the satirical news source *National Report*. On October 5, 2013, the co-hosts of *Fox & Friends Saturday* worried over the closure of the World War II Memorial, which had actually resulted from the Republican-led shutdown. During the discussion, co-host Anna Kooiman claimed that while the memorial is closed, "President Obama has offered to pay out of his own pocket for the museum of Muslim culture."[13] Well, the source for that statement was a satirical website, but they never bothered to fact check. Kooiman later tweeted she was sorry, but one suspects that most Fox News viewers—given their advanced age demographic—are not following her Twitter feed. And, as if that were not enough, in 2010, *Fox Nation*, the online presence for Fox News that allows user comments and interaction, excerpted several paragraphs from *The Onion*'s satirical piece, "Frustrated Obama Sends Nation Rambling 75,000-Word Email," eliciting a flurry of negative and indignant comments from the site's readers.[14] Possibly shamed by the reports mocking *Fox Nation* for taking *The Onion*'s piece seriously, the site quickly took the article and its comment thread down. But no apology was offered, and no correction was posted. As *Raw Story* reported: "For a news outlet to retain credibility, standard industry procedure dictates that reporters and editors not only correct mistakes, but acknowledge them as well. *Fox Nation* had done neither at time of this writing."[15] Instead, Fox News simply made the story disappear.

As this brief little foray into the world of Fox News and its relationship to satire has revealed, television news bears little resemblance to the network era of either Walter Cronkite or Peter Jennings. In addition to the sensational, ideological angle of most television news today, the increased corporatization of news has brought great change as well. But while these trends explain the added commercialization and politicization of news, they don't quite account for the rise in the role of satire news in informing the public. While satire news was once expected to be consumed *after* an audience took in the traditional news, that is no longer the case. Today it is satire news that sets trends, informs audiences, and shapes public debate. If Fox News changed the landscape when it was first launched, one could argue that it has been satire news—along with citizen-journalism—that has created the latest shift. What is important to note is that the impact of satire can actually be measured, so we will share with you some of the surveys and data that help explain the state of news media today. Our goal is to help you understand how changes in news media have affected public thinking on today's political issues. We've broken the chapter down into six sections that cover (1) the connection between news media and democracy, (2) the rise of "fake" news, (3) the rise of satire news, (4) the role of satire news as that of a "faithful watchdog" for the public, (5) some key examples of satire news, and (6) the role of satire in offering a space for "spectacular dissent"—that is a public form of critical thinking that takes the shape of entertaining spectacle.

Democracy and the Information Society

You don't need to be a scholar to understand that the health of a democracy depends on active and informed citizens. A democracy is only as good as its citizenry. As we explained in chapter 2, one key component of strong citizenship is education. Schooling teaches young citizens to understand their role in their government and in society, and this is done not only through civics classes, but also through the various ways in which schools train students to understand the world in which they live. While schooling provides the critical infrastructure within which the citizen develops, it is the media that provides the key information that citizens use to make decisions. Even if citizens are trained to be critical thinkers and to question the status quo, if the media misinforms them, then their decisions are grounded on falsehoods. But, if the media presents them with the key issues of the time in a way that lets them develop informed decisions, then they are able to actively participate in the development of a healthy democracy.

It all seems pretty simple until you recognize that what constitutes information has itself become a topic of great debate. As Colbert famously quipped during his speech before President Bush at the White House Correspondents' Association Dinner, "Reality has a well-known liberal bias."[16] To simplify a fairly complex process by which even the basics of reality came to be the subject of confusion in our nation, we can highlight two key factors that made the whole "reality thing" a mess. The first was the left-progressive move to complicate the notion of truth associated with postmodernism, and the second was the increasing fundamentalism of the right. Taken together they combined to make the simple decisions of citizens a lot harder.

Let's start by thinking about the left notion that truth is complex, subjective, and biased. This idea was developed as a critique of the way that many notions of truth—what some call master narratives—were developed by those in power so that they could stay in power. If what we came to take for granted was in fact biased against large segments of the population, then such ideas need to be questioned. To spin this in a way that might seem familiar, there was once a day when teachers and professors were the voice of the truth in the classroom. But progressive scholars, working under the theoretical concepts connected to postmodernism, thought such hierarchies needed to be questioned. So, they insisted that there was no logical reason why the teacher was always right, just like men were not smarter than women, white people were not smarter than black people, and so on. The goal was to ask questions about the social truths that had created society. And, when you think about it, it was a pretty good idea and one that was very important for a healthy democracy, since there was no reason why, up until the election of Barack Obama, a white man had always held our nation's highest role.

There was a downside to the progressive, postmodern take on truth, though, and that was that it made it easier for those that wanted to twist the truth to get away with it. These same notions allowed President Bush to refer to the Geneva Conventions as "vague" when he didn't want to admit that water-boarding was torture.[17] After 9/11, a vague notion of truth reigned in the administration and allowed us to be taken to war with two nations, neither of which was responsible for the attacks on our country. It was this very same vague notion of truth that became the core of Colbert's "truthiness"—the neologism he used to launch his very first episode.

The facts of 9/11 are so often forgotten, hidden beneath the spin of rhetoric and political positioning, but the majority of the men on the planes that attacked the United States on 9/11 were from Saudi Arabia, and yet, there was never any discussion of invading that nation. And those weapons of mass destruction that were the motive for the war in Iraq were a total fabrication too. Bush took his "vague" notion of truth and coupled it with an aggressive "us-versus-them" logic. The same logic, incidentally, that most call "jihadi" in other contexts. Writer Paul Auster recently gave an interview where he explained the "jihadi" nature of Republican politics: "I think of the right-wing Republicans as jihadists; they're as crazy as those people. They want to destroy the country that we want to save. And you know they're not doing it with machine guns and bombs, but they're doing it by electing insane people to enact insane legislation that is going to do as much damage to us as bombs would in the long run."[18] What of course has to be mentioned, though, is that for Republicans it is people like Paul Auster that are the "jihadis." We live in a time when there always seems to be many sides to a story and where the facts are often forgotten, hidden, or misrepresented.

Not only are the facts lost, they are turned into partisan opposition that often becomes completely removed from any sense of reality. It is worth remembering that in response to the terrible massacre of twenty school children and six teachers in Sandy Hook, Connecticut in the winter of 2012, Sarah Palin reacted to the extraordinary gun violence of that day by going out and buying her husband a "nice, needed, and powerful" gun for Christmas. It was a "small act of civil disobedience," Palin writes in her memoir, prompted by "the anti-gun chatter coming from Washington" (Introduction). As Dan Savage explains, "before the grieving mothers and fathers of Newtown, Connecticut, could put their dead children in the ground, Sarah Palin ran out gun shopping."[19] One first-grader at Sandy Hook was shot eleven times, leading some to think that it was time for a law restricting automatic weapons. But such "chatter" made Palin feel threatened.

All of this is to say that the "truth" on which a citizen's decisions should be based is no longer a simple matter, if it ever was. We can have an event like the Sandy Hook massacre, the facts of which don't seem in dispute. We have the number of dead bodies, the bullets, the weapon—the details seem clear. But for some reason former Vice Presidential nominee Sarah Palin does not see that event as cause for concern over gun access in our country; instead she seems to have no ability at all to link the facts of our gun laws to the facts of the dead bodies. And it is in this disconnect that the citizen is caught. Who is the victim here? Palin and her guns? Or the children of Sandy Hook? Or does that connection make sense? How is a citizen to tell?

That is where the media should step in, helping to sift the hype from the helpful information, providing much-needed perspective, context, and facts. As Russell Peterson explains, "Maintaining an informed electorate is one of democracy's daunting challenges" (22). And if that democracy is supported by a news media more inclined to hyperbole and hysteria such as that found on Fox News, then citizens are less likely to be able to function as they should. As we explained in the introduction, though, it gets even more complicated since citizenship itself is undergoing transformation away from the duty-bound, rational citizen toward one that is also influenced by entertainment and spectacle and only sometimes by reason and truth. Jeffrey Jones suggests that entertaining political programming is a legitimate location for public discourse. He explains that former separations between "serious" information and "entertainment" programming no longer make sense. According to Jones, such a model,

> advocates a strict separation between the "serious" information needed for citizens to be informed, deliberative, interrogational, and empirically reasoning thinkers, and the "entertainment" programming that is threatening because it is supposedly none of these things. Yet this normative ideal, I contend, is rarely found in the practices of modern citizenry and is an unrealistic standard for the types of behavior that currently hold much interest for many citizens. What's more, it does not represent the multitude of ways in which people exchange, process, and engage political material in their day-to-day lives, ways that just as easily can be crude, limited, dismissive, trivial, playful, and emotional as they can be thoughtful, wide-ranging, generous, complex, rational, serious, and high-minded. Nor does it accurately represent the ways in which people attend to politics—in passing, cursorily, mixed in with other activities, from various media and across numerous subjects. In short, holding onto a conception of citizenship born from a rational-critical standard is perhaps noble, but it is an inappropriate means for assessing the relationship of television to politics. Instead, I agree with Schudson when he argues, "We require a citizenship fit for our own day." (25)

We think Jones makes an important point. Like it or not, entertainment and emotion affect citizenship at least as much if not more than reason and critical engagement. The trick, though, is the difference between such programming when it happens on a news channel that bills itself as "fair and balanced" and on a satire show on Comedy Central. While Jones is quick to point out that it is time to open up our notions of the proper sources for "news," it would be fair to say that it is exactly due to the way that news sources themselves have morphed into broadcasts of opinion, spectacle, and misinformation that the valid sources of news have changed. These changes opened the news mediascape for non-traditional news sources to fill in the gap. We agree with Jones that the current state of news media requires that we consider political entertainment programming as one of its most central sources. As Jones puts it, "what if such programming is actually an alternative form of reporting—another way of producing useful, informative, or meaningful materials with just as much value to citizens as that provided by television news? Are such criticisms of the genre merited in that case? And what if citizens maintain a meaningful relationship with the genre, using it for forms of civic engagement beyond simple information acquisition?" (xi). Thus, while the news media plays a key role in informing the citizenry, there is little doubt that its function as a source of information has morphed into one that is only partially connected to information. What the rest of this chapter will show is that in the wake of these changes, audiences of satire news are more likely to have a grasp of the facts behind an issue than those watching so-called "fair and balanced" news sources like Fox News.

Will the Real "Fake" News Please Stand Up?

Do a quick web search for "fake news" and you will inevitably see the term linked to satire news. The website of *The Onion* is the first link and the second is a Wikipedia article on "news satire." Stewart has been repeatedly referred to as a fake newsman and he gets some of the top hits. But scroll a little farther and you will see wholly different "fake" news. These are the sites that are functioning as watchdogs for the mainstream news media and for them, "fake" news is propaganda posing as news. According to Peterson, "the nutritional value of the news itself has come into some doubt. News programming is, according to the consensus, becoming almost indistinguishable from entertainment programming" (2). But the worries over the "fake" nature of the real news are not only limited to its connection to entertainment programming and the rise in opinion programming over information programming; they are also linked to its propagandistic function.

One of the biggest threats to credible news since 9/11 has been government-sponsored news programming. In 2006, Amy and David Goodman reported that, "Since coming to power, the Bush administration has engaged in a systematic campaign of covert propaganda aimed at subverting both domestic and foreign media. The Government Accountability Office estimates that between 2003 and 2005, the administration spent $1.6 billion on advertising and public relations to promote its policies" (62–3). $1.6 billion! And it gets worse. They go on to explain that "Iraqi journalists were paid stipends of up to $500 per month, depending on how many pro-American pieces they published. This secret program is run by a relatively unknown defense contractor called the Lincoln Group, which in 2005 landed a multiyear $100 million contract to produce pro-American, anti-insurgent TV, radio, and print messages" (63–4). The Goodmans state that these practices lead the public to mistake the illusion of news for reality as journalists trade truth for their own success: "Instead of learning from the media what is actually going on in the world, we get static—a veil of distortion, lies, omissions, and half-truths that obscure reality" (12–13). As our democracy came under fire after 9/11 with a series of policies that threatened civil liberties at home and human rights abroad, the news media offered little resistance. Instead, they became the conduit through which these "fake" news stories were able to circulate.

According to the Goodmans, "Under the Bush administration, at least twenty federal agencies have spent $250 million creating hundreds of fake television news segments that are sent to local stations" (74). One of the best sources for information on these fake news segments is The Center for Media and Democracy's website *PR Watch*, which covers corporate and government-funded video news releases (VNRs). These pre-packaged news segments look and sound like "real" news segments, but they have been produced by corporations or the government to provide information that supports their goals. And in many cases television stations disguise the sponsored content and pass it off as legitimate news, almost never offering their viewers any information to balance the propaganda they have just consumed. *PR Watch* explains that more than one-third of the time, stations simply aired the entire VNR with no editing of any kind. If, as they report, 75% of US citizens rely on local news programming and 70% turn to network or cable news daily or near-daily, then the constant presence of these packaged news segments is of great concern. Their key findings include:

- VNR use is widespread.
- VNRs are aired in TV markets of all sizes.
- TV stations don't disclose VNRs to viewers.
- TV stations disguise VNRs as their own reporting.
- TV stations don't supplement VNR footage or verify VNR claims.
- The vast majority of VNRs are produced for corporate clients.[20]

In the sample studied by the Center for Media and Democracy over half of the US population (52.7%) had seen a VNR in a ten-month period of time and the broadcasting station hid it from them.

The substitution of "fake" news for "real" is not just limited to canned video footage. The Goodmans report that the Bush administration regularly paid for pro-government op-eds. "An Education Department investigation in 2005 revealed that at least eleven newspapers had run op-ed pieces written by education advocacy groups that were paid for by the federal government, but never identified their government funding" (80). And that same year conservative columnist Armstrong Williams took $240,000 from the Department of Education to write in support of No Child Left Behind (78). So exactly how strong can our democracy be if we citizens live under a government that pays news media to run pro-government stories? And that is just the news assault from the government; corporations regularly provide VNRs as well. Coverage of new drugs, new products, and most other news linked to the commercial world has been influenced by corporate sponsorship of one sort or another.

This all means that the material presented as "real" is often actually propaganda. But as we pointed out in the story of Fox News, the presentation of "real" news has other limitations in the current mediascape as well. Geoffrey Baym in *From Cronkite to Colbert: The Evolution of Broadcast News* explains that much has changed in broadcast news from the sort of serious reporting associated with a trusted newsman like Walter Cronkite. The transition from the network era of three main stations to the multichannel/cable era brought a number of shifts. First, television broadcast news now competes with other non-news programming that offers alternative options for viewers with cable. This directly leads to more efforts to make news entertaining. One direct consequence of this, as we saw in the case of Fox News, was the turn to more visual graphics and away from verbal information. Baym reports that coverage of the Bill Clinton affair with Monica Lewinsky "contained some 70% more visual images than those during Watergate" (34). He goes on to explain that "One story . . . contained thirty-five different images in less than two and a half minutes, an average of less than four seconds per picture" (ibid). Not only were viewers barraged with sensationalist images, these flashed on the screen with no real time for analysis of what was being seen, a practice that disallows viewer reflection. Baym notes these images were accompanied by "a variety of postproduction effects such as slow motion or the altering of color and tone to complicate imagery, an approach virtually non-existent in the

Watergate coverage" (35). Today news media increasingly offers entertainment over information and analysis. Baym suggests that today's news no longer works to present information to the public, preferring instead to "construct engaging, reality-based stories" (37).

Added to the barrage of special effects and images, another new development has shaped the news: the appearance of the analyst over the participant. Baym explains that in place of participants in the political process, the networks have tended to turn increasingly to analysts who provide their views on topics. These are academics, lawyers, former government insiders, and other paid pundits who work for the network. Baym notes that in the coverage of the Clinton/Lewinsky affair "the analyst sound bite averages eleven seconds longer than those of lawmakers" (38). An even greater shift, though, is the time spent showing conversation between anchors, across commentators, and between pundits.

As explained above, with the advent of Fox News, 24/7 news channels moved toward greater and greater time for opinion programming over straight news (See Figure 3.2). Thus the rise of the pundit also marks a real attack on "real" news. According to Darrell M. West in *The Rise and Fall of the Media Establishment*, the 1980s ushered in a substantial rise in punditry. It is worth noting that the term— pundit—was not originally a derogatory word. Pundits were experts and they offered commentary and context that journalists were not expected, or trained, to provide. In *The Political Pundits*, Dan D. Nimmo and James E. Combs explain that "one of the oldest and most cherished public forums for punditry in the history of print journalism is the column" (12). That sort of punditry, though, where a learned public intellectual shares opinions in print, is a far cry from the right-wing hysterical, fear-mongering punditry of figures like Bill O'Reilly, Glenn Beck, Lou Dobbs, Ann Coulter, and Sean Hannity. These types of pundits have played a major role in creating a post-9/11 media intent on whipping up public hysteria, fostering intolerance and bigotry, and creating a sense of the United States as a

Figure 3.2 Bill O'Reilly suggests that the "liberal media" has turned news into propaganda[21]

nation in constant peril. According to François Debrix, "Since 9/11, the conservative, populist, loud-mouthed Fox News network talk-show host and pundit Bill O'Reilly has taken it upon himself to represent and protect American lives" (145–46). He explains that what makes these shows dangerous is that they are "intent on producing the impression of news reporting, information providing, facts revealing, and truth declaring," but what they really do is allow pundits like O'Reilly to "convince his audience of the moral superiority and greater commonsensical value of his punditry" (145). The problem is that shows like these report unsubstantiated opinion and biased ideology as factual, true, and objective: think, for instance, of O'Reilly's "No Spin Zone." Moreover, they are organized around a constant sense of fear and a never-ending state of crisis: "The shock-value of O'Reilly's interventions (or interpretations) is aimed at gathering popular support or triggering public scandal by unleashing waves after waves of fear among his audience members" (145–46). None of these developments is a good sign for the public deliberation essential to a healthy democracy.

So, thus far, we have surveyed a series of reasons why the "real" news may be more fake than the "fake" news: we have the increasing politicization of news, the connection between Republican Party politics and news hype, the rise in paid propaganda passed off as news, the advent of spectacle-heavy news formats, the increase in opinion programming over news programming, and the rise in vitriolic punditry over reasoned debate. All this combined in the post-9/11 era with the culture of fear connected to the never-ending war on terror, marking a moment in US history where the nation always seemed in crisis and at risk. Over a decade after the terrorist attacks we are now able to note how political discourse after 9/11 has favored affect over reason. Lauren Berlant calls this "visceral politics": it describes a political sphere whose "dominant rhetorical style is to recruit the public to see political attachments as an amalgam of reflexive opinion and visceral or 'gut' feeling" (47). Certainly President Bush was the poster-boy for thinking from his gut, but the same sort of emotional "thinking" drives much news media as well. In some ways, the fear and anxiety that followed from the 9/11 attacks had some basis in fact—lives were lost, terrorists had succeeded, and the future was unclear. But whatever sort of ground that justified the sense of fear in the early days after 9/11 quickly gave way to the hype, hysteria, and anxiety caused by a permanent war that has no boundaries, no clearly defined enemy, and no end in sight. As Austin Sarat explains, "Since September 11 'fear again threatens reason.' Aliens have been imprisoned for months on the flimsiest grounds. The attorney general of the United States moved to deport people on the basis of secret evidence. The president authorized military tribunals to hold trials under special rules, and Congress passed the USA PATRIOT Act" (6). The point is that fear was mobilized after 9/11 in ways that specifically weakened our democracy. It is not possible to watch a few hours of any of the major news networks and not see stories aimed at producing anxiety, stress, and fear, often in ways that are wholly illogical and with no basis in reality. It is exactly this sort of free-floating fear that Colbert parodies in his recurring segment "The Threatdown" where the #1 threat to us is usually bears.

While the news media was busy making us worry over non-existent threats, we were distracted from something that should have really worried us: the deregulation of the news media which led to the increasing control of all mainstream news by a small number of media conglomerates. Beginning during the Reagan presidency and highlighted by the Telecommunications Act of 1996, most regulations that governed news and public affairs programming disappeared. The deregulation of news media led to the transformation of news media from a service to citizens to a product for consumers. Media ownership became concentrated in the hands of multinational corporations and most major news outlets fell into the hands of only five corporate sources.[22] Baym notes that these changes meant that "the primary tilt of the new corporate landscape was toward commodification, the reconceptualization of all media products packaged for maximum profit" (*From Cronkite to Colbert* 14). This meant that news became market-driven and news producers looked to attract consumers rather than inform citizens. As Jones notes, the move to entertaining political news may not be such a terrible thing, but this is only true if the audience is able to discern enough reality from the programming to make informed choices. One thing is clear; in today's world of news media the main goal is to hook the consumer. Such practices lead, as Baym notes, to an "absence of a commitment to truth" where political proclamations that "bear little resemblance to the reality they claim to represent" take the place of "democratic insight" (*From Cronkite to Colbert* 15).

As mentioned before, one of the central arenas for the development of a vibrant and engaged public sphere is the media, since the media is the primary source through which citizens come to be informed about issues affecting our nation. According to Baym, "It is axiomatic that the vitality of democracy depends on an informed citizenry . . . Today, more than ever, news media serve as a primary link connecting individuals to the political process" (*From Cronkite to Colbert* 7). But changes in the mediascape, including deregulation, paid propaganda, the 24/7 news cycle, the multichannel era, the cult of punditry, the hype of fear, and more have influenced the quality, depth, and caliber of the material presented as news to the public. And these changes have paved the way for the so-called fake news, i.e. satire news, often to seem more real than the "fair and balanced" reporting of cable news channels like Fox. But as we said at the start, we'll report; you decide. Here is a matchup of some "real" news versus some satire news (see Table 3.1 and Table 3.2).

Yeah, we know that's eleven for satire, but we couldn't resist. As you line up these examples, though, even if we gave one more to the satirists, it is really hard to see which of the two deserves the term "fake" news. Sure the satirists are doing some crazy things—swearing, dressing up, exaggerating, running parodies. But, as we will explain further in our chapter on the art of satire, satire is comedy; it is not news and it does not want to appear as news. In fact, if anything it is harder for satirists to do their silly, playful stunts when the real newsmen are so busy being silly themselves. But if you take out the silly parts, which of these lists actually mentions real issues of concern to the public and which list distracts the public from the key issues central to our democracy? Which list helps us to see when we are being duped? And which dupes? As Megan Boler explains, Stewart is not simply a classic court jester, goofing around. She points out that "A recurring theme in the online discussions is that, in the current climate, truth can only be

Table 3.1   Fox News Highlights from 2013

1. Anchor Heather Nauert said a Muslim girls' swim class at a YMCA was evidence that "Sharia law is now changing everything."
2. Megyn Kelly declared without any shadow of a doubt that Santa Claus is white.
3. Bill O'Reilly backed her up.
4. Brian Kilmeade asked a Nicaraguan co-host during Hispanic Heritage Month if she "grew up on tacos."
5. The government shutdown became the "government slimdown."
6. *Fox & Friends* said the day of Obama's inauguration was the "most depressing day of the year."
7. Bob Beckel of *The Five* said, "I would not have another mosque built in this country until we got it worked out who was not a terrorist."
8. Fox News psychiatrist Dr. Keith Ablow told Steve Doocy he thought Obama was victimized by his parents and was taking it out on America.
9. Bill O'Reilly says Asians aren't liberals because they're "industrious and hard-working."
10. Geraldo Rivera says jurors would have shot Trayvon Martin sooner than Zimmerman did.

Sources: "The 20 Worst Fox News Moments of 2013." BuzzFeed Politics. *http://www.buzzfeed.com/andrewkaczynski/ worst-fox-news-moments-of-2013*; "Fox News' 5 worst moments of 2013." Salon. *http://www.salon.com/2013/12/26/ fox_news_5_worst_moments_of_2013/*

Table 3.2   Satire News Highlights from 2013

1. Jessica Williams of *The Daily Show* does a stop-and-frisk parody. In "Frisky Business," *The Daily Show* correspondent exposes the hypocrisy and racism of Mayor Michael Bloomberg's stop-and-frisk program.
2. Aasif Mandvi interviews a racist GOP leader. Mandvi uncovered a national scandal in the form of North Carolina GOP leader Don Yelton, who said he supported controversial voter ID laws because "If [the law] hurts the whites so be it. If it hurts a bunch of lazy blacks that want the government to give them everything, so be it." The segment caused such an uproar that Yelton resigned from his position nearly overnight, and went on air to defend himself the next day.
3. Jon Stewart covers how "weird" it was for Megyn Kelly to insist that Santa was white.
4. Jon Oliver covers the government shutdown calling it a "Shitstorm" and refers to House Republicans as a bunch of "self-righteous Orwellian zebra queefs."
5. Jason Jones of *The Daily Show* makes a fool of Republican Gina Loudon when he interviews her on the Affordable Care Act, telling her "You are so much better than [the Democrats] at reducing complicated ideas into meaningless phrases."
6. One week after the 2013 government shutdown started, Stephen Colbert plays the "Not a Game" board game with an eight-year-old where he explains, "I go first and I refuse to take my turn." Colbert would only agree to take his turn if his opponent would concede the whole thing.
7. *The Daily Currant* runs a story called "Obamacare Website Accidentally Enrolls Thousands in Sex Offender Registry" that highlights the conservative hysteria over the new law.
8. The Yes Men ask the US Chamber of Commerce to reconsider their decision to withdraw the lawsuit they had filed against them four years earlier. The case was caused by a Yes Men prank where they posed as Chamber of Commerce officials and claimed that they were doing an "about-face on climate change."
9. Stephen Colbert was so excited to see the CNN show *Crossfire* return that he hosted a parody of the program with Oscar the Grouch and Big Bird. *Crossfire*, says Colbert, "practically invented people yelling incoherently at each other." On his mock show, "Pointless Counter Pointless," the *Sesame Street* characters debated important topics such as the letter S.

(Continued)

Table 3.2 *(Continued)*

10. Jon Stewart finds an article in *Bloomberg Magazine* about questionable business practices through which a private equity firm (Blackstone) structured a strange financial agreement to pay a company to force it to miss a debt payment, resulting in a credit default swap where they would make over $15 million. Stewart and correspondent Samantha Bee wondered why the media wasn't covering the story.

11. *The Daily Show* and *Colbert Report* both report on CNN's terrible inaccuracy. And Jon Stewart's team of correspondents parody it with a segment by Samantha Bee, Jason Jones, John Oliver, and Aasif Mandvi billed as "The Best F#@king News Team Ever."

Sources: What Happens Next: A Gallimaufry. *http://fozmeadows.tumblr.com/post/62896706344/sandandglass-jason-jones-talks-to-gina-loudon*; "The 10 best segments from 'The Daily Show' and 'Colbert Report' this year." Salon. *http://www.salon.com/2013/12/24/the_10_best_segments_from_the_daily_show_and_colbert_report_this_year/*; "Chamber of Commerce Drops Lawsuit Against Parodists The Yes Men, Who Ask The Chamber To Reconsider." Techdirt. *http://www.techdirt.com/articles/20130616/18233023499/chamber-commerce-drops-trademark-infringement-suit-against-activistparodist-group-yes-men-group-asks-chamber-to-reconsider.shtml*; PoliticalMinute. *http://politicalminute.org/best-daily-show-colbert-report-2013/*; "Blackstone Unit Wins in No-Lose Codere Trade: Corporate Finance." Bloomberg. *http://www.bloomberg.com/news/2013-10-22/blackstone-unit-wins-in-no-lose-codere-trade-corporate-finance.html*; Political Minute. *http://politicalminute.org/the-daily-shows-jon-stewart-and-samantha-bee-report-on-questionable-business-practices-that-the-media-ignores-video/*;

achieved through this kind of humor: 'Jon Stewart and the excellent writers of *The Daily Show* have also given anyone paying attention an essential piece of strategy: sometimes the truth can ONLY be delivered through comedy. While "real" news shows refuse to check political claims against reality, it has taken a "fake" news show to do actual research necessary to prove many of the lies politicians tell'" (*Digital Media* 32). Boler and Stephen Turpin point out that central to the success of satire news is "the widely-shared frustration and perception that the news media is failing democracy" (388). Even independent journalist Amy Goodman of *Democracy Now* describes The Yes Men, Stewart, and Colbert as examples of "good" journalism, especially in contrast to that found on cable news (*Static*). And if these examples aren't helping make the point, there are numerous surveys that show that viewers of satire news score higher in knowledge of current events than viewers of cable news. For instance, a 2007 study by the Pew Research Center for the People & the Press showed that viewers of *The Daily Show* and *The Colbert Report* were among the most informed, scoring much higher than viewers of cable news networks.[23] So will the real "fake" news please stand up? Or is there still confusion?

Satire News and "Real" News

In Mark K. McBeth and Randy S. Clemons's essay "Is Fake News the Real News?" from Amarnath Amarasingam's edited volume *The Stewart/Colbert Effect: Essays on the Real Impacts of Fake News,* they argue that "fake news shows are not only at least as real as the mainstream news, . . . they contribute more to the type of deliberative discourse essential to genuine democracy and public policy" (79). Not only is there significant evidence, as highlighted above, that the "real" news is not that real, but it also seems clear that satire news has moved in to overtake "real" news as a source of legitimate, timely information and critical reflection useful to deliberative democracy. According to McBeth and Clemons, "much of American political coverage is inauthentic (fake) and . . . the programs of Jon Stewart and Stephen Colbert both represent authentic (real) discourse that breaks through the shell of the real (fake) news" (81). All of this suggests that we are living in a unique era when satire news may be more important than the real news as a source for political information central to our democracy. Today it is common to have satire news items included on mainstream news coverage. Can you imagine a newscaster like Walter Cronkite covering what happened on *The Smothers Brothers* or *All in the Family* as though the satire was relevant for his news report? McBeth and Clemons point to a time when CNN fact-checked a 2009 *Saturday Night Live* sketch about President Obama (79). In another example, Colbert was flabbergasted when the mainstream news covered his comedic interview with Robert Wexler in 2006, when he got the congressional candidate to say silly things that then were intensely scrutinized by the news media as serious statements. Again and again, satire news provides content for mainstream news—a fact that highlights the radical ways that news media has changed in the last two decades.

In addition, it is noteworthy that satirists are regularly interviewed on serious political news programs with little to no attention to the fact that they are actually comedians and not pundits or politicians. *The Daily Show* correspondents received press passes to cover the 2000 Republican National Convention (and have been at every convention since then). Back in 2000 Bill Hilary, the executive vice president of Comedy Central, was surprised by the development, stating: "People are taking us seriously, even though we're a comedy show. For the first time, they're saying 'The Daily Show' has a place in social commentary." But as Jones notes, Stewart was less amazed about his supposed new role: "The whole point of our show is that we're a fake news organization. What's more appropriate than going to a fake news event? Everybody knows it's a trade show" (72). But what Stewart does admit here is that his show is on par with the mainstream news—making satire news and "real" news overlap and intersect. One of the most famous highlights to this sort of crossover happened when Stewart appeared on CNN's *Crossfire* in a showdown that led to the show being canceled. In addition, Colbert did a number of interviews in 2012 after launching his "fake" candidacy for president of South Carolina, including with figures like ABC's George Stephanopoulos; he later was interviewed by David Gregory on *Meet the Press* to offer his views on the 2012 election. Bill Maher is also a regular visitor to so-called "real" political news programs. The reverse is true too: politicians appear all the time on comedy shows attempting to get "serious" interest. The impact of these appearances, most visible in the "Colbert Bump," has been documented so much so that commentators wonder if a politician can get elected if they *don't* appear on satire television. John Edwards even announced his candidacy on *The Daily Show* in 2003. As Jonathan Gray, Jeffrey Jones, and Ethan Thompson explain in their introduction to *Satire TV,* "satire TV forms a key part of televised political culture" (6). You simply can't understand news today without it.

One of the main features of satire's power over contemporary news is its ability to draw attention to key news items in ways that most straight coverage does not. David Marc explains in his essay for *Satire TV* that the current power of satire has been decades in the making. During the McCarthy era the comedy-show *Laugh-In* "demonstrated conclusively that making jokes about The News was more popular on television than was The News itself" (xiv). *Laugh-In* then led the way for *Saturday Night Live,* showing producers that satire news could be profitable and powerful. Other important precursors to today's satire news include the highly innovative work of Michael Moore, whose program *TV Nation* was launched after the success of his documentary *Roger and Me* about General Motors CEO Roger Smith's closing of several auto plants in Flint, Michigan. *TV Nation* ran from 1994–95, airing first on NBC and later on Fox (not Fox News). Structured as a newsmagazine, the show offered satirical and humorous stories such as "The Corporate Challenge" where CEOs were asked to use the products their companies created. In one segment they paid a lobbyist $5,000 to get Congress to declare "TV Nation Day," which they then did.[24] Despite incredible success, the show did not get a third season, since, even though BBC wanted to run it, Moore could not find a US-based channel to air the show. Relatively tame by today's standards of satire, Moore clearly hit a nerve by linking citizenship to trustworthy media. So *TV Nation* morphed into *The Awful Truth*, a show with a similar format that aired on British Channel 4 in 1999. As Jones explains, "Moore crafted a fine satirical edge with his programs, demonstrating how fake news could be used to penetrate the façades of power and make a pointed political critique, all with a laugh and devious smile" (64). Even though *The Awful Truth* aired in Britain, the show focused on problems in US government, business, and society. Emphasizing the power bloc that controls most news media, *The Awful Truth* would open with animated cartoons of five CEOs of media corporations (Ted Turner, Rupert Murdoch, Bill Gates, Sumner Redstone, and Michael Eisner). The viewer would then hear: "In the beginning, there was a free press. Well, not really, but it sounded good. By the end of the millennium, five men controlled the world's media. Yet there was one man who operated outside their control (showing a shot of Michael Moore). He and his motley crew were known as the People's Democratic Republic of Television. Their mission: to bring the people the Awful Truth."[25] Here we can note echoes to the sort of language that is used by The Colbert Nation. In one bit that Colbert fans will find familiar, Moore responded to legislation to display the Ten Commandments in public schools by asking the bill's co-signers to state the eighth commandment, which most failed to do.[26] Colbert would later ask Congressman Lynn Westmoreland, who was supporting a similar bill to display the Ten Commandments publicly, to name all ten; he failed as well.[27] What both examples illustrate, though, is the power of satire to draw attention to the hypocrisy of politicians. These comedians were educating the citizenry on vital issues while the mainstream news media looked the other way.

A further influence on the current significance of political satire media was the talk shows of figures like Dennis Miller and Bill Maher, whose respective programs *Dennis Miller Live* (1994–02) and *Politically Incorrect* (1993–02), set the stage for a new era in political talk programming. Both programs took the comedian interview to a whole new level. Certainly politicians and public personalities had been interviewed by comedians in the past, especially on programs like *The Tonight Show,* but Miller and Maher interviewed with a dose of cynicism and sharp wit that was new to the genre. They really grilled their guests, while making the interview fun and funny. Viewers were educated and entertained. As Jones notes, "*Dennis Miller Live* and *Politically Incorrect* were pioneers in the development and eventual critical acceptance of the merger of entertainment talk shows with political talk" (71).

This trajectory would take a rapid turn after 9/11, when, as explained above, a series of forces combined to radically change the nature of news media. David Gurney analyzes these shifts in his contribution to *A Decade of Dark Humor: How Comedy, Irony, and Satire Shaped Post-9/11 America* where he emphasizes the extraordinary power of comedians in shaping the focus of today's news coverage: "By choosing to satirize particular stories and events from the already parsed field of news media, comedians play a crucial role in determining which news items become more widespread topics of conversation" (3). According to Gurney, the late night comedy television hosts "have become high-profile critical commentators, using humor to show the public that the major events and players of the day are not beyond reproach, and that, in fact, the foibles of the powerful are in dire need of the exposure and critique that a cutting joke can bring" (4). This process is even more heightened by the way that these items can circulate in social media. Viewers take clips and share them, allowing satirical interventions to have an impact far greater than satire from earlier generations. Rather than simply consume the news, viewers of satire are able to engage with it, by taking the clips that they like and sharing them with their communities. Such practices allow satire to help create an active and engaged citizenry, since most of the time those "shares" include viewer comments and opinions. Roughly two-thirds of the US public uses Facebook and half of those users get news there.[28] These changes represent a real shift in how the US public gets the news it uses to form opinions and make decisions.

Beyond the influence of satire news on content, on form, and on the media practices of politicians and mainstream news, it is important to note that another key factor in determining which genre is the "real" news is the way that satire news does its research. One major feature of today's satire news is that it works as a fact-checker for the mainstream news. The field of journalism is shrinking, with numbers down by 30% in newspaper newsroom journalism since 2000.[29] In local TV, sports, weather, and traffic account for 40% of content and on CNN produced-story packages dropped by almost half from 2007–12. As Pew reports, "this adds up to a news industry that is more undermanned and unprepared to uncover stories, dig deep into emerging ones or to question information put into its hands."[30] Meanwhile, catching the mainstream news making mistakes, misrepresenting facts, and distracting the public has become the major business of satire news. As we will explain in the next section, it is the trust satire news has developed with the public that accounts for a lot of its power today.

Our Faithful Watchdog

One important change in satire news is that it is often perceived to be more trustworthy than the so-called real news. All of the factors described above have combined to make viewers suspicious of the mainstream news. Too often, in fact, they are reminded by satirists that the mainstream news is inaccurate, hyperbolic, and sometimes outright misleading. The Pew Research Center for the People & the Press reported in 2005 that 45% of Americans polled said they believed "little or nothing of what they read" in their daily newspapers. And a Harris poll from the same year found that only 12% of the public reported "high confidence" in the media—ranking it only ahead of law firms. In addition a 2003 Pew poll found that 32% of those surveyed considered news organizations to be immoral. As Susan D. Moeller explains, this sense of distrust is connected to the ongoing revelations of plagiarism, fabrications, and all-around sloppy journalism (quoted in Boler 174).

It should come as little surprise that as faith in the mainstream news has gone down, faith in the satirists has risen. In 2009 *Time Magazine* did an online poll that named Jon Stewart as the most trusted newsman since Walter Cronkite. Compared to Brian Williams, Katie Couric, and Charlie Gibson, Stewart logged 44% of the vote.[31] While Stewart was quick to dismiss the poll, stating that he is a comedian and not a newscaster, it is clear that he embodies something important for the public that they are not finding on mainstream news. And one of those things is that he is *not* claiming to be an accurate source of news; he is just doing it. His viewers understand the issues better and, in comparison to the mainstream news, he is able to communicate complex ideas in a way that is clear and nuanced. As Douglas Moran explains on the Salon.com blog, "Stewart is funny, absolutely; often hilariously so. But even more, he's *clear*. He distills topics that are the subject of incredibly tortured writing in places like the *New York Times* and the *Washington Post* into simple, easy-to-understand pieces that are, yes, funny, but also (God help us) clear and informative."[32]

Part of this trust derives from the fact that viewers simply believe that satire news is more truthful than corporate, ideologically-biased news. As Megan Boler and Stephen Turpin note, *The Daily Show* is appealing in large part because it is seen as more real or more truthful than the mainstream news (392). The only push back on the status quo comes from satire, which tends to make the "fake news" seem more truthful about the reality of US politics than the straight news. And as Jones notes, today the failures of the news media to perform a watchdog role for our democracy do not surprise: "the public is well aware that both television and politics are spectacle performances, and indeed, that the press and government are two mutually reinforcing and constituting institutions" (182). And as he points out, one of the problems is the highly emotive, irrational nature of much news presentation: "News media are part of the political spectacle, including journalists cum talk show pundits who act more like lapdogs to power than watchdogs of it, cheerleading embedded reporters, and patriotic news anchors who wear their hearts on their sleeve" (182). Think here of all the times Glenn Beck has cried on his show out of love for his nation.

But added to the increased trust audiences have of satire news, we also have increased accuracy. In some ways because satire news sources don't claim to be "fair and balanced," they are perceived as more so. Jones does a close study of the CNN coverage and *The Daily Show* coverage of the 2004 presidential campaign and finds that not only did Stewart's show offer equivalent degrees of information, he also went further in "helping viewers 'add things up,' that is, in helping citizens construct meaning from what may seem to be isolated or random events in traditional news reporting" (18). So added to trust and accuracy, we also have satire news offering their audiences better forms of critical reflection that help them sort through material, ask meaningful questions, and draw knowledgeable conclusions from the information presented. As McBeth and Clemons point out, the lack of focus on the cognitive side of satire news may be what makes it work more as a source of critical engagement (83).

All of these elements work together to make satire news perform more of the functions of the fourth estate than the fourth estate itself. In fact, some refer to it as the fifth estate. The term "fourth estate" usually refers to the press. Originating in 1787 Britain, the term was coined to refer to the "fourth" estate that would supervise the political power blocs of 18th-century Britain. The term suggested a free, independent press able to report on politics in unbiased ways. But, as we have explained, the fourth estate has been falling down on the job, which is why we have the new term the "fifth estate," which often refers to the watchdog of the watchdogs. Once the news media lost its independence and seemed increasingly controlled by the power elite, the fifth estate emerged as an outside, independent group that offered refreshing, uninfluenced information and opinion on pressing social issues. Today, the fifth estate is commonly seen as an alternative to the mainstream media. It includes not just satire news, but also the world of bloggers, independent reporters, and citizen-journalists that attempt to courageously report information that is being repressed or misrepresented. Thus, one excellent example is the work of Julian Assange and Wikileaks, which led to a film entitled *The Fifth Estate* that traced their story.

Resources like Wikileaks, Media Matters, factcheck.org, and a host of other alternative, independent news watchdog sites are now effectively doing the work that the supposed independent media in a democracy is meant to do. For citizens, though, the process is complex, since they have to filter the political bias of politicians in addition to the multiple biases of the news. And while our democracy depends on the newsgathering of these alternative venues, one difference between satire news and the work of Wikileaks is that the satire news is engaging, enlightening, and entertaining. We get the intrepid nature of alternative news in a package that amuses us at the same time. And this is why news satirists like Jon Stewart can reach a broader audience than the drier, more serious versions of fifth estate reporting. According to Gray, Jones, and Thompson, "satire TV often says what the press is too timid to say," but it does so in a way that audiences find enjoyable as well: "Satire can energize civic culture, engaging citizen-audience, inspiring public political discussion, and drawing citizens enthusiastically into the realm of the political with deft and dazzling ease" (4). Moreover, as we will explain in chapter 5 on the art of satire, satire is a unique form of comedy that encourages critical thinking and promotes reflection. It questions sources of power and the ways that they construct their versions of the truth. But in contrast to news channels like CNN and Fox News, it never claims authenticity or legitimacy—a move that in today's age of duplicity and hype allows viewers to trust satirists much more than mainstream news reporters. It is not just what satire news does; it is how it is perceived over and against the mainstream media. Understanding the fact that the public has lost faith in the watchdog ability of the news media is critical to understanding why many US citizens trust satirists more. Think about it: if a scandal breaks in politics, which news source are you more likely to trust to give you the real issues: CNN, Fox News, or *The Daily Show*?

The Satire News Top Five

OK, so the title for this section is tongue-in-cheek since there is no way to decide on the top five. In fact we had a list of about 20 options, which would have been too long. Then we decided to take out other excellent examples, like Colbert's Super PAC, since that was already covered in chapter 2. Brilliant satirical interventions like some of the work of Andy Borowitz, College Humor's excellent parody of the Gagnam Style video—Mitt Romney Style—and public satire events connected to Billionaires for Bush, all ended up out of the lineup. There's even more, but rather than go through a list of what we are not including we will just dive in and run down five of our favorite examples of important satire news.

The Onion, "Freedoms Curtailed in Defense of Liberty"

The satirical newspaper *The Onion* was founded in 1988 and added an online presence in 1996. In the first months after the 9/11 attacks on the United States it would be *The Onion* that was consistently a source of valuable critical thinking. In those first days after the attacks most television comedians, apart from Bill Maher, were circumspect. Paul Achter explains that, "For almost three weeks after the terrorist attacks of 2001, comedians in the U.S. embarked on an unusually serious assessment of comedy and its proper role in public life" (274). Leno and Letterman, true to form, "told fewer and safer jokes, mostly at the expense of easy targets like the Taliban and Osama bin Laden. *The Daily Show*'s Jon Stewart was so shaken he cried."[33] But *The Onion* responded quickly with a heavy dose of satire to help offer an alternative to the emotional nature of most post-9/11 news. They issued a special edition of their magazine a week after the attacks, with the slogan: "Attack on America: Holy Fucking Shit."[34] In their next issue they ran a story: "Shattered Nation Longs to Care About Stupid Bullshit Again." Achter describes the post-9/11 pieces in *The Onion* as a "useful public deliberation over proper emotional responses to a news-saturated moment" (299).

The news environment after 9/11 was one of the worst in the history of our nation. It was dominated by hysteria, misrepresentation, and scare tactics. But what was worse was that almost all mainstream media simply regurgitated the claims and ideologies of the Bush administration. Bush et al. cast post-9/11 America as a nation at war with an enemy. Everyone was divided into friend or foe and the quest for victory was wrapped in what Jamie Warner calls "prophetic dualism." The news media simply followed suit, repeating the party line and often working hard to prove loyalty. She notes that the editorial pages of 20 major US papers continued to repeat the same framing of the 9/11 events as the Bush team

(60). Even news anchor Dan Rather told David Letterman a few days after the attacks that he was fully behind the president: "George Bush is the President, he makes the decisions and you know, as just one American wherever he wants me to line up, just tell me where."[35] Such statements revealed the extent to which the news media had abdicated their fourth estate role. Thankfully, as Warner shows, *The Onion* refused to allow the rhetoric of the Bush administration to reign: "*The Onion* used satire to plant ambiguity into the carefully drawn and policed dualism of Good versus Evil, thus prompting the reader to reevaluate the frame. By introducing a little levity into the unflinching gravity of prophetic dualism, *The Onion* successfully reframed Bush administration policies for their readers and talked back to the powers that be" (62).

While there was a flurry of pieces released by *The Onion* in the post-9/11 era, we want to highlight one that we feel best shows how *The Onion* worked to remind citizens of the ways that their rights were being threatened by the post-9/11 culture of fear. Their piece "Freedoms Curtailed in Defense of Liberty" appeared in their October 10, 2001 issue, almost two weeks before President Bush signed the USA PATRIOT Act into existence—legislation that has had a major effect on privacy, due process, and other constitutional protections. In their piece, *The Onion* does an excellent job of portraying the lack of debate, reason, and democratic dialogue of those early post-9/11 days—a lack which effectively made it possible for the administration to push through legislation that curtailed citizen rights, to take us into an unjust war based on lies and deceptions, and to unravel most of the core values of our nation. The piece starts by covering a fictitious press conference by then-Press Secretary Ari Fleischer:

> Responding to the threats facing America's free democratic system, White House officials called upon Americans to stop exercising their democratic freedoms Monday. "In this time of national crisis, a time when our most cherished freedoms are threatened, all Americans—not just outspoken talk-show hosts like Bill Maher—must watch what they say," White House press secretary Ari Fleischer told reporters. "Now more than ever, if we want to protect democracy for future generations, it is vital that nobody speak out about the issues of the day."[36]

Unlike most mainstream news coverage of the plans to pass legislation limiting civil rights, *The Onion* was quick to remind the public that we should not submissively acquiesce to everything the Bush administration wanted to do. Most importantly, they reminded us that our democracy depends on our civil liberties and that we should be quick to reject any government efforts to take them away.

> Fleischer's sentiments echoed those of many executive-branch officials, who, in the wake of the Sept. 11 attacks, have called for broad-based limitations on civil liberties—and urged all patriotic, freedom-loving citizens to support those restrictions—in defense of the American way of life. "We live in a land governed by plurality of opinion in an open electorate, but we are now under siege by adherents of a fundamentalist, totalitarian belief system that tolerates no dissent," Attorney General John Ashcroft said. "Our most basic American values are threatened by an enemy opposed to everything for which our flag stands. That is why I call upon all Americans

to submit to wiretaps, e-mail monitoring, and racial profiling. Now is not the time to allow simplistic, romantic notions of 'civil liberties' and 'equal protection under the law' to get in the way of our battle with the enemies of freedom."[37]

The piece offers a refreshing and clear rebuttal of the twisted rhetoric used at the time to explain incursions into civil liberties as the only way to protect our freedom. And, despite a few variations, the quotes from Fleisher and Ashcroft were fairly true to form.

In 2011, in honor of their 1,000th issue, *The Onion* launched a movement to win the Pulitzer, even setting up its own website, "Americans for Fairness in Awarding Journalism Prizes," (AFAJP) which describes itself as a non-profit watchdog group committed to "exposing those who engage in improper journalism award giving": "We at AFAJP are asking how much longer the Pulitzer Board can turn a blind eye to what is, year in and year out, the most in-depth, comprehensive, elegant, and masterful reporting in the United States of America. How much longer must *The Onion* endure this grave injustice?"[38] So what do you think? Should *The Onion* win a Pulitzer? After all, according to *The Onion*'s tagline it is "America's finest News Source."

Michael Moore's Fahrenheit 9/11

We've talked a bit about Michael Moore's satirical interventions on television, but it is in the world of documentary filmmaking where he has really made his mark as a satirical innovator. Arguably, Moore's success with the genre has sparked a host of other satirists, like Morgan Spurlock of *Supersize Me*, to consider making satirical documentaries intended for widespread commercial release. Amber Day notes that this genre really depends on Moore as its iconic figure and she explains that the satiric documentary "combines a playful, satiric style with unabashed polemic, resulting in a product rooted simultaneously in mass culture entertainment and political activism, guerilla theater and documentary exposé" (99). But what also distinguishes Moore is the way that his films are grounded in a deep commitment to US democracy. As David Holloway explains, "*Fahrenheit 9/11* welded liberal culture-war positions to a republican vision rooted in Jeffersonian assumptions about citizenship and participatory democracy" (102).

Fahrenheit 9/11 was released in June of 2004, five months before the presidential elections and Moore was not shy about saying that his goal with the film was to see Bush lose reelection.[39] Beginning by showing the questionable, if not outright illegal, way that George Bush won the 2000 election against Al Gore, the film focuses on providing key information about the so-called War on Terror, the shady dealings of the Bush administration, and the failures of news media coverage on these issues. Moore insists again and again that what ails the nation is the corporate-power elite that constantly bypasses procedure, due process, and our legal system to acquire more and more power. He draws attention to the fact that the right may speak about its commitment to core values, but that that is simply empty rhetoric since the real attack on our nation stems from corporate assaults on citizens and conservative attacks on civil rights. When it was released, *Fahrenheit 9/11* gave the public a refreshing look at the ways that we had been consistently duped by our elected officials, it covers the signing of the USA PATRIOT Act, the decision to go to war in Afghanistan, and the war in Iraq—all events that were not in the best interest of the US public. It also suggests that when Fox News called the 2000 election for Bush before the full results had come in from Florida, it tilted the outcome in an election scandal that gravely affected public trust in our democratic process.

As Holloway notes, one of the central successes of the film is the way that it helps build a collective, populist community that is linked by their refusal to accept the mainstream narratives about 9/11 as valid: "Moore's depiction of the U.S. as a deeply divided society governed by incompetent, self-serving, authoritarian elites gave the film a populist, dissident chic that undercut prevailing representations of 9/11 as an assault on civilization, freedom, and democracy" (103). Moore uses satire at the service of democracy, staging fast-paced montages of images of Bush on vacation against information about all of the pressing issues he was ignoring. Using agitprop humor, caustic voice-overs, and other techniques of cognitive dissonance, Moore's thesis is that the greatest casualty on 9/11 was our democracy. The film mocks the logic that allowed us to accept those assaults on our national values, but it also uses a tone and critical mode that is at once sarcastic and serious. The combination is sharp and entertaining and it works to create a bond between the audience and the filmmaker—a bond meant to re-instantiate an engaged and committed civic community.

But perhaps what makes the film one of the best examples of satire news in the post-9/11 era is not just its ability to speak truth to power, but rather its ability to motivate public debate. As we mentioned in chapter 2, immediately upon its release it sparked controversy. Debate raged over whether all of its facts were right, over its narrative shortcuts, and its caustic tone—and these critiques came from both the right and the left (Day 106). Democratic Mayor of New York City, Ed Koch, who had endorsed Bush for president, called the film "propaganda" and British journalist Christopher Hitchens contended that the film contained "distortions and untruths."[40] The other side to the story, though, is that the film won not just a Palme d'Or at Cannes but also the People's Choice Award for Favorite Motion Picture, an unprecedented honor for a documentary.[41] The fact that the film won an award voted on by the general public tells us that behind the media critics there was a public that enjoyed the film and thought its message was significant.

The Yes Men and The New York Times Parody

The Yes Men are an activist duo that self-describes as culture-jammers. Culture-jamming is a term coined in 1984 by anti-consumerist social movements that employ tactics of disrupting or subverting media culture. One of the best-known culture-jamming groups is AdBusters, which played a major role in Occupy Wall Street. As we mentioned in chapter 2, The Yes Men take culture-jamming to a new level by impersonating major players in media, corporations, and government—a practice they call "identity correction." They came to fame by creating fake websites that often led to invitations for public speaking where one or both of the duo show up impersonating the organization they are spoofing. In their first stunt, they created a fake website for the World Trade Organization, which many thought was authentic, and they eventually were invited to speak in Austria. In one of the most famous stunts they posed as representatives of Dow Chemical and claimed that Dow was going to compensate victims of the Bhopal incident, and the story was picked up on BBC.

In The Yes Men hoax we want to cover they worked with a large group of collaborators including the Anti-Advertising Agency, CODEPINK, United for Peace and Justice, Not An Alternative, May First/People Link, Improv Everywhere, Evil Twin, and Cultures of Resistance. On November 12, 2008, one week after the election of Barack Obama to his first term, The Yes Men and their collaborators released a "fake" special issue of *The New York Times*. Approximately 80,000 copies of the special issue dated July 4, 2009 were handed out for free on the streets of New York, Los Angeles, and other major cities. Substituting the famous tagline "All the News That's Fit to Print" with "All the News We Hope to Print," the paper imagined the world the activists hoped to read about in the future. As Steve Lambert, one of the main contributors explains, "After the 2008 election of Barack Obama much of the United States population was excited about the future for the first time in years. With the Special Edition, we wanted to find a way to celebrate what we wanted, rather than criticize what we didn't. We wanted to create our own vision instead of responding to others."[42] The headline read "IRAQ WAR ENDS" (see Figure 3.3). Other articles included "Nations Sets its Sights on a Sane Economy," in addition to announcements of dozens of new initiatives, including an establishment of national health care, a maximum wage for CEOs and an article wherein George W. Bush accuses himself of treason for his actions during his years as president.[43] Consisting

Figure 3.3   The parody of *The New York Times* hits the streets
Photo Credit: Steve Lambert

of 14 pages of text and a supporting website the paper included World, National, Business, and Local sections with hypothetical headlines like "Maximum Wage Law Passes Congress," "USA Patriot Act Repealed," and "All Public Universities To Be Free." Lambert explains that "each story provided a fictional history of how such a thing could happen on such a timeline through grass-roots pressure using real-world details. A replica of the *New York Times* website mirrored the stories online and was visited by over 300,000 people in the first two days."[44]

While *The New York Times* was mainly flattered by the spoof, it is worth remembering that the mainstream newspaper had been involved in a number of scandals over its inaccuracies and war-mongering in the 9/11 era. One of the most egregious cases was that of Judith Miller who was caught in a controversy over her coverage of weapons of mass destruction in Iraq, even after the information had been proven to be false. Later the paper found a number of her stories to be inaccurate, but it was her involvement in the Valerie Plame affair—where Plame's identity as a member of the CIA was leaked—that was the most damning. Miller refused to reveal the source that had leaked the information. Later in court, that source was exposed to be Scooter Libby, Vice President Cheney's Chief of Staff. The case had many twists but to most in the public it was evidence of the way that the Bush administration used the mainstream press to its ends. And it proved that *The New York Times* was not above the fray.

This is why one of their most well-known columnists was represented in the hoax version of the paper. As The Yes Men describe it on their website where they list the pieces on the spoof: "Less momentous, but poignant, Tom Friedman's letter of resignation, full of remorse for his consistently idiotic and fact free predictions about the Iraq war."[45] A direct link to the failures of *The New York Times* to present accurate information in the midst of a national crisis, the paper imagined a brighter future. While it took a jab at the failures of the mainstream news, it did not do so with sarcasm or negative snark; instead, one of the remarkable features of this satirical stunt was its utopic vision and hopeful tone.

Jon Stewart Takes On Jim Cramer of CNBC

The news media generally failed to help inform our citizens about the key issues revolving around the attacks of 9/11, but many hoped those failures were tied to the fears generated by such a traumatic event. Those hopes were dashed when the news media failed again to help educate the citizenry in the face of the economic collapse of 2009. As Jones explains, "television news media have been implicated in two of the most egregious public failings of the new millennium—the fabricated reasons for the Iraq War and the American banking and financial sector crisis in 2008–2009" (117). Even though we dedicate a chapter just to the comedy of Stewart and Colbert, we had to include this one in our lineup since it was one of the best examples of the way that satire news called attention to news media failures during the financial crisis.

As you may recall, the financial crisis really hit the wall at the end of Bush's second term and was in full swing when Obama took office. Rather than offer a change in course, Obama effectively continued the bailouts that Bush had initiated. Banks, insurance companies, and automakers all lined up for government hand-outs and Obama did not disappoint. But where he differed from Bush was in his plan to also support those that lost their mortgages. This then quickly led to media frenzy over the "losers" who were now mooching off of government. News media channels like CNBC were at the forefront of this frenzy, quickly pegging the US citizens caught in the mortgage crisis as idiots who had bought a more expensive house than they could afford. Meanwhile, the banks, corporations, and Wall Streeters who actually caused the crisis were spared.

While *The Daily Show* had aired some segments critical of the news coverage of the financial crisis and bailouts, it would not be until March 4, 2009 when Stewart would really focus in on the topic. That evening he had planned to interview CNBC's Rick Santelli, who actually didn't show, but that didn't stop Stewart from airing an eight-and-a-half minute segment mocking the way that CNBC had covered the crisis. The clip starts by reminding viewers that CNBC's motto is that it is "the only business network that has the information you need." There are then a series of clips that show reporters making claims that turn out to be patently false. In one we see images from *Mad Money* on March 11, 2008, with a clip of the show's host, Jim Cramer, stating "Bear Sterns is fine," followed by a black screen and then the text: "Bear Sterns went under six days later."[46] The segment continues to show a series of clips where CNBC misleads the public, telling them about the financial security of institutions that were anything but secure and touting the strength of a market that was in the midst of a collapse.

Cramer didn't like the critique and he quickly responded by stating that *The Daily Show* was little more than a "variety show."[47] And thus the feud between Stewart and Cramer picked up steam, leading to a face off on *The Daily Show* on March 12, 2009. The confrontation was much publicized, making the episode one of the most watched in *The Daily Show*'s history, with 2.3 million viewers and a front page article in *USA Today*. Stewart began by pointing out the "fake" news of CNBC's coverage of the crisis, claiming that Cramer had simply accepted the information fed to him by corporations and had not fulfilled his duty as a reporter. Following some of the same claims he had made previously on *Crossfire*, Stewart then called Cramer out for allowing entertainment value to overtake serious reporting: "I understand you want to make finance entertaining, but it's not a fucking game. And when I watch that, I get, I can't tell you how angry that makes me. Because what it says to me is: you all know. You all know what's going on. You know, you can draw a straight line from those shenanigans to the stuff that was being pulled at Bear, and AIG, and all this derivative market stuff that is this weird Wall Street side bet."[48] Cramer responded by mostly agreeing with Stewart on his assessments and the interview ended with Stewart suggesting, "Maybe we can remove 'In Cramer We Trust' and go back to the fundamentals and I can go back to making fart noises and funny faces." To which Cramer responded: "I think we make that deal right here."

The impact of the interview was widespread. Clips from *The Daily Show* were instant memes and Stewart was hailed in the media as having "won" the debate.

The interview was covered all over the mainstream media. As *Newsweek* reported on the showdown: "Cramer's excuse: CEOs lied. Stewart's retort: act like a real journalist. Stewart did."[49] In almost all coverage of the interview it was clear that Stewart was being treated like a serious journalist and Cramer was coming off as a buffoon. James Fallows of *The Atlantic* wrote a piece entitled "It's True: Jon Stewart has become Edward R. Murrow."[50] Not only was the media relieved to see Stewart finally doing the work of serious reporting, even Obama's press secretary Robert Gibbs responded by saying he was pleased to see somebody asking "a lot of tough questions."[51] Perhaps as an even greater sign of Stewart's impact, viewership of CNBC dropped by 10% in the first three days after the interview.[52] Once again the US public had satire to thank for helping offer insightful information on issues central to our nation.

Tina Fey Does Sarah Palin

On August 29, 2008, presidential candidate John McCain announced that Alaska Governor Sarah Palin would be his running mate. The selection of Palin goes down in history as one of the worst choices for running mate, surpassing even the mockery that arose from the candidacy and election of Dan Quayle. Quayle ran with George Bush Sr. and was constantly characterized in the media as incredibly uninformed, offering the US public fun quotes like: "I love California, I practically grew up in Phoenix."[53] And of course Bush Jr. offered his own set of disturbing bloopers. Palin, though, took things to a whole new level. Not only was she full of language gaffes, not only did she seem woefully unprepared to hold the second-highest position in our government, but she unabashedly relished her "maverick" identity, which allowed her to boldly say things that had no grounding in reality. Having been chosen based on her sassy, nonconformist personality, a trait the campaign thought matched well with McCain, she had barely been vetted before the announcement was made. But even in haste McCain's advisors nailed what would become some of the greatest problems with McCain's running mate in a report meant to explore her weaknesses: "Democrats upset at McCain's anti-Obama 'celebrity' advertisements will mock Palin as an inexperienced beauty queen whose main national exposure was a photo-spread in *Vogue* in February 2008. Even in campaigning for governor, she made a number of gaffes, and the *Anchorage Daily News* expressed concern that she often seemed 'unprepared or over her head' in a campaign run by a friend."[54]

From the start the McCain-Palin campaign tried to carefully control press access to Palin. But despite the limited access, it would be her interview with CBS Evening News anchor Katie Couric that would begin the trouble for Palin's public image. Couric asked a series of questions that Palin seemed unprepared to handle including the now infamous one on why Alaska's proximity to Russia would help her foreign policy experience. But one of the best zingers came when Couric asked her about the proposed economic bailout:

COURIC: Why isn't it better, Governor Palin, to spend $700 billion helping middle-class families, who are struggling with health care, housing, gas and groceries, allow them to spend more and put more money into the economy instead of helping these big financial institutions that played a role in creating this mess?

PALIN: That's why I say, I, like every American I'm speaking with, we're ill about this position that we have been put in where it is the taxpayers looking to bail out, but ultimately, what the bailout does is help those who are concerned about the health care reform that is needed to help shore up our economy, helping tho—it's got to be all about job creation too, shoring up our economy, and putting it back on the right track, so health care reform and reducing taxes and reigning in spending has got to accompany tax reductions and tax relief for Americans. And trade, we've got to see trade as opportunity, not as—competitive—scary thing, but one in five jobs being created in the trade sector today, we've got to look at that as more opportunity. All those things under the umbrella of job creation. This bailout is a part of that.[55]

In a certain sense, then, no one needed any help mocking Palin, she did it on her own with no assistance at all. And that is where Tina Fey of *Saturday Night Live* fit in. The late night comedy show had a long history of political impersonations so as soon as Palin was nominated, it was clear Fey would be tapped to imitate her. And then there was the fact that they bore an uncanny resemblance. The first impersonation took place in September of 2008 when Fey as Palin paired up with Amy Poehler as Hilary Clinton for "A Nonpartisan Message from Governor Sarah Palin & Senator Hillary Clinton." The sketch began to lay out the characterization of Palin as an unqualified upstart: At one point Fey/Palin exclaims "I can see Russia from my house!"[56] Enough said.

Fey's impersonation signaled a new moment for entertainment television, since it quickly became an essential component of Palin's public image. As Jones explains, "while the McCain-Palin campaign and the news media were simultaneously attempting to 'define' Sarah Palin for the voting public, *SNL* took this nationally unknown politician and through its satirical commentary on news footage, cemented a largely negative and damning public perception of the candidate" (4). The momentum would just continue as Fey reprised her impersonation shortly after the Couric interview. While Couric's interview had exposed all the public needed to know about Palin's lack of qualifications, it opened the door for a host of queries about whether or not Couric had "gone after" Palin. Rather than focus on the ridiculous answers Palin gave, media attention wondered whether Couric had been unfair. Conservative filmmaker Joseph Ziegler said that Couric was "obviously trying to trap Governor Palin into saying something stupid or extreme."[57] Regardless of the partisan hype, Couric had laid the groundwork in what McCain's senior strategist, Steve Schmidt, later called the "most consequential negative interview that a candidate for national office has gone through."[58] Next up was Fey who performed Palin by simply repeating her words. In that sketch Poehler impersonated Couric and Fey quoted nearly verbatim the words and gestures of Palin: the result was devastating. Taken out of the serious news realm of the Couric interview, Palin's words seemed even *more* absurd. As Jones points out, "Fey and SNL transported the viewer out of the serious context associated with journalism—one that offered the viewer little recourse beyond befuddlement or disbelief—and recontextualized the encounter through a comedic lens, thereby granting the viewer a different perspective from which to view the event" (4).

Even though Palin would later appear on *SNL* attempting to recover her image, it was too late and each of the subsequent interactions between the McCain/Palin campaign and the comedy show proved more damning to their credibility—both McCain and Palin appeared on the show, each time to greater absurd effect. The Fey/Palin impersonations are credited with putting the final nails in the campaign coffin. And they are also credited with boosting the ratings of *SNL* to a level not seen since 1994 (Jones 4). Reaching segments of the voting public that might not have tuned into the Couric interviews, the parody riffed on Couric and made the interviews far more politically powerful. Moreover, the parody revealed the increasing power of satire entertainment to shape public discourse about politics (see Figure 3.4).

We have run down five top examples of the ways that satire news has been more powerful than the so-called serious news since 9/11. In each example you have seen the way that entertainment has combined with politically relevant news coverage to help inform the public about the issues at stake in our democracy. And in each case these comedic interventions have made a difference. Across a range of genres—from documentary to print, from comedy television to internet newspaper, from culture-jamming hoax to impersonation—satire has become one of the primary ways that the public understands politics and acts politically. But isn't such a development a frightening prospect? Do we really want citizens to form opinions about political candidates from watching *SNL*? Should we really be learning about the financial crisis from a comedian? And wouldn't it be better if *The New York Times* really were "all the news that's fit to print"? Well, as we've pointed out, the trouble with such thinking is the idea that critical thinking and entertainment are oppositional. What we are witnessing today is a blurring of pleasure and politics, and when that connection happens through satire, it turns out that the outcome can have extremely positive effects for our democracy.

Figure 3.4   Fox News mistakes Tina Fey for Sarah Palin[59]

Spectacular Dissent: Satire News as Ethical Spectacles

This chapter has pointed to a number of key ways that the mediascape changed after 9/11 transforming satire from not only a comment on news, but also an actual source of it. And key to that transformation was the sense that satirists were more trustworthy than mainstream news figures. Connected to these shifts was the progressive entertainment value of all news sources, a fact that Jones and Baym point out shows no sign of reversal. With the rise of satire, though, came the logical concern that satire had no place being the source of news. Instead, news should be the source of news, right? Even if news has more entertainment value, it should inform citizens instead of the comedians. While it is absolutely essential to continue to struggle to make the news media accountable to the public and committed to informative reporting, we believe that there are special features of satire that offer unique opportunities for activating an engaged and informed citizenry.

We discussed changes in citizenship in the introduction and will return to it in future chapters, just as we will also describe specific features of satire that position it as a distinctive feature of democratic deliberation, but we wanted to conclude this chapter by pointing to the way that satire news works as a form of "ethical spectacle." Media scholar and activist Stephen Duncombe works on the idea of an "ethical spectacle" in *Dream: Reimagining Progressive Politics in an Age of Fantasy*. Duncombe argues that progressive politics lost its claim to utopic thinking, to dreaming, when it became largely dominated by negative politics. He urges a return to the sort of passionate engagement that fires up citizens to fight for causes in which they believe. For Duncombe, the ethical spectacle can challenge the contemporary era of spectacle-heavy politics. It makes political information both informative and fun and takes away from the circus of distracting politics that is full of lies and misinformation. In this way, satire news is ethical spectacle since it marries showmanship with a heavy dose of reality. He explains, "For spectacle to be ethical it must not only reveal itself as what it is but also have as its foundation something real" (154). In this way a media event like Fey's rendering of Palin reveals and amplifies "the real *through* spectacle" (155). What Duncombe explains is that political engagement is activated through "people's fantasies and desires through a language of images and associations" (121). Anger and outrage over Palin's selection motivates a population to vote, just as disgust at the poor reporting of Cramer will turn people away from CNBC and towards *The Daily Show*.

Building on Duncombe's theory Angelique Haugerud develops the idea of "spectacular dissent" in her study of Billionaires for Bush. She explains that the spectacle of satire today performs important democratic dissent and critique. Analyzing the theatrical stunts of the Billionaires, she shows how they "contrast two protest modes: an older, 'traditional' form that involves marches, chants, and speeches, and an ostensibly new and playful theatrical form" (42). In a similar fashion, all of the satire news examples we have covered here follow the flow of spectacular dissent. Rather than angrily decrying the pathetic quality of today's news media, these satirists correct the story in a way that is lively and fun. The jabs here are cloaked in humor, a move that makes them not just more palatable, but also more meaningful. Viewers can engage with the humor, sharing it, repeating it, and enjoying it in ways that add much more political power than we had previously been willing to consider. As Gournelos and Greene point out in their analysis of the Couric/Palin interview, the public has greater accessibility to the text and to multiple versions of it; specifically, Gournelos and Greene point to "the ability of audiences to see it online, the subsequent negotiation of the text by *SNL*, audiences watching the *SNL* clip, and its continued life on news outlets, blogs, and comedy shows" (xv). For them we are witnessing an era when "political action and activism are quantitatively and qualitatively different from simpler concepts of performance and consumption" (xv).

And here is where the joke really counts. Because satire offers a specific sort of joke, one that demands audience participation and reflection; it engages the viewer in a way that standard news does not. As Duncombe explains, the key to the ethical spectacle of satire news is not just its entertaining wrapper of fun; it is also that the satire is not complete without audience participation. As he puts it, what is so magical about satirical comedy is that, when it works, "the audience and the comic create something together" (132). A bond is developed of trust and hope and knowledge. Today that process happens more in satire than in the "real news." If news at one time served the citizenry as a faithful fourth estate, that role is now played by the satirical fifth estate.

4

The Dynamic Duo: Jon Stewart and Stephen Colbert Redefine Political Satire

Did you ever go to a taping of *The Colbert Report*? Well, if you had, you would have heard that as an audience member you had a job to do. Many of us who joined the audience over the last years heard that it was our job to cheer Colbert to an Emmy victory. Why? Because *The Colbert Report* was tired of all of the Emmys going to *The Daily Show*. The Emmy, which is the television equivalent of an Academy Award, has a number of categories for awards, and programs like *The Colbert Report* and *The Daily Show* compete in the category of "Outstanding Variety, Music, or Comedy Series." From 2003–12 *The Daily Show* won the Emmy in this category, beating out *The Colbert Report*, which was nominated from 2006–12. Thus Colbert began a rivalry between the shows as he plugged for *The Colbert Report* to win the coveted award. Each year that *The Daily Show* won, Colbert would bemoan Stewart's success on the *Report*.

But that would all end in 2013 when Colbert turned the tide and his show won two Emmys for "Outstanding Variety, Music, or Comedy Series" and "Outstanding Writing for a Variety, Music, or Comedy Program," thereby ending the ten-year winning streak of *The Daily Show*—the longest winning streak of any program in the award's history. In typical in-character egotistical fashion, the on-air Colbert boasted about his award. In fact, he began his bit by saying that he had no idea what came over him at the awards ceremony when he thanked his staff—since, of course, he was the only person responsible for the show. He then phoned Stewart to rub in his victory, actually using his award statues to dial the phone. But Stewart wasn't going to let Colbert call all the shots and he surprised Colbert by answering the phone while popping out in a surprise visit to the show. He then refused to humor Colbert by acting upset, congratulating him instead on an award well deserved. As the two dueled over whether Stewart would demonstrate sadness over Colbert's win, thereby satisfying Colbert's desire to see Stewart jealous, Stewart offered the ultimate twist: he is executive producer of Colbert's show, so, in essence, the award is *really* his anyway and he has just won for the eleventh time (see Figure 4.1).

Figure 4.1   Stewart celebrates Colbert's win by pointing out that as Executive Producer he really gets the credit[1]

All silliness aside, and there has been lots of silliness between these two shows, the story of Jon Stewart's *The Daily Show* and Stephen Colbert's *The Colbert Report* is central to understanding the ways that satire has radically changed our nation's politics. One telling factoid is that these shows have not only been nominated for and won in the category of "Outstanding Variety, Music, or Comedy Program" for Emmys; they have also been nominated for and won Peabody Awards. Peabody Awards recognize distinguished and meritorious public service by radio and television stations, networks, producing organizations, and individuals. Reflecting excellence in quality rather than popularity or commercial success, they are awarded to about 25–35 winners out of a pool of about 1,000 nominees. *The Daily Show* has won for election coverage twice, in 2000 and 2004. The citation for the 2004 award reads: "Through the momentous weeks of the 2004 Presidential Campaigns, Jon Stewart and cohorts provided the kind of cathartic satire that deflates pomposity on an equal opportunity basis. Somehow this sharp commentary made the real issues more important than ever."[2] *The Colbert Report* also won twice: In 2007 for its excellence in news and entertainment and in 2011 for its Super PAC related coverage. The 2007 citation reads: "What started as a parody of punditry is now its own political platform. Whether serving as a campaign site or 'merely' mocking television itself, the result is a program that inspires viewers to laugh, think, and sabotage Wikipedia. Colbert elicits fear from members of Congress, expands our vocabulary, and skewers personality-driven journalism— all while maintaining his composure as an egotistical, but lovable, uber-patriot."[3]

As these citations show, both programs have gone well beyond traditional comedy and entertainment; they signal a new era of political satire that is highly entertaining and also highly significant in shaping the way that the public thinks about major new stories. As testament to the degree to which this form of entertainment is performing a public service, Jeffrey Jones, author of *Entertaining Politics* and a scholar whose work has influenced many of the arguments in this book, became the director of the Peabody Awards in 2013. While the awards are for "excellence" and go to the "best of the best," meaning that entertainment is not ruled out as a category of evaluation, historically the awards have gone to serious programming that has brought important information to the public; overall, they are considered to be the "most prestigious and selective awards in electronic media."[4] The fact that *The Daily Show* and *The Colbert Report* have won these awards shows how seriously satire is being taken these days.

Spanning Emmy Awards and Peabodys, *The Daily* Show and *The Colbert Report* highlight the bizarre world where the most entertaining satirical news can be the most informative, and where programs on Comedy Central do more to inform the citizenry than programs on all-news stations. As we've explained thus far, today's satire emerges at a unique moment in US history where a variety of factors have all converged to challenge the way that the public gets information central to making informed decisions. That said, though, it would be fair to say that it was the combined punch of satire's dynamic duo—Jon Stewart and Stephen Colbert—that took the possibilities for satire to a whole new level. As the many other satirical examples we cover in this book show, these two comedians are not alone: there is more public satire today than ever and it is created by both citizen-satirists and professionals. Nevertheless, as this chapter will show, Stewart and Colbert played a specific role in advancing public discourse and democratic possibility through their own unique versions of political satire. This chapter focuses on the dynamic duo of contemporary political satire and shows how their distinctive version of political advocacy and comedy opened the door to an especially potent form of US satire—one which has become a model in other parts of the world. After giving background on the two shows and the comedians behind them, we then discuss the role they have played as media makers, especially vis-à-vis the mainstream news media. We then discuss a paradigmatic Stewart-Colbert collaboration—the Rally to Restore Sanity and/or Fear that took place on the National Mall in 2010. Next we describe differences between the two shows in an effort to highlight their satirical synergy. While *The Colbert Report* ends in 2014 and *The Daily Show* will go on without its counterpart, there can be little doubt that the intersection of these two shows played a major role in advancing political satire.

A Tale of Two Satire Shows

The Daily Show first aired in 1996 with host Craig Kilborn. In those early years the show was shaped as a mockery of entertainment news and early segments included "This Day in Hasselhoff History." Kilborn's version of the program was much less politically focused than Stewart's and it created lots of segments that were aimed at making US citizens look uninformed and stupid. Jeff MacGregor, a reviewer from *The New York Times,* called the show a "not-quite parody of a not-quite newscast" and criticized it for being cruel and for lacking a central editorial vision or ideology. He described it as "bereft of an ideological or artistic center…precocious but empty."[5] That lack of focus would all change when Stewart took over the show in 1999.

Before taking over *The Daily Show* Stewart had hosted *Short Attention Span Theater* on Comedy Central and two shows on MTV. His career began with stand-up comedy—a skill he continues to use on his show today. Many of the staff under Kilborn remained with Stewart, including Colbert who had joined the show in 1997 as one of four on-location reporters. Colbert was able to observe firsthand how the show changed when Stewart took over as host. In an interview after Stewart had assumed the host position, Colbert explained the difference between the two hosts: "The field pieces we did were character-driven pieces—like, you know, guys who believe in Bigfoot. Whereas now, everything is issue- and news-driven pieces, and a lot of editorializing at the desk. And a lot of use of the green screen to put us in false locations. We're more of a news show; we were more of a magazine show then."[6] Colbert noted that one of the most significant shifts was that Stewart wanted to intersect with current headlines: "The first thing I noticed, was that our field pieces were coming out of the news, and not in sort of opposition to them."[7]

The show shifted to a more biting and politically motivated form of satire while continuing to work on excellent writing that could pop the entertainment value of the program. Supported by a brilliant cast of comedians, Stewart's program had a number of recurring segments that allowed the show to mock current news media practices. Among them was the hilariously funny and intensely biting series "Even Stevphen," which placed Colbert alongside Steve Carrell. In a parody of the sorts of opinion-driven content that gluts up cable news stations, the two comedians would begin debating an important topic and then would end by lobbing insults at one another. In a retrospective series on the show entitled, "10 F#@king Years" Stewart explains, "In our ten years on the air we have tried hard to further the state of public discourse. Of course we have failed and never more nobly than when 'Even Stevphen' came along, a heated discussion on the issues of the day."[8] Regardless of the issue that was meant to frame the debate, the two comedians would quickly devolve into hurling invectives and shouting at each other.

The general format for the show has Stewart run down headlines with clips of media coverage to illustrate his points. Often all he has to do is show a ridiculous news segment and point at it while looking perplexed to make his point. Again and again Stewart emphasizes that the current news media is not doing its job of offering valuable information to the public. This rundown is usually followed by a bit that includes one or more of the staff of correspondents either on location or in the studio. The last part of the show is the interview. Guests are often recent authors but Stewart also speaks with entertainers, media figures, and politicians regularly.

The momentum for the political edge of the program would jump with its move to cover the Democratic and Republican National Conventions in 2000, when Colbert reported from the floor, astonished he had been given a press pass. And then with the election of George W. Bush the show switched into high gear as it became one of the most significant sources of counter-information to the mainstream news and to administration rhetoric that the public had available. Stewart became laser-focused on exposing the lies of the administration and the failures of the news media to point them out. As Jones explains, "Illuminating such lies became central to the show's moral mission" (75). "What we try to do," Stewart contends, "is point out the artifice of things, that there's a guy behind the curtain pulling levers" (quoted in Jones 75). "But," as Jones points out, "it was the conflu-ence of these two forces—masterful information management techniques and fear-mongering by the Bush administration and a television news media that helped facilitate these political deceptions and ruses through its weak reporting and tendency toward patriotic spectacle—that made TDS the perfect vehicle for interrogating the truth" (75). One of the central features of the show that made it a groundbreaking satirical show was the way that it combined comedic fun, sharp political critique, and view of another reality—one which seemed increasingly absent in most other forms of media. As Stewart explained in 2002: "There are times when it's not about making a joke, it's about having to acknowledge what is going on, so you can feel like you're still in the same world as everyone else."[9]

As *The Daily Show* became a source for entertaining satire and incisive political commentary, Colbert's role on the show became increasingly central and he filled in as anchor for Stewart on a number of occasions, including the full week of March 3, 2002, when Stewart was scheduled to host *Saturday Night Live*. Then the day after the 2004 Emmys in Los Angeles, when *The Daily Show* won both the Best Writing and Best Variety Series awards, Colbert met with Doug Herzog, the head of Comedy Central.[10] At that time Herzog was interested in expanding *The Daily Show* franchise, and Stewart and Ben Karlin (*The Daily Show*'s executive producer) were looking for a TV series for their production company, Busboy. Colbert was the logical lead for such a project since Steve Carrell had already left the program and they did not want to lose Colbert's talent as well. So, at the meeting with Herzog, Stewart and colleagues made a one-line pitch: "Our version of the *O'Reilly Factor* with Stephen Colbert."[11] After the meeting, Herzog agreed to an eight-week run without even asking for a pilot.

But the idea for the show did not exactly come out of nowhere. In 2004, before pitching *The Colbert Report* to Herzog, a series of spoof commercials had appeared on *The Daily Show* announcing an "exciting new *Daily Show* spin-off." The ads showed Colbert channeling his own version of an angry O'Reilly shouting at guests, threatening to cut their mics, and aggressively insisting that he was right. Thus the show's core concept was centered on Colbert playing a bombastic pundit-like character that would be familiar to cable-news junkies—a role he had often channeled on *The Daily Show*. In an interview with *USA Today* before the first show aired Colbert explained: "Shows like *O'Reilly* or *Scarborough* or even to some extent Aaron Brown's are more about the personality of the host and less about the headlines," He went on to say: "My show is really about opinions; it's about bluster and personality."[12] Thus, *The Colbert Report* would hinge on the development of his persona, an opinionated pundit based on "the manliness of Stone Phillips and his 'thick lacrosse-player's neck' and Geraldo Rivera's 'sense of mission' as a 'crusading warrior' of journalism." But Colbert explained, "Bill O'Reilly, an 'admirable' talent—'I watch (him) with my mouth open,'" would be "clearly the model for his satire."[13]

Much of the context for the show reflected its historic moment. Years after Stewart had set the tone for incisive political satire, and over four years after

George W. Bush assumed office and then led the United States into war in Iraq as part of an ongoing and permanent "war on terror," *The Colbert Report* was imagined as a complement to the sort of satire available on *The Daily Show*. Colbert's character was envisioned as "right-wing, egomaniacal, fact-averse ('factose intolerant'), God-fearing, and super-patriotic." The Colbert persona "claims to be an independent who is often mistaken for a Republican, but uniformly despises liberals and generally agrees with the actions and decisions of George W. Bush and the Republican Party."[14] The idea was to parody the so-called independent thinking of a figure like O'Reilly, while also exposing the critical flaws and logical fallacies that underpin conservative punditry. This was evidenced by one of the questions that Colbert used to enjoy asking of many of his guests: "George W. Bush: great President, or the *greatest* President?"[15]

Perfecting the One-Two Punch: Stewart and Colbert Conquer the Infotainment World

How common is it for you to think of today's news as infotainment? As we've explained, this process has been decades in the making, but the transition today is almost complete—and it signals a shift that is still troublesome for many media scholars. Is infotainment fundamentally bad for our democracy? Or is it merely a new sign of how citizens engage with the news? What are we to make of these changes? Well, while the answer may be tricky, one thing is clear: it can't be considered without attention to the satire of Jon Stewart and Stephen Colbert, who, as we will argue here, are the preeminent infotainers in the world today. Angelique Haugerud describes a 2009 political cartoon in her book on the Billionaires for Bush that exemplifies how satire has come to offer the public a source of trustworthy information in a format that is attractive to them. The ad imagined a world with no more newspapers and a woman asking "Without newspapers, who would hold people in positions of power accountable?" The man walking beside her replies, "Jon Stewart" (31). The joke, of course, is how it came to be that a comedian has earned that degree of public trust. How did an entertainer become more trusted than a news reporter? Well, the only way to answer that question is to better understand infotainment.

The terms "infotainment" and "infotainer" were first used in September 1980 at the Joint Conference of The Association for Information Management (ASLIB), the Institute of Information Scientists, and the Library Association in Sheffield, UK. Perhaps, given the term's largely negative associations today, it will come as a surprise to learn that infotainment actually first referred to scientist-comedians who self-designated as "the infotainers." Offering a combination of entertainment and information, the infotainers were a group of British information scientists who put on comedy shows at their professional conferences between 1980 and 1990.[16] We find it important to remember that the term was first used for comedians who had the purpose of educating their audience. Today the phrase has mostly moved out of the space of direct live performance to describe media practices, and the phrase is mostly used in a derogatory fashion. In today's vocabulary infotainment designates "information-based media content or programming that also includes entertainment content in an effort to enhance popularity with audiences and consumers" (Demers 143). And usually the idea is that that mix of entertainment and news is a bad thing.

But what if the real infotainment is not news with an entertaining spin, but rather the reverse—entertainment with a news spin? From the start both Stewart's and Colbert's shows had a clear interest in combining topical news items of significance to US citizens, but perhaps more than anything both shows have wanted to be fun and funny. It is worth remembering that while we might be pointing out their serious impact on contemporary politics, they have always denied their interest in being a source of the news. They consistently reject the idea that their shows are news programs, pointing out that they air on Comedy Central, and that it is not their responsibility to inform the public about anything. And they deny any interest in influencing politics as well. That is not their intent, they insist: according to them, their intent is to be entertaining—nothing more, nothing less.

Should we believe them, though? As we will explain in more detail in the next chapter on the art of satire, crying pure entertainment is one of the common moves for the satirist. Satirical comedians always use the cover of comedy to hide from accusations of slander or worse. As Megan Boler explains, "The appeal of satire and irony is in large part the frank admission of complicity with the spectacle. Beginning with the self-assignation of 'fake news' (*The Daily Show* is known as 'the most trusted name in fake news'), both Jon Stewart and Stephen Colbert insistently assert that their shows are merely comedy and not news, have no partisan agenda, and do not claim to be outside of the spectacle of commodity. They assert this complicity in the following ways: by referring to their corporate owners; by dismissing their own authoritative claims; by recognizing the immediate contradiction of the very fact that they exist and appear through broadcast at all ['I would not exist but for the corporation that feeds me']" (386). Again and again they try to tell us not to take them seriously and not to confuse them with news reporters.

The satirist does not want the burden of responsibility of the reporter. But the satirist also does not want to be linked to the news reporter because such a move ignores the art of satire and its status as comedy. In an interview with *The New York Times Magazine* that appeared shortly before the first episode of *The Colbert Report*, Colbert played with the idea that what Stewart and he are doing is serious:

> *Will you continue the tradition of political satire that allowed "The Daily Show" to inject so much welcome gravity into the light, goofy realm of late-night TV?*
> Jon would be so happy as a comedian to hear that he injected gravity. Can I be the one to tell him?
> *Seriously, what do you have against gravity?*
> If we thought we added gravity to anything, we would feel that we had failed. We're just trying to ease the pain of people who feel the world is going insane and no one is noticing. We're like Cortaid, something not too heavy that is used for a rash or a bug bite. I wouldn't use it for a wound.
> *I think you're underestimating the influence the show has had. People might perceive it as substantive because the jokes happen to be political.*
> But I guarantee you that it has no political objective. I think it's dangerous for a comedian to say, "I have a political objective." Because then they stop being a comedian and they start being a politician. Or a lobbyist.[17]

Colbert may have jokingly opposed comedy and politics, but effective satire bridges these two realms in a way that is critically productive as well as artfully entertaining, thus becoming a paradigmatic case of infotainment. As Colbert mentioned during the rundown of upcoming pieces during the show's premiere episode, "Finally, a new show premieres, and changes the world."[18] While the phrase mocked the idea of a television show changing the world, the joke sets him up only to win, since if he actually does change the world, he can claim that he never intended to. And if he doesn't change the world, he can at least have fun trying. To confuse matters, in a few of their published interviews Stewart and Colbert admitted to the fact that they are interested in engaging their audiences in ways that help them practice more informed political decision-making. In an interview with Terry Gross for NPR Colbert spoke about how *The Daily Show* had made his comedy more political, mentioning that Stewart pushed him to go beyond humor for laughs to humor with a political opinion. He explained that up until that moment he had mostly done frivolous comedy, jokes about Ted Kennedy drinking too much for *Second City*, or comedy free of references to people, places, or politics with Amy Sedaris. According to Colbert it wasn't until he worked with Stewart on *The Daily Show* that he began making politically engaged comedic choices.[19]

All joking aside, there is plenty of evidence that Stewart and Colbert are having an effect on the public's understanding of issues, on the definition of news media, and on political accountability—and we will detail some specific examples of these activities below. One of the most significant effects of these shows is in the realm of trust. Both comedians have been considered by the public as trustworthy news sources. As we've mentioned already, in a 2007 Pew study, Stewart landed in fourth place tied with Brian Williams, Dan Rather, and Anderson Cooper as the journalist that Americans most admired. This adds to the polls that show viewers of these shows as more knowledgeable than those of mainstream news programs. Baym, for instance, says that they should be considered an example of "alternative journalism" rather than fake news ("The Daily Show" 261). Jones also eschews the "fake" moniker for Stewart's work: "*The Daily Show* is fake only in that it refuses to make claims to authenticity. But being "fake" does not mean that the information it imparts is untrue. Indeed, as with most social and political satire, its humor offers a means of reestablishing common sense truths to counter the spectacle, ritual, pageantry, artifice, and verbosity that often cloak the powerful" (182). The public has lost trust in the mainstream news and the gap has been filled by the satirists. For Boler, "Jon Stewart is offering a reality check in the otherwise apparently absurd theater of media and politics" (390).

What is perplexing about their modes of delivery is that they operate on two levels at all times: they are trustworthy news sources, dedicating significant program time to covering major news items, while simultaneously delivering this information in a package full of silliness, wit, and comedy. When we watch these shows we get more information from more trustworthy sources than the mainstream news. That should make them news then right? Not exactly. Because what we have is still infotainment, it is information in a package of comedy and performance. As Russell Peterson explains, "Colbert offers incisive analysis, though it is coated in silliness" (3). One of the most intense face-offs on the debate over whether Stewart and Colbert are a source of news or a problem for it took place when Ted Koppel interviewed Stewart for *Nightline* in 2007. The exchange indicated for some the generational gap between a baby-boomer idea of duty-bound citizenship and trust in authority and a generation-X attitude of engaged citizenship and skepticism of authority. Koppel, who would later reverse his attitude and applaud Stewart and Colbert for "doing a better job than the real journalists,"[20] could barely disguise his disgust for his comedian guest. Koppel began by critiquing the way that *The Daily Show* had accused the media of being "stage managed" and the debate got intense:

> KOPPEL: the reality of it is—and it's no joke anymore—there are a lot of people out there who do turn to you for . . .
> STEWART: Not for news.
> KOPPEL: Well . . .
> STEWART: For an interpretation. A comedic interpretation.
> KOPPEL: To be informed. They actually think they're coming closer to the truth with your . . .
> STEWART: Now that's a different thing. That's credibility. That's a different animal.
> . . .
> KOPPEL: Alright, so you have found an answer through humor . . .
> STEWART: No. It's not an answer.
> KOPPEL: Well, an answer that . . .
> STEWART: I found an outlet. I found a catharsis. A sneeze, if you will.
> KOPPEL: It's not just a catharsis for you, it's a catharsis for your viewers. Those who watch say, at least when I'm watching Jon, he can use humor to say BS, that's a crock.
> STEWART: But that's always been the case. Satire has always been . . .
> KOPPEL: Ok, but I can't do that.
> STEWART: No, but you CAN say that's BS. You don't need humor to do that because you have what I wish I had which is credibility and gravitas. This is interesting stuff, and it's all part of the discussion and I think it's a good discussion to have, but I think it's important to take a more critical look. You know, don't you think?
> KOPPEL: No.
> STEWART: And certainly not from me.
> KOPPEL: No, not from you. I've had enough of you.
> STEWART: I know my role, I'm the dancing monkey.
> KOPPEL: You're finished. (Smiles)[21]

So which is it? Are they trying to make us laugh or make us think? Are they dancing monkeys or infotainers interested in educating the citizenry and sparking democratic deliberation? The answer, of course, is both. And, moreover, the answer is that the idea of separating these spheres is nonsense. We are describing the power of these shows as a one-two punch. And the core of this is the idea that there has been a fundamental synergy between the satirical comedy on each show that is powerful taken separately but was dynamite taken together. Stewart's amazement at the failures of media reporting and the shortcomings of politicians combined with Colbert's exaggerated in-character punditry to allow viewers to have an especially potent combination of satire that invigorated our democracy. Stewart's show demands accountability, honesty, and truth for the public through a satirical method that asks the audience to scratch its head and question the stories we are fed. Colbert enacts the insanity by taking the pundit, opinion-driven world of news media to an exaggerated level that exposes all of its flaws. By being in-character he was able to ask the audience to recognize that what the comedian Colbert thinks is different from what the character Colbert thinks. The gap between what he said and what he meant opened a space for the critical reflection of an audience that was simultaneously laughing and learning. In contrast, Stewart wants us to see what he sees. He wants to pull back the veil and expose the artifice posing as reality. Stewart would begin by unmasking those in power, then Colbert would put the mask back on, but this time it was bigger and more ridiculous. The audience finished the hour enlightened and engaged.

Many scholars have noted the synergy between these shows, and we recommend the works by Amarasingam, Baym, Holt, Jones, and McClennen for greater detail than we can offer here. Jones uses the combination of Stewart and Colbert as a foundational feature of his argument that details the shift to entertaining politics. Rather than the boxing metaphor we have invoked, Jones opts for evidence and calls them Exhibit A and Exhibit B. According to Jones, "*The Daily Show* became a serious (though humorous) arena for interrogating power, and in the process, Stewart left the jester persona behind. In short, Stewart and *The Daily Show* became Exhibit A for the ways in which political entertainment television (especially the satirical kind) could play a positive, important, and critical role in communicating politics, especially in the seeming absence of such from traditional news media" (x-xi). Jones notices the way that Stewart reverses the traditional quality of much humor. Rather than entertain the audience so that they don't have to think about the abuses of power—i.e. as a court jester—Stewart does not let the audience distract themselves from the world in which they live. Instead, he finds a way to make "getting it" fun. Next Jones describes Exhibit B: "Colbert too announced the seriousness of the genre and its location as a place for substantive political commentary and critique when he appeared as the featured entertainment at the White House Correspondents' Association dinner in 2006 . . . Colbert became an almost overnight sensation as the video of his performance spread quickly across the internet by viewers hungry for just such a critique. In sum, here then was Exhibit B of how the power of satire and parody could play an important role in enunciating critiques that were difficult to articulate (or be effective) in other ways" (xi).

There are two important takeaways here: the shows were very much in conversation but they did not offer the same version of satire. If you look at our top ten lists below you will note an obvious difference. Much of the impact of Stewart's comedy comes from the incisive effects of his satirical interrogations of the media and his engaged and heartfelt connection to the health of our democracy. Colbert, in contrast, opted often for a more flamboyant style and for events and stunts that took place outside of the confines of his show. Colbert, trained as a serious actor and with experience singing on Broadway, uses satire mixed with showmanship. Stewart uses his sharp wit and stand-up savvy to engage in intense exchanges with media figures, politicians, and other public personalities—usually on his own show. Each of them, though, has had a successful career speaking truth to power in a highly entertaining fashion. Here are some highlights of their careers (see Tables 4.1 and 4.2 and Figures 4.2 and 4.3).

Table 4.1   The Stewart Top Ten

1. **Indecision 2000:** As George W. Bush claimed victory over Al Gore through a lengthy recount and a controversial Supreme Court verdict, *The Daily Show*'s "Indecision 2000" was virtually the only cable show to express outrage. The election coverage earned *The Daily Show* a permanent place as a serious (but entertaining) source of American political coverage.

2. **Post-9/11 Reflection:** On his first show after the September 11 attacks, a visibly upset Stewart took a somber tone and showed his audience his heartfelt concern for his nation. "I'm sorry to do this to you," he said. "It's another entertainment show beginning with an overwrought speech of a shaken host, and television is nothing if not redundant. So I apologize for that. It's something that unfortunately we do for ourselves so that we can drain whatever abscess is in our hearts and move on to the business of making you laugh—which we haven't been able to do very effectively lately."

3. **From Screen to Page:** Stewart and his *Daily Show* cohorts took their satire to the reading masses with *America (The Book): A Citizen's Guide to Democracy Inaction* in 2004. A parody of a high school textbook—including activities and discussion questions—the book reminded the nation that we were all in dire need of civics education. Tom Carson, reviewing the book in *The New York Times*, wrote it was "not only more informative about how American government and culture work than the textbooks it burlesques, but gives us a keener sense of having a stake in both." And it features naked Supreme Court Justices. *Publisher's Weekly* named it Book of the Year.

4. **Crossfire Under Fire:** In October 2004, Stewart appeared as a guest on CNN's debate show *Crossfire* and expressed his concerns about the program. When asked to "be funny" he responded that he wasn't there to perform. "It's not so much that it's bad as it's hurting America . . . Stop hurting America," Stewart said in reference to the "partisan hackery" that he critiqued *Crossfire* for perpetuating. In January 2005, CNN canceled *Crossfire* and most credit Stewart's shaming of the hosts for the decision.

5. **Stewart Out Becks Beck:** In March 2009, Stewart dedicates almost half of an entire show to parodying Glenn Beck's pundit performances. Beck has always tried to show how his views are logical and true, often using a black board and suggesting he is "teaching" his audience. Stewart mocked this and exposed the faulty logic and hyperbole at the center of Beck's attacks on the "secular progressive agenda."

6. **A Real Health care Debate:** In 2009, as most mainstream media allowed conservatives to frame the narrative over health care, Stewart confronted anti-health-reform activist Betsy McCaughey and exposed the basic fallacies in her anti-health care spin. Revealing his inner geek, Stewart referred to life-expectancy statistics, Medicare reimbursement policies, physician incentives and average health-insurance costs to refute McCaughey's claims about the health-reform bill. Stewart called her "dangerous" and said, "I like you, but I don't understand how your brain works." More of the same hard-hitting counters to Republican fear-mongering over health care would appear after the passage of the Affordable Care Act.

7. Stewart vs. Cramer: In the wake of the Wall Street meltdown and the lack of useful coverage of those events, Stewart and his staff did a number of pieces exposing the truth behind the economic meltdown. The most visible confrontation took place between Stewart and Jim Cramer of CNBC's *Mad Money* on March 12, 2009 on *The Daily Show*. Stewart quickly exposed the hypocrisy behind many of Cramer's claims and chastised him for encouraging viewers to stay in the market when he knew it was risky. The interview was the second most-viewed episode in the show's history with 2.3 million viewers.

8. **Stewart Champions Care for First Responders:** The First Responders on 9/11 quickly had a series of health concerns that required special medical attention, but they weren't getting it. In 2010 as support for a bill to provide them with care was stalling, Stewart dedicated half of his show to their story. Lawmakers and journalists would later credit Stewart with helping to pass the bill and *The New York Times* referred to him as the "modern-day equivalent of Edward. R. Murrow."

(Continued)

Table 4.1   (*Continued*)

9. **Stewart vs. O'Reilly:** Both O'Reilly and Stewart have faced off on each other's shows dating back to 2001. Each time the encounter is highly provocative, but it is the debate they held in 2012 in the midst of the presidential election debates—The Rumble in the Air Conditioned Auditorium—that best epitomizes their showdown (see Figure 4.4). Eclipsing the presidential candidates, the two went head-to-head on some of the most significant policy issues facing the nation, from health care to foreign policy to entitlements—and they did so with the goal of educating and entertaining their audience.

10. **Stewart Stands Up for Veterans' Rights:** Stewart has been a staunch advocate for veterans' rights and in 2013 he zeroed in on their health care needs. Coverage of problems with attending to veterans' claims began in April with a piece called "The Red Tape Diaries." Then in May *The Daily Show* decided to call attention to the massive backlog of veterans' health claims with a bit called "Zero Dark 900,000." That piece was followed in September 2013 with one called "Ignoring Private Ryan." Together they offered the public the best coverage of this massive failure to protect the health and welfare of our veterans. Could there be anything more patriotic?

Sources: "Top 10 Jon Stewart Moments." TIME. Web. http://content.time.com/time/specials/packages/completelist/0,29569,2028143,00.html; "The Book of the Year:
  The Daily Show with Jon Stewart Presents America (The Book): A Citizen's Guide to Democracy Inaction." Publishers Weekly. 6 Dec. 2004. Web. http://www.publishersweekly.com/pw/print/20041206/24997-the-book-of-the-year.html; Carter, Bill, and Brian Stelter. "In 'Daily Show' Role on 9/11 Bill, Echoes of Murrow." The New York Times. Web. 26 Dec. 2010. http://www.nytimes.com/2010/12/27/business/media/27stewart.html; O'Reilly vs. Stewart 2012. Web. http://www.therumble2012.com/; "Zero Dark 900,000." The Daily Show. 3 May 2013. Web. http://www.thedailyshow.com/watch/thu-may-2-2013/zero-dark-900-000

Table 4.2   The Colbert Top Ten

1. **Truthiness:** On his first episode of the *Colbert Report*, Colbert launched a recurring segment entitled "The Wørd." "Truthiness" was The Wørd that launched that first show and it became an overnight sensation, becoming the "word of the year" for Merriam-Webster and the American Dialect Society in 2006. It encapsulated the post-9/11 turn away from facts—especially in the rhetoric of George W. Bush, who often spoke of making decisions based on his "gut." And it epitomized Colbert's ability to satirically play with words in a way that made the public recognize the lack of rational decision-making that had come to dominate national politics.

2. **The Bush Roast:** Colbert performed at the 2006 White House Correspondents' Association roasting President Bush, literally, to his face. The performance went viral as fans found great pleasure in seeing Colbert speak "truthiness to power." Stewart would later refer to the performance as "ballsalicious." The performance catapulted Colbert into international fame as a satirist to watch.

3. **Better Know a District:** One of the most famous recurring segments of *The Colbert Report* became a victim of its own success. Colbert would interview members of Congress, often exposing their limited intellectual abilities. Famous examples were when he interviewed Georgia Rep. Lynn Westmoreland who had sponsored a bill to publicly display the Ten Commandments but could only name three of them himself, and when New York Rep. Yvette Clark claimed that the Dutch had slaves in 1898. His interview with Robert Wexler, who was running unopposed in Florida, went viral when he convinced Wexler to say something that would surely ruin his election if he had an opponent. The silly statement then was aired as serious on mainstream news—setting off a feud with Colbert and leading politicians, like Nancy Pelosi, to suggest to House members that they avoid the show.

(*Continued*)

Table 4.2   (*Continued*)

4. **Colbert for President:** On October 16, 2007 Colbert announced on his show that he would run for President of the United States. Originally the plan was to run for both the Republican and the Democratic nomination in his home state of South Carolina. But when he learned the filing fee for the Republicans would be $35,000 he opted to run only on the Democratic ticket, but was eventually denied a place on the ballot. His Facebook page for the campaign had more than 1,000,000 likes within one week and polls had him as high as 13% against Rudy Giuliani and Hilary Clinton. He resumed his bid in 2011, asking voters to vote from him as President of South Carolina, using the ballot spot slotted to Herman Cain (who had dropped out of the race by then) as a vote for him.

5. **Colbert Goes to Iraq:** For one week in June of 2009 Colbert shot his show from Iraq as a way to raise support for our troops. Riffing on comedian Bob Hope's visits to the front, Colbert engaged in a variety of theatrics meant to entertain the troops and help connect their experiences to the US public. He also used the shows to help raise funds for the Yellow Ribbon Fund that assist injured veterans.

6. **Colbert Edits Newsweek:** The same month he went to Iraq, he guest-edited an issue of *Newsweek*. Colbert used the issue to shame the media and the administration over the Iraq War. "I know what you're thinking: 'Isn't the Iraq War over?' That's what I thought, too," he wrote in his editor's introduction. "We stopped seeing much coverage of the Iraq War back in September when the economy tanked, and I just figured the insurgents were wiped out because they were heavily invested in Lehman Brothers."[1] The issue was mixed with serious pieces on the war and some fun Colbert contributions.

7. **Colbert and Campaign Finance:** Outraged by the effects of the Supreme Court's Citizens United decision, which allowed corporations to give unlimited and anonymous amounts to campaigns, Colbert decided to start his own Super PAC so that he could teach his audience how the scam worked. Operating from June 2011-November 2012 the Super PAC inspired citizen-activists to start their own Super PACs, and Colbert used his own to finance a series of ads and teach the public about the effects of big money on campaigns.

8. **Colbert Shows Us How to Give:** Beginning with a broken wrist on the show in 2007, Colbert has used his persona and power to get his fans to raise money for causes. Some have been silly—like the wrist strong effort—but many have been serious. Colbert led a major effort to raise money for tsunami victims, used his Super PAC money to help victims of Hurricane Sandy, and has also gotten fans to contribute to DonorsChoose.org, which supports teachers across the nation.

9. **Colbert Goes to Congress:** After participating in the "Take Our Jobs" program meant to help the public understand the plight of undocumented workers, Colbert appeared before Congress to talk about immigration reform. He began in-character, but then he broke character to make a heartfelt plea on their behalf "I like talking about people who don't have any power," he said, the bravado gone from his voice as he worked his way to a downer of a punch line. "It seems like the least powerful people in the United States are migrant workers who come here. . . . And at the same time, we invite them here *and* ask them to leave. . . . I don't want to take anyone's hardship away from them [but] migrant workers suffer and have no rights."

10. **Colbert Tweets:** Colbert is active on Twitter and often uses it to move his comedy outside of the confines of his TV show. In 2010 he won the "Golden Tweet" for the most retweeted tweet. Then in 2011 he responded to claims made by representatives of AZ Senator John Kyl that the senator's fabrications about Planned Parenthood were "not intended to be factual statements." Hearing that the senator's staff thought such a response made sense, Colbert decided to invent the hashtag "#notintendedtobeafactualstatement" and encouraged his audience to tweet round-the-clock non-facts about the senator. That first night there were more than a million tweets per hour using that hashtag. Then Colbert staffers created a twitter bot with the handle @RealHumanPraise in response to news that Fox News encourages staffers to prop up fake online accounts to anonymously combat negative stories about the channel (see Figure 4.5). The automated, nonsensical tweets appear with the hashtag #PraiseFox.

(*Continued*)

Table 4.2 *(Continued)*

Sources: "Top 10 Colbert Moments." TIME. Web. http://content.time.com/time/specials/packages/completelist/
0,29569,2027834,00.html; Colbert, Stephen. "Why I Took This Crummy Job." Newsweek. 5 June 2009. Web. http://
www.newsweek.com/why-i-took-crummy-job-80621; "Stephen Colbert: Charity Work, Events and Causes." Look to
the Stars: the World of Celebrity Giving. Web. https://www.looktothestars.org/celebrity/stephen-colbert; Zak, Dan.
"Stephen Colbert, in GOP pundit character, testifies on immigration in D.C." The Washington Post. 25 Sept. 2010.
Web. http://www.washingtonpost.com/wp-dyn/content/article/2010/09/24/AR2010092402734.html; Luippold, Ross.
"Colbert Trolls Fox News By Offering@RealHumanPraise On Twitter, And It's Brilliant." HuffPost Comedy. 5 Nov.
2013. Web. http://www.huffingtonpost.com/2013/11/05/colbert-trolls-fox-news-realhumanpraise_n_4218078.html

Figure 4.2 Stewart and O'Reilly go head-to-head at their debate[22]

Figure 4.3 Colbert announces the launch of @RealHumanPraise on Twitter[23]

As these highlights reveal, the shows had a lot of synergy with distinct differences. Clearly Colbert engaged far more with off-show stunts that encouraged fan participation. Both, though, directly participated in a lot of public works, indicating their clear commitment to their nation. For instance, each comedian has been a strong advocate for veterans. They have used their shows to educate the public about specific ways that our government—under both Bush and Obama—has not done enough for veterans' rights. Their satire combines a philanthropic, patriotic passion with intense and hard-hitting comedy that exposes the folly of mainstream news media coverage of major political issues. But more than just critique and satirize media coverage, they have each shown considerable concern for the way that democratic deliberation in this nation has been stymied by a shrill discourse of opposition and partisanship—and it was their combined concern for this issue that led them to stage their greatest collaboration to date.

Stewart and Colbert Face Off at the Rally to Restore Sanity and/or Fear

Given the fact that *The Colbert Report* was a spin-off of *The Daily Show,* it is logical that the two shows had a fair amount of synergy. In the early seasons of *The Colbert Report,* Stewart ended with "the toss"—a segment where he interacted and bantered a bit with Colbert while he was on-screen at his set (see Figure 4.4). The intersection was always fun and was a good way to get viewers of *The Daily Show* to stay tuned for Colbert.

Eventually, the work it took to produce "the toss" wasn't worth the trouble as *The Colbert Report* had solid enough ratings to stand on its own, and the connecting segment was dropped. That didn't mean though that the two comedians did not interact a fair bit on their programs. There were many times when

Figure 4.4 Colbert tells Stewart he will have to do the toss by himself since he has a headache[24]

Stewart or Colbert appeared as a guest, or one phoned the other, during their shows for increased comedic effect. In one especially fun example, Colbert passed over control of his Super PAC to Stewart during his run for president of South Carolina in 2011.

Arguably, though, their most significant comedic collaboration took place in the lead-up to and during their Rally to Restore Sanity and/or Fear that took place on the National Mall in Washington DC on October 30, 2010. Initially, they were announced as separate events: Stewart's "Rally to Restore Sanity" and Colbert's "March to Keep Fear Alive." The rally was a chance for what Stewart said were the 70–80% of Americans who try to solve our nation's problems rationally and be heard above the more vocal and highly visual 15–20% who "control the conversation." "You may know them," Stewart said. "They're the people who believe that Obama is a secret Muslim planning a socialist takeover of America so he can force his radical black-liberation Christianity down our throats. Or that George W. Bush let 9/11 happen in order to pass Dick Cheney's Halliburton stock portfolio."[25] Somewhat ironically, satirist Stewart focused on the idea that our nation needed more "reason" in order to thrive. His motto for the rally? "Take it down a notch for America." After he made the announcement on his show, rally signs were proposed for the event including one that read "I disagree with you, but I'm pretty sure you're not Hitler."[26] In-character Colbert countered by claiming that things were not nearly hysterical enough. Colbert's call? "Now is the time for all good men to freak out for freedom!"

The event was staged in the midst of the build-up to the 2010 mid-term election and on the heels of Glenn Beck's "Restoring Honor" event at the Lincoln Memorial on August 28, 2010, which had been billed as a "celebration of America's heroes and heritage." Beck's event had stirred up quite a bit of controversy since it fell on the 47th anniversary of Martin Luther King Jr.'s "I Have a Dream" speech and took place shortly after Beck accused President Obama of being a "racist" and not holding "true" Christian values.[27] While Stewart and Colbert would deny that their rally was in response to Beck's it was clear that Tea Party rhetoric like Beck's was one of the prime targets of their rally. As fear-mongering Beck tried to position himself as a voice for "civil rights," and as he tried to label Obama's health care initiative as "reparations," it was clear that the nation needed a big dose of sanity. Beck wasn't offering sanity, and nor were his invited guests. Guess who was one of the featured speakers at Beck's event? Sarah Palin. Only days before she appeared at the rally she had defended "Dr. Laura Schlessinger's dropping of the n-bomb 11 times on constitutional grounds."[28] *Daily Beast* writer John Avalon claimed that the Beck event should have been more aptly called "I Have a Nightmare" not "I Have a Dream," since the prime motive for the event was to ramp up the divisions that were haunting the democratic process and the deliberative possibilities of our nation. Avalon cautioned that what made Beck and Palin dangerous was their language of hope and unity mixed with their fierce commitment to divisiveness: "the self-righteous conservative populism that Beck and Palin have pumped up and profited from is predicated on a fundamental vision of division—'real Americans' versus subversive secular socialists; true patriots versus the president."[29]

He points out that Tea Party rhetoric depends on the idea that the nation is under threat and that the true "unity" of it is one that excises the voices of democrats: "By dividing our country into us against them, sowing the seeds of hate and condemning the concept of a big tent, Beck and Palin represent the opposite tradition in American history as Lincoln and King—they are dividers, not uniters. We can take them at their word: They want to take our country back, not help it move forward."[30] It was this sort of political position-taking that was the backdrop for Stewart and Colbert's call for something different.

So, in the midst of rhetoric that masqueraded as promoting civil rights but actually promoted some of the deepest political divisions in this nation since the Vietnam War, Stewart called for sanity. The promotional website for the event stated: "We're looking for the people who think shouting is annoying, counterproductive, and terrible for your throat; who feel that the loudest voices shouldn't be the only ones that get heard; and who believe that the only time it's appropriate to draw a Hitler mustache on someone is when that person is actually Hitler. Or Charlie Chaplin in certain roles." In complete contrast to the hyped-up language used by Beck about how his rally was meant to be a "wake up call" for America, Stewart urged that his would be low key: "Think of our event as Woodstock, but with the nudity and drugs replaced by respectful disagreement; the Million Man March, only a lot smaller, and a bit less of a sausage fest; or the Gathering of the Juggalos, but instead of throwing our feces at Tila Tequila, we'll be actively *not* throwing our feces at Tila Tequila."[31]

The brilliance of the Stewart/Colbert pairing lay in the way that Stewart's call for reason was reversed and exaggerated by Colbert's in-character out-Becking of Beck. As his promotional website read—this nation needs more fear, not less:

America, the Greatest Country God ever gave Man, was built on three bedrock principles: Freedom. Liberty. And Fear—that someone might take our Freedom and Liberty. But now, there are dark, optimistic forces trying to take away our Fear— forces with salt and pepper hair and way more Emmys than they need. They want to replace our Fear with reason. But never forget—"Reason" is just one letter away from "Treason." Coincidence? Reasonable people would say it is, but America can't afford to take that chance.[32]

Riffing on Tea Party and post-9/11 conservative language that obsessed over the idea that our nation's freedom is under threat, that people hate us for our freedom, and that we are fighting a war to defend our core values, Colbert's own words were only slight exaggerations of the sorts of things that Beck, Palin, Coulter, Limbaugh, and other high-profile fundamentalist Republicans uttered on a regular basis. Here are just a few highlights of the sorts of comments that Colbert was parodying:

Glenn Beck: "Al Gore's not going to be rounding up Jews and exterminating them. It is the same tactic, however. The goal is different. The goal is globalization . . . And you must silence all dissenting voices. That's what Hitler did. That's what Al Gore, the U.N., and everybody on the global warming bandwagon [are doing]."[33]

Sarah Palin: "(Barack Obama) is not a man who sees America like you and I see America. Our opponent is someone who sees America, it seems, as being so imperfect that he's palling around with terrorists who would target their own country. Americans need to know this."[34]

Ann Coulter: "Whether they are defending the Soviet Union or bleating for Saddam Hussein, liberals are always against America. They are either traitors or idiots."[35]

Rush Limbaugh: "Look, I know Pope Francis thinks he knows something about religion, but he obviously doesn't. God and religion are tools meant to stir up fear, hate, anger and paranoia within people so they're easier to manipulate. And I'll tell you what, this hopeful demeanor this new Pope has seems very similar to that of President Obama's 2008 presidential campaign. And we all know President Obama is the anti-Christ. The last thing Americans need is hope."[36]

Each of these quotes highlights the paranoia, fear mongering, and downright lack of reason that has been dominating much right-leaning rhetoric for the past decade. Stewart tries to get his audience to see how crazy such language is, by basically saying, "isn't that crazy?" Colbert, in contrast, exposed the craziness by exaggerating it in-character. Rather than call for calm, he revealed how the hype for hysteria was ridiculous by enacting its folly and mocking its false logic.

After the rally was announced, there was an immediate media buzz and public response. The night of the announcement there were already 69,000 attendees signed up on Facebook—a number that far exceeded the estimated 25,000 that had been the basis for getting a permit to use the National Mall.[37] Sister events were planned in a number of major cities and Arianna Huffington appeared on *The Daily Show* to offer to fund as many buses as needed to take attendees from New York to DC. Media representatives from across the nation and the globe scrambled to get press attendance and even Obama, who was out helping campaign for Democrats at the time, referred to the rally as a welcome antidote to the vitriolic nature of most cable television: "What happens is these cable shows and talk show hosts, a lot of them figure out that, 'The more controversial I can be, and I'm calling Obama this name or that name and saying he wasn't born in this country, that will get me attention.'" Obama wanted to remind US citizens that the country does not need to be polarized by stark divisions and irreconcilable opposition. He then mentioned the rally as a welcome opportunity for US citizens who were looking for reason: "Use Jon Stewart, the host of *The Daily Show*. Apparently he's going to host a rally called something like, 'Americans Who Favor a Return to Sanity,' or something like that." He described the event as something that would reach out to the majority of the nation that "don't go around calling people names, they don't make stuff up, they may not be following every single issue because they just don't have time, but they are expecting some common sense and some courtesy."[38] As Obama battled ongoing attacks about his citizenship, his patriotism, his religion and his love of terrorists, the idea of an event that advocated reason and respect was obviously appealing.

The rally began with a duel between Yusef Islam's "Peace Train"—sponsored by Stewart—and Ozzy Osborne's "Crazy Train"—sponsored by Colbert. The opposing messages in the songs led the comedians to face off on their different ideas about what our nation needed most. Stewart awarded "Medals of Reasonableness" and Colbert countered with "Medals of Fear" and much of the back-and-forth between the comedians was fairly silly. Stewart broke the entertaining quality of the event, though, to pause and offer a moment of sincerity and to reflect on the mere idea that a comedian would be attempting to pull an event like this off: "And now I thought we might have a moment, however brief, for some sincerity, if that's ok; I know there are boundaries for a comedian, pundit, talker guy, and I'm sure I'll find out tomorrow how I have violated them."[39] He reminded the audience that the rally was not meant to ridicule people of faith or to suggest that there is nothing to fear; the goal, rather, was to gain perspective and clarity in "hard times." But more than anything the idea was to correct the misrepresentation of political conflict that dominated so much contemporary news media and threatened to destroy the viability of our democratic process: "We can have animus and not be enemies. But, unfortunately, one of our main tools in delineating the two broke. The country's 24-hour, politico, pundit, perpetual, panic conflict-a-nator did not cause our problems, but its existence makes solving them that much harder. The press can hold its magnifying glass up to our problems, bringing them into focus, illuminating issues heretofore unseen. Or they can use that magnifying glass to light ants on fire, and then perhaps host a week of shows on the sudden, unexpected, dangerous flaming ant epidemic. If we amplify everything, we hear nothing."[40] Sounding more like a politician or a visionary leader than a comedian he ended his speech urging the people at the event to work together to create their own version of the nation, one that was not dominated by division and hype: "Because we know instinctively as a people that if we are to get through the darkness and back into the light, we have to work together."[41]

Perhaps even more interesting than the idea of these two comedians appearing on the National Mall in an effort to host a rally aimed toward returning our nation to reasonable discourse is the fact that their call to come together was heard loud and clear. The audience that day numbered around 215,000 (compared with Beck's turnout of about 80,000), Comedy Central broadcast live with two million viewers and an additional 570,000 viewing online (see Figure 4.5).

Stewart and Colbert reached about 2.8 million people that day in real-time with many more seeing the event subsequently. Despite the impressive audience pull of the event, there was still considerable criticism of the rally's success in later media coverage, especially as Stewart and Colbert had to finesse the media's anxieties over being one of the main sources of democratic distress in our nation. Others claimed that the event was not well managed (since the audience was bigger than anticipated) or that the performances were not that entertaining. Three days later the nation voted in mid-term elections, and while GOP made gains and turnout was lower than hoped for, it is worth considering the impact that Stewart and Colbert had on getting out the vote for reason. Neither one of them would admit that the timing of the rally was linked to the election, but then again they won't admit that they are interested in influencing politics either. Clearly, it's up to you to decide.

Figure 4.5   Huge crowds attend the rally on the National Mall
Photo Credit: Amy Marash

E Pluribus Unum: In Satire We Trust

We've talked about their synergy and their major publicly staged collaboration at the rally, but now we would like to turn briefly to explain some of the ways that the comedy of Stewart and that of Colbert on *The Colbert Report* are different. Interestingly, when Colbert is out of character, he and Stewart seem to both share a strong sense of commitment to our nation and compassion for our citizens—as evidenced by the way they use their comedy to support causes. As Peterson explains, "What really sets Jon Stewart apart from the mainstream hosts [is] his faith in the political process. . . . Jon Stewart actually *cares* about politics—which distinguishes him not only from other late-night hosts, but from most citizens. He's different enough from the anti-political evolutionary line to be considered a representative of a different species: *Homo satiricus*" (118). Colbert clearly is part of the same species too. The key difference is that Colbert's in-character satire is all a performance of something he does not believe. In an interview with Neil Strauss for *Rolling Stone* Colbert explained the distinction between how he and Jon Stewart satirized the news: "Jon deconstructs the news in a really brilliant comedic style. I take the sausage backwards, and I restuff the sausage. We deconstruct, but then we don't show anybody our deconstruction. We reconstruct—we falsely construct the hypocrisy. And I embody the bullshit until hopefully you can smell it."[42] In an interview with Charlie Rose where Rose asked him to comment on a *Rolling Stone* issue that featured him alongside Stewart on the cover, Colbert similarly suggested that "Jon deconstructs the news and he's ironic and detached. I falsely construct the news and am ironically attached . . . Jon may point out the hypocrisy of a particular thing happening in a news story or a behavior, or somebody in the news. I illustrate the hypocrisy as a character."[43]

That role as a character added challenges for viewers who could find themselves confused over what Colbert really thought and who might have been overly charmed by his grinning charisma. As Adam Sternbergh explains, Colbert's fans would occasionally find themselves in the awkward position where they are laughing at his rendition of an extreme view that sometimes felt eerily similar to laughing at a non-satirical version: "Colbert's on-air personality, so distinct from Stewart's, leads to a peculiar comedic alchemy on the show. During one taping I attended, Colbert did a bit about eating disorders that ended with his addressing the camera and saying flatly, 'Girls, if we can't see your ribs, you're ugly.' The audience laughed. I laughed. The line was obviously, purposefully outrageous. But it was weird to think that this no-doubt self-identified progressive-liberal crowd was howling at a line that, if it had been delivered verbatim by Ann Coulter on *Today*, would have them sputtering with rage."[44] The trouble, as Sternbergh explains, is that no one would want to associate Colbert with Coulter: Coulter is really a hateful person and Colbert merely offered a simulation of her shrill behavior. But still the fact remains that Stewart's satirical comedy doesn't run the risk of getting us to laugh while he makes offensive remarks. Sternbergh makes his point by offering readers a test where he lists ten offensive statements and asks readers to guess who uttered them: Coulter or Colbert? Here is one comparison:[45]

"Even Islamic terrorists don't hate America like liberals do. They don't have the energy. If they had that much energy, they'd have indoor plumbing by now."

"There's nothing wrong with being gay. I have plenty of friends who are going to hell."

Could you tell which is Colbert and which is Coulter? We can't either and we are experts! The first is Colbert and the second is Coulter. Sternbergh's exercise makes an important point about Colbert's in-character satire and it's one that can't be dismissed. But there is a crucial difference—and that difference is comedy. Colbert said these sorts of comments on a comedy show and in the context of his satirical silliness. Colbert tells his audience things like, "Opinions are like assholes, in that I have more than most people."[46] He certainly offered his audience sufficient clues that he was not serious.

There is more that differentiates *The Daily Show* and *The Colbert Report* than we have time to analyze in detail but it is important to recognize some real ways that their comedy differs. Beyond the distinctions between in-character satire and straight satire, Colbert's program was far more focused on engaging his audience. He often encouraged his viewers to do silly things that just promoted his ego. But he also called on them to become more active members of society. Colbert reached out to youth culture via green screen challenges posted on YouTube, the use of Wikipedia and other internet venues, cartoon segments, hashtag fun on Twitter, hip musical guests, and other gimmicks like Colbert's dance off with Korean pop icon Rain—activities that surely influenced his landing *The Late Show* gig. As we detailed in our chapter on satire and civics lessons, Colbert used his own Super PAC not just to educate the public, but he also issued a challenge to his viewers to become directly engaged in the process themselves.

This is why the run to be president of South Carolina, the launch of his own Super PAC, and the bid to moderate the presidential debates were more than just publicity stunts. Colbert in-character as a bloviating pundit had the luxury of being able to play with the idea of promoting his oversized ego while also encouraging his fans to engage in civic participation. Colbert's viewers learned how our democratic process worked by playing along with him, learning in the process, and laughing all the way. Similarly, his word plays—from the puns that he used in the opening rundown, to the words that swirled around him on the opening credits, to his segment "The Wørd"—all combined to allow his audience to have fun while reflecting on the connections between language, politics, and public opinion. He was able to parody the personality-driven books of conservative pundits like O'Reilly by spoofing them and out-besting them with his own books: *I Am America* and *America Again*. He even had fun releasing a parody of a patriotic children's book, in the satirical vein of books like Lynn Cheney's *A is for Abigail*.

Another key difference between the shows was due to the difference in the on-air talent. Colbert was on his own, while Stewart has had the support of an extraordinary cast working with him. When Colbert wanted to expose the flaws in logical thinking and the breakdown in political logic that dominated much coverage of major issues, he had to engage in series like "The Wørd" segment or "Formidable Opponent," that allowed him to debate himself. Spoofing O'Reilly's use of text that reiterates what he says on his show, Colbert's "Wørd" segment had him speaking a monologue while text appeared on his right that at times agreed with him, but at others mocked and critiqued him. The effect was sheer satirical brilliance since the audience had to parse a variety of sources of information. Stewart, on the other

Figure 4.6   Stewart has the benefit of a great supporting cast of comedians[47]

hand, has the luxury of calling on his cast (see Figure 4.6). In one amazing bit from August 2010 he went after Fox News for covering over the fact that the very same sinister mosque builder that troubled them at Ground Zero was one of their co-owners, Saudi Prince Al-Waleed bin Talal. Showing a photo of the prince shaking hands with Rupert Murdoch, Stewart exclaimed, "That's right, the guy they're painting as a sinister money force OWNS Fox News." But to drive the craziness home he then called on John Oliver and Wyatt Cenac to explain to him how Fox News could have done this story. Were they evil or just stupid? Wearing "team evil" and "team stupid" t-shirts the pair offered Stewart their thoughts:

> JOHN OLIVER: Jon, do you know what? I'm going to go with "they didn't know."
> Remember, things are hectic on the morning show, plus Gretchen isn't there, and she's the only one who knows how to use Google. More so, it was probably a Hooters Freedom Monday. I just think at the end of the day, they didn't know.
> JON STEWART: So, so, you . . .
> OLIVER: Exactly. I'm with stupid.
> WYATT CENAC: Nobody's that stupid. They're deliberately hiding the truth. If Al-Waleed wasn't part-owner of Fox News, they'd have gone to *town* demonizing this guy. They would've said his full name over and over again. Al-Waleed bin Talal! Al-Waleed bin Talal!! And look at these villainous pictures.[48]

Stewart, of course, has plenty of fun pointing out logical fallacies, faulty reasoning, and downright terrible reporting when he runs down headlines at the top of his show, but the fact that he can rely on a strong cast to support his show reveals a significant difference between *The Daily Show* and *The Colbert Report*.

Where Stewart has really grown as a satirical comedian is in the interview segment, which has increasingly become a prime source of information for the public. Stewart has the pull at this point to get an impressive slate of interviewees—politicians from Obama to Pakistani President Pervez Musharraf, and pundits and journalists from O'Reilly to Peter Jennings, and an endless list of other political guests and entertainers are on his interview roster. One of the key features of the interview is the way that Stewart has become famous—as evidenced by his encounter with Jim Cramer—for asking unexpected questions, for taking the gloves off, and for refusing to swallow the spin he gets. Such was the case when he grilled Nancy Pelosi on why she couldn't help change Washington.[49] He refused to allow her to simply blame Republicans and continuously pushed her to own her responsibility for the process and work harder to reassure the public that they could trust their politicians. Stewart's ability to conduct interviews that barely, if ever, happen in mainstream news venues has earned him not just the trust of the public, but also its attention. Since he breaks down the typical line of questions and really interacts and engages with his guest, the viewer is able to see the guest in a different light. Often barely attempting to inject humor into his interviews, Stewart instead uses the time on his show to offer his viewers knowledge they wouldn't gain otherwise.

In one of the Peabody citations that the show received, his achievements in interviews were highlighted as a central feature of the show's public impact:

> Much has been made of the fact that growing numbers of viewers, old as well as young, turn to *The Daily Show with Jon Stewart* for "news." Mr. Stewart, however,

repeatedly reminds those viewers that his program is "fake news." Nevertheless, the program applies its satirical, sometimes caustic perspective to the issues of the day, on those engaged with the issues, and on the everyday experiences that will be affected by them. In the context of *The Daily Show with Jon Stewart* serious, even-handed interviews with significant political figures including many presidential candidates, commentators, reporters, and authors took on new significance and reached new audiences.[50]

Key here is to remember that much of Stewart and Colbert's demographic is a younger sector of the population that is not likely to tune in to Charlie Rose or Terry Gross, so Stewart's ability to engage these figures on his show allows this information to reach a younger audience in desperate need of civic training. As Jones notes, "Stewart's interviews with guests also depart from traditional journalistic practice as he engages in a sincere deliberative exchange aimed at airing agreements and differences of opinion between two people, not engaging in shouting matches or partisan polemics for spectacle display. Though humor might be employed in both, the outcome is that a comedy show has been instrumental in introducing important changes to the public conversation made available through television through its quite serious and earnest insistence on arriving at honest truth" (17). This is how Stewart has used interviews to change the public conversation.

In contrast, the key to the interview for Colbert was his character, which allowed him to make outrageous claims as he tried to "nail" his guest. As Geoffrey Baym explains, he often tried to "out right-wing" his conservative interviewees, a move that on occasion led the conservative guest to move to a more moderate position ("Parody" 132). On occasion, however, it actually led to the revelation of a guest's extreme views. For example, Colbert managed to rile up Harvard professor Harvey Mansfield, author of *Manliness*, enough to give him a high five in camaraderie when Colbert suggested that women were bad drivers.[51] His gloves were softer with left-leaning guests who often got the expected pedantic questions, but were at least able to expose the absurdity of them. In an out-of-character interview about the Colbert persona as it appeared on *The Daily Show*, Colbert explained "I'm essentially a very high-status character, but my weakness is that I'm stupid."[52] He explained that a central part of the character was that he was a fool, or more specifically, "a fool who has spent a lot of his life playing not the fool."[53] This fool persona was quite disarming in the interview segment and it allowed Colbert to get in quite a few zingers unavailable to Stewart's sharp-tongued straight satirical mode. Colbert got to play the pundit, allowing him to cut off interviewees and insult them. But the goal was always to reveal that that sort of dialogue was not a real "rapport"—a word that was parodied by the way that Colbert pronounced the title word "Report" with a silent "t." Colbert confessed to Terry Gross in an out-of-character interview that: "One of sort of the unintentional puns of our show is that it is called the Colber(t) Repor(t), and it unintentionally plays on the word 'rapport' . . . which is a sense of understanding between the speaker and the listener. We're the same people you and me, we get it. The rest of the people out there they don't understand the things that we understand. The show is like an invitation to the audience to be part of the club."[54] Colbert's interviews, in their parody of the ways that most news channel interviews are not conversations of significance at all, asked the audience to strive harder for a better dialogue. Stewart, in contrast, refuses to let his interviewees dish him sound bites. He demands that they really talk to him. Both shows use different interview tactics, but their goals of advancing public dialogue intersect and overlap. As Day puts it, "their work functions as political speech in and of itself" (81). One thing is certain, our nation benefitted from almost ten years of the combined satirical punch of Stewart and Colbert. While Colbert's move to *The Late Show* means the end of his character and the end of his on-screen connection to *The Daily Show*, we can only hope that he will continue to interact with Stewart on political satire for many more years to come.

5

When I Mock You, I Make You Better: How Satire Works

Two weeks before the 2004 presidential election, *New York Times* reporter Ron Suskind quoted a Bush administration aide dismissing what he termed the "reality-based community." The aide explained to Suskind that "a judicious study of discernible reality [is] . . . not the way the world really works anymore. We're an empire now, and when we act, we create our own reality. And while you're studying that reality—judiciously, as you will—we'll act again, creating other new realities, which you can study too, and that's how things will sort out. We're history's actors . . . and you, all of you, will be left to just study what we do."[1] The statement was meant to mock reporters, who, according to the aide, were in the business of studying and reporting on the "realities" that politicians create.

We need to stop and pause for a moment to digest that exchange since it is easy to overlook how outrageous it was. Here was a presidential aide telling a *New York Times* reporter that politicians had no interest in reality; that they "created" it, and that reporters were simply to report on what they created. Shouldn't a statement like that have caused a flurry of reaction when it appeared in a major newspaper? Sadly, it didn't. Surrounded as it was by a host of insulting comments that had been leveled at the press and the public in those years, it only resonated with those few that continued to expect more from government and news about government. Then after Bush was inaugurated for his second term, Stephen Colbert satirized the same crisis in his speech before President Bush at the White House Correspondents' Association Dinner when he mocked the fact that reporters too often accepted the version of events offered by the White House: "But, listen, let's review the rules. Here's how it works: the president makes decisions. He's the Decider. The press secretary announces those decisions, and you people of the press type those decisions down. Make, announce, type."[2] When Colbert satirically said almost the same thing as Bush's aide—the world listened. They listened because the critique was in the form of satire and they listened because the satire was launched right in the face of the president.

Satire like Colbert's only works if there is something to satirize. When the comedians we are studying in this book emerged on the scene we had a government accustomed to lying, misinforming, and manipulating truth. And we had a press that too often yielded to scandal, sensation, and entertainment rather than practicing an aggressive pursuit of evidence, information, and reasoned critique. Even worse, we had a public caught between the fear of terrorist attack, the manipulation of big business, and a culture of division and conflict. When Bill Moyers interviewed Jon Stewart in 2003 he started by saying: "I do not know whether you are practicing an old form of parody and satire . . . Or a new form of journalism." Stewart replied by refusing to separate satire from news: "Well then that either speaks to the sad state of comedy or the sad state of news. I can't figure out which one. I think, honestly, we're practicing a new form of desperation. Where we just are so inundated with mixed messages from the media and from politicians that we're just trying to sort it out for ourselves."[3] Stewart emphasized the point that we are in a unique historical moment. Even though satire almost always emerges in force when societies are in crisis and when leaders are failing them, the conditions in this nation after 9/11 severely limited public access to the truth and frustrated public debate of major social issues. Part of this was due to the way that the news media gave the Bush presidency a pass on critical reporting, often just lining up behind the president and his team, notably, for instance, in its reporting of Bush's "Mission Accomplished" publicity stunt that had him land on an aircraft carrier announcing the end of the Iraq War years before it actually ended. As Frank Rich illustrates in *The Greatest Story Ever Sold*, "about the only discouraging words to be found in the American mass media about America's instant victory in Iraq was on a basic cable channel. . . . *The Daily Show* [was] one of the few reliable spots on the dial for something other than the government line" (87).

9/11 did not only herald a crisis for critical thinking; it was also a tough moment for comedy. The shock and fear that reigned in the United States after the attacks created a strange moment for comedy. At first, comedians found it hard to be funny and then the nature of the event was such that some comedy simply failed to work either as helpful therapy or as much-needed critical corrective. Exemplifying the paralysis of some comedians, Mayor Giuliani appeared on *Saturday Night Live* surrounded by firefighters and police officers eighteen days after the attacks on the Twin Towers. Producer Lorne Michaels asked the mayor: "Can we be funny now?" To which Giuliani replied: "Why start now?"[4] The joke was light and self-deprecating, but it wasn't satire. Paul Lewis notes that shortly after 9/11 there was a lot of dark humor that was often sadistic in its brutality (17). Labels, put-downs, and mean mockery led to a comedy of attack and to what Lewis terms as "killing jokes" (17). Lewis uses as evidence the smiling images of the prison guards torturing Iraqis at Abu Ghraib. He references testimony by Spec. Sabrina Harman who explained that she attached electrical wires to an Iraqi detainee's fingers, toes, and penis because she was "just playing with him" (10).

Against this sort of dark humor, Russell Peterson notes the way that much humor after 9/11 was simply flat and unengaged: "the aftermath of 9/11 did reveal the limits of late-night's anti-political approach. Suddenly, glimmers of strident, showbiz patriotism kept popping up in what had previously been a no-reverence zone. Flag pins sprouted on hosts' lapels" (196). Peterson references Dan Rather's appearance on David Letterman on September 17, 2001 when he told the comedian that he was ready to line up behind the president whenever he asked him. For Peterson this showed the extent to which late-night comedy had become woefully disconnected from any form of political critique: "Not only was irony apparently dead, it looked for the moment as if even good old-fashioned American skepticism were on life support" (195).

Taken together, this means that satire was only one of the many versions of comedy that circulated after 9/11. As Lewis points out, humor can be damaging and mean or it can draw us together and help us understand our world:

> Humor can help us cope with problems or deny them, inform or misinform, express our most loving and most hateful feelings, embrace and attack, draw us to other people who share our values or fallaciously convince us that they do when they don't. Beyond this, a joke can highlight a point or blow smoke on it, call attention to a problem or cover it up. Especially at times when what we're joking about is important, the good news about humor (that it is absorbing, delightful, relaxing, and dismissive) is frequently also the bad news. (7–8)

All humor is not equal, though, and all humor does not divide society. According to Lewis, when humor is at its best it "can aid in (re)solving problems by helping us calm down, lighten up, and think clearly and creatively" (15). Peterson focuses on the specific value of satirical humor and points out its direct benefit for democracy: "Genuine satire can give us information and insight that enhances our ability to fulfill our role as citizens in a democracy" (22). It is important to bear these distinctions in mind since spiteful mockery is quite different from socially engaged satire. The humor at the heart of satire is never meant to be destructive; it is meant to help the audience have a corrective to misinformation and spin. In the post-9/11 era the crisis in critical thinking and the crisis in comedy intertwined to create an especially fragile moment for public discourse and it was satire that stepped into the mix and offered the public an alternative way of thinking about key political issues within a productive critical framework that was both fun and politically insightful.

That's not how everyone sees it though. It is common to suggest that satire is damaging to democracy. Too often it seems easy to suggest that the satirists themselves have made a mockery of our nation, but they can only mock what actually exists. Moreover, satirists are often criticized for cultivating apathy or cynicism or distrust in politics. But, this again, is a problem of cause and effect. The satirists did not create the sad state of politics nor are they responsible for the crisis in our news media: they are only drawing attention to it. But how exactly do they draw attention to it? And why is Colbert's critique of the relationship between the Bush administration and the news media different from Ron Suskind's? What is it about satire that makes it work in a special way? How can we distinguish satire from other forms of comedic critique? Even more importantly, we need to understand how satire works to figure out the specific ways in which it can help strengthen our democracy and save our nation. To do this we begin by examining the specifics of satire and how it intersects with and differs from other forms of comedy and critique like irony, parody, cynicism, and snark. This chapter helps explain how we can tell the difference between being sarcastically mocked and being asked to think critically. The second section of this chapter gets to the heart of this dilemma by explaining how satire never tells us what to think. We then move on to explain why satire today is at a very unique historical moment when it is often taken to be a discursive mode more commonly understood as "true" and "trustworthy" than the words of politicians and reporters. It no longer is only a commentary on our democracy but rather a source of its vibrancy and health. This means that understanding satire may be more important for the health of our nation than ever before.

What Is Satire, and Why Should We Like it?

Satire is one of the oldest forms of comedy and there are numerous scholarly studies on the specifics of how it varies over time and in particular contexts. While we can't get into all of the details of these nuances, we do want to point out a few key characteristics about post 9/11 satire. First, given the overall decline in progressive political discourse and given the contentious and aggressive nature of most news media, satire is a communicative mode that often is less aggressive and negative than the objects of its critique. This is somewhat of a reversal from previous modes of satire. Second, given that so much speech today seems like a parodic performance, satire and satirical parody often feel more real than what they caricaturize. And third, satire has become a central mode of political engagement often superseding more "serious" political interventions and also commonly becoming a featured part of the very same modes of communication it is meant to mock. We will explain these three points in detail below, but this is all to say that today's satire is unlike its historical predecessors in many ways.

Satire is dedicated to exposing human folly and its goal is to inspire critical thinking and reasoned social engagement. It is often accompanied by irony, parody, and word play. It is regularly confused with mockery, cynicism, and sarcasm. Frequently these different comedic and critical modes exist side-by-side, meaning that a comedian may make a sharp satirical point one moment to turn around and sarcastically attack someone the next. Our goal in this section is to give you a brief, but useful, breakdown of these differences since understanding their nuances is necessary for being able to distinguish between satire and other forms of comedy that are simply negative and demoralizing.

One of the tricky issues that complicates understanding satire is its relationship to *irony*. Almost all satire uses irony, but not all irony is satirical. So let's start with unpacking the meaning of irony since it may actually be a term even less understood than satire. At a basic level, irony means saying something and meaning the opposite. According to Sean Hall "irony is about opposites" (44). When people say the opposite of what they mean "they are expressing a belief or feeling that is at odds with what they are saying on the surface" (44). And they often indicate that they are being ironic by either using extreme understatement or overstatement. The key to irony, then, is the double layer between what is said and what is meant. Claire Colebrook points out that such a practice can often smack of elitism since ironic speech suggests two audiences: one that gets the irony and one that doesn't (20). That gap between understanding irony and being confused by it often leads to the notion that irony is negative for democracy since it seems to create a sense of intellectual superiority. The problem, though, is the "reality" that lies behind the ironic statement. Even if we concede that the concept of reality is slippery, the only members of our society threatened by the use of irony to expose fallacies in public discourse are those that attempt to depend on fallacies for their social power and rhetorical persuasion. One of the key merits of irony for a healthy democracy is the fact that it asks the audience to decode, decipher, and deconstruct the message. Such practices have real benefits for the health of a democracy where the public is constantly negotiating meaning in a field of misrepresentations, deceptions, and political performance.

Irony, though, has always been under suspicion and this was especially true after 9/11 when a number of critics enthusiastically announced the "death of Irony." The idea was that irony is divisive, filled with unspoken derision, and too obtuse. The concept of irony was often confused with cynicism and silliness. Or, if we were to listen to Alanis Morissette's famous pop song "Ironic," irony simply refers to things that are just unpleasant. As Zoe Williams of *The Guardian* notes, you may regularly hear "Isn't it ironic?" But, in fact, mostly it isn't "ironic" at all: "Hypocritical, cynical, lazy, coincidental, more likely. . . . We have a grave problem with this word (well, in fact, it's not really grave—but I'm not being ironic when I call it that, I'm being hyperbolic)."[5] Suffering from public misrecognition of what the term really means, irony was often cast as either too negative or too self indulgent to be a useful mode for post-9/11 communication. Ironically, after 9/11 many assumed that we would enter a time when language really meant what it meant. There were celebrations that the critical nature of irony would give way to a return to positive language. As linguist Geoffrey Nunberg pointed out two months after the attacks,

> Some people see this as the sign of a reevaluation of American priorities. "The Age of Irony died yesterday," wrote Andrew Coyne in Canada's *National Post* on Sept. 12, a report confirmed a few days later by no less an authority than *Vanity Fair* editor and *Spy* co-founder Graydon Carter: "There's going to be a seismic change. I think it's the end of the age of irony." Roger Rosenblatt came to the same conclusion in a *Time* essay that decried the intellectuals and "pop-culture makers" whose detachment and unseriousness now seems a dangerously empty pose: "The ironists, seeing through everything, made it difficult for anyone to see anything."[6]

It was no longer the time for figurative or artful or layered language. The idea was that irony was an inadequate mode for discussing the attacks; it lacked the gravitas needed. But that notion was ironic for the simple fact that the nation was already being fed a series of misleading, non-factual statements by both the government and the press on a daily basis. Even if we read the statements by the administration in the most generous light, they were sending mixed messages to the public in a way that defied a literal use of language. As Nunberg reminds us, "These really are unprecedented times, when the administration tells us that the most patriotic thing that most of us can do now is to get on with our normal daily lives, but to remain alert for terrorists at the mall and anthrax in the mail."[7] Thus the attacks on irony after 9/11 reveal more about the way that the concept is often misunderstood than they do about the limits of irony for democracy. As Nunberg explains, "irony has always been a natural response to the condition of trying to live a normal life in ominous times."[8] Irony doesn't make the times ominous, nor does it distance the public from a commitment to their nation; it does, however, ask us to question received messages, to think about how language is used, and to wonder at the links between words and what they are meant to represent. "Irony is a way of seeing things and seeing through them at the same time."[9] And that, Nunberg reminds us, was a pretty rare practice well before 9/11.

Luckily the claims to irony's death were greatly exaggerated. As Williams points out, despite the excitement with which some critics looked forward to the end of irony, it was impossible to repress it in an era when the actual realities of the time were so steeped in double-layered meaning and contradiction: "Naturally, irony was back within a few days, not least because of the myriad ironies contained within the attack itself (America having funded al-Qaida is ironic; America raining bombs and peanut butter on Afghanistan is ironic)." She goes on to explain why we need irony in moments of crisis: "The end of irony would be a disaster for the world—bad things will always occur, and those at fault will always attempt to cover them up with emotional and overblown language.... Irony can deflate a windbag in a way that very little else can."[10] The key point here, and one that can't be forgotten, is that irony only works with what there is. If there is no windbag, no falsehood, no rhetorical authoritarianism, and no human folly, then irony has no hold.

Irony, then, is an eye-opener. It allows the audience to perceive hidden or obscured meaning. And it is different from satire because it is not a form of comedy, but rather is far more specifically a mode of critical thinking. Much—almost all—satire uses irony, but the reverse is not true. Irony is not comedy. Also irony may simply be aimed at exposing deception and hypocrisy. It does not necessarily carry with it the same degree of social critique that is at the core of satire. Irony does not have the performance quality of satire. Both irony and satire attempt to instill awareness and correct misperceptions of reality, but satire is typically understood as more socially engaged and more aimed at change than irony. Irony can just be a form of derision in the face of folly. Many of the pieces that appeared in *The Onion* after 9/11 exemplify this sort of irony, since their critical mode is almost too straightforward for them to be seen as comedic satire. One such piece appeared just over two weeks after the attacks. In "U.S. Vows to Defeat Whoever It Is We're at War With" *The Onion* practiced a key form of post-9/11 irony:

> In a televised address to the American people Tuesday, a determined President Bush vowed that the U.S. would defeat "whoever exactly it is we're at war with here." Flanked by Condoleezza Rice and Donald Rumsfeld, President Bush pledges to "exact revenge, just as soon as we know who we're exacting revenge against and where they are."
>
> "America's enemy, be it Osama bin Laden, Saddam Hussein, the Taliban, a multinational coalition of terrorist organizations, any of a rogue's gallery of violent Islamic

fringe groups, or an entirely different, non-Islamic aggressor we've never even heard of . . . be warned," Bush said during an 11-minute speech from the Oval Office. "The United States is preparing to strike, directly and decisively, against you, whoever you are, just as soon as we have a rough idea of your identity and a reasonably decent estimate as to where your base is located."[11]

The brilliance of this piece is that today it feels more like satire. It is funny. But on September 26, 2001, it really wasn't funny; it was just ironic. What makes it different is that at the time of its release it signaled indignation over an administration poised for war when they were not clear on our enemies or the goals of the war. There was very little funny about watching a nation declare war in such a manner. And while satire is almost never roll-on-the-floor-laughing funny, there still is a difference between being able to read a piece like the one above with a wry smile and reading it with an angry glare. On September 26, 2001 it would have likely promoted the angry glare; today we might manage a wry smile. This means that one of your best tests for whether a bit is ironic or satirically ironic is your reaction, since a perfect division between them is impossible and since so much of what they do overlaps.

Satire is often indistinguishable from *mockery*—or what Peterson dubs *pseudo-satire*. Real satire may be silly and fun, but it always has a clear intent to promote critical thought, while mockery and pseudo-satire stop short of delivering a message: "Satire nourishes our democracy, while the other stuff—let's call it pseudo-satire, since it bears a superficial resemblance to the real thing—is like fast food: popular, readily available, cheap; tasty in its way, but ultimately unhealthy" (23). The point is that not all contemporary forms of satire are equal: programs that are primarily focused on politics, like *The Daily Show*, should not be confused with other late-night comedy that is aimed more at apolitical irony than actual political satire. The litmus test is intent, not how funny the bit is. If the program has an intention to stimulate critical thinking, then what you have before you is satire; if the goal is to mock a stupid situation, then what you have is pseudo-satire, mockery, or cynical irony. Think of it as the difference between shows like *South Park* or *The Simpsons*, which Gray, Jones, and Thompson describe as being "willing to attack 'everything,' thereby not amounting to any form of 'meaningful' political discourse" and shows that attack with a goal of promoting critical reflection like *The Colbert Report* (7). As Jones describes it in his contribution to *Satire TV*, after 9/11 there was a vast difference between the type of humor on a show like *SNL* and that found on *The Daily Show*. According to him, *SNL* "had become little more than a community theater troupe's interpretation of political advertisements on TV, and perhaps even played an unwitting role in reinforcing the political messages that both campaigns wanted embedded in voters' minds." Pseudo-satire in this context was nothing more than an accomplice to power. He explains that as *SNL* was retreating from any real satirical intervention productive satire could be found elsewhere on cable: "Rather than recoiling after 9/11, another show written and produced in New York, *The Daily Show with Jon Stewart*, found its legs with an aggressive critique of the Bush administration's wars and terror(izing) campaigns" (46).

The point is that some ironic comedy is just intensely, critically, negative critique that offers little, if any, of the hope and radical imagination necessary for stimulating effective public discourse. Negative, merely cynical satire, then, is quite different from politically productive satire. Even though both types of comedy play with social norms and both lead to critical responses, politically productive satire is not satisfied with cynicism, apathy, or disillusionment as a response. Gray, Jones, and Thompson outline key features of satire in their essay "The State of Satire, the Satire of the State." They point out that one of the essential elements of satire is that, through the performance of scrutiny and critique, the audience is asked to perform their own scrutiny and critique. Thus, one key characteristic of satire that differentiates it from apolitical irony, pseudo-satire, and cynical mockery is its call for an active audience. News may seem to offer viewers information and pseudo-satire may make it funny, but satire does more. Satire asks the audience to take a piece of news and play with it, test it, reflect on it, and question it, "rather than simply consume it as information or 'truth' from authoritative sources" (11). Another key feature of satire is that it asks the audience to question sources of authority and to refuse to take the status quo for granted. But, just as it asks the audience to think critically, it does so in a form that is highly entertaining and pleasurable. In contrast with dry political commentary, satire can communicate with a general, educated public and it can demonstrate, in a way that combines silliness with seriousness, that commonly accepted truths require reconsideration and resistance. While political satire always has political goals and always comes with an intent to mock human stupidity, its inherent critique is fun which allows the audience a chance to "get it" without feeling humiliated. Thus, unlike nasty mockery and the comedy of put-downs, satire ultimately works to create a sense of community among those that bond together since they get the joke. The collective experience of getting the joke together stimulates the social bonds necessary for a commitment to democracy, showing how satire plays a direct role in strengthening the public sphere.

This is why satire should also not be confused with *cynicism, sarcasm,* and *negative mockery.* Each of these forms has a common practice of derision—a comedic form that does not unite the audience, but rather makes someone a clear "butt" of the joke. These modes of communication share with irony layered meaning and playful language. Using hyperbole, understatement, double entendre, and wit, these forms of figurative language—where the speaker says something different from what is meant—do ask the brain to work harder to process meaning since it has to analyze the relationship between literal and figurative meanings. The trick, though, is that these modes of communication may be at the service of making the speaker feel smart, superior, or self-righteous. Much of Bill Maher's comedy falls into just this sort of derision, even though he can also be a great source of critically powerful satire. Similarly, Lewis Black often appears to just hate all of humankind for the inane things it does and he often ends his bits in a screaming frenzy, literally spitting bile at the audience, who mostly feels on his side, but may also feel yelled at. While it may be fun to watch these comedians, they don't have the same sort of political energy that Stewart, Colbert, and groups like The Yes Men have. They might inspire some critical distance in their viewers, but it is hard to imagine them gathering a large audience on the National Mall to rally for democracy. As Gray, Jones, and Thompson explain, "Satire is provocative, not dismissive—a crucial point that critics typically ignore when assessing its rôle in public discourse" (13).

So one of the best tests that can help distinguish between satire and pseudo-satire is that of intent and inspiration. That should make identifying true satire easy, right? Well, sort of. To make things even more confusing even the best political satirists can occasionally lapse into apolitical cynicism. Stewart can launch a sharp barb that has the sole goal of making its object seem idiotic. Even the gregarious and charismatic Colbert can come pretty close to moving into the realm of cynical invective. In one case where he spoofed Mika Brzezinski's frustrations over having to cover Sarah Palin he wavered between extremely smart satire and biting sarcasm (see Figure 5.1). After running a clip of an exasperated Brzezinski asking her co-host Joe Scarborough when exactly Palin was going to stop being news, Colbert launched in to give her a pep talk:

> I know you think this story has no purpose other than keeping Sarah Palin's name in the headlines for another news cycle. I know you think she has nothing to offer the national dialogue and that her speeches are just coded talking points mixed in with words picked up at random from a Thesaurus.
> I know you think Sarah Palin is at best a self-promoting ignoramus and at worst a shameless media troll who will abuse any platform to deliver dog-whistle encouragement to a far right base that may include possible insurrectionists.[12]

He went on about how hard it was to cover Palin only to end by telling Brzezinski to suck it up and do her job. The brilliance of the bit was that Colbert did little to disguise his disgust for Palin, but he wrapped his visceral loathing of the former

Figure 5.1   Stephen Colbert lectures Mika Brzezinski on how to cover Palin[13]

vice presidential candidate in a smart piece of satire that reminded his audience of the very real ways that Palin's politics represent a true threat to our democracy. So not only can the same comedian mix satire and pseudo-satire; the same bit might as well.

As if those messy combinations were not enough to make it seem impossible to tell when comedy hurts our democracy and when it helps, we also have critics that refuse to see the satiric potential of some comedy and just dismiss it outright as cynicism. Drawing the distinction between *skepticism* and *cynicism*, Roderick Hart and Johanna Hartelius argue that Stewart has "engaged in unbridled political cynicism" (263). They argue that one of the things they most deplore is that Stewart "makes cynicism attractive [. . . and] profitable" (263). According to them,

> [Stewart] saps his audience's sense of political possibility even as he helps AT&T sell its wares. Stewart urges them to steer clear of conventional politics and to do so while steering a Nissan. Mr. Stewart is especially attractive to young people, so his website offers them portable cynicism in the form of CDs, DVDs, clothes, books, and collectibles. Stewart knows there's money to be made in cynicism. (263)

While the tone of their piece borders on the satirical, and certainly seems cynical, they suggest that Stewart is a "fundamentally anti-political creature" (264). They point specifically to his use of the diatribe as an example of what makes him more a cynic than a satirist. And they claim that the goal of the show is to "make people feel bad about politics" (268). In contrast, they suggest, our nation needs skeptics, not cynics: "Skeptics are buoyed up by the need to know. Because life is complex, an enlightened politics requires a considerable amount of skepticism. But unlike the cynic, the skeptic can have faith in human institutions because they are fashioned by group effort, not by lone individuals, and because the ravages of time rarely vanquish them" (271). It seems that the authors of the piece paid no attention to Stewart's rally on the National Mall or to his push for supporting veterans' health claims and a First Responders Health Care Bill.

The point is that even among scholars of satire, there is great disagreement over who is the "real" satirist. The attention that Stewart and Colbert have received for their satirical success has often made them a target of critique by those that suggest that their satire is too soft, too cynical, or too silly. One piece by Steve Almond, "The Joke's on You" in *The Baffler*, exemplifies this sort of critique. According to Almond, "What Stewart and Colbert do most nights is convert civic villainy into disposable laughs. They prefer Horatian satire to Juvenalian, and thus treat the ills of modern media and politics as matters of folly, not concerted evil."[14] It seems Almond missed the 2010 segment we analyzed in chapter 4 when *The Daily Show*'s John Oliver and Wyatt Cenac take opposing sides while debating a Fox News story that mocked and criticized Alwaleed bin Talal, a businessman who wanted to fund the mosque near Ground Zero, who, ironically, also happens to be part owner of Fox News. John Oliver represents Team Stupid, while Cenac argues for Team Evil in a bit that literally demonstrates the way that it can be difficult to determine if coverage like that of Fox News is a sign of stupidity or evil, and that shows that satire's goal is to expose both the evil and the stupid (see Figure 5.2).

Figure 5.2   Cenac and Oliver play out evil versus stupid[15]

Stewart ends the bit by asking the two if there could be another option, another way to understand Fox News's failure to mention that the person they were attacking was actually one of the owners of their network. The exchange proves beyond doubt that *The Daily Show* is engaging in exactly the sort of satire that exposes how folly and evil overlap and intersect:

> STEWART: Guys, this is obviously a very polarizing debate. There's lots of contradictory evidence. Is there a chance there is perhaps a third, less explosive, explanation? Something else?
>
> CENAC & OLIVER: No, no, no, no.
>
> OLIVER: Absolutely not, Jon. These are the only two possible explanations, because if they're not as stupid as I believe them to be, they are *really* fucking evil.
>
> CENAC: And if they're not as evil as I think they are, they are stupid. We're talking potatoes with mouths.
>
> OLIVER: No, no, not even potatoes, Wyatt. A potato can still power a digital clock.
>
> CENAC: Ooh, that's a good point, that's a really good point.
>
> OLIVER: Rocks. You're talking about rocks with mouths.
>
> STEWART: I'm glad you two could come to some agreement. Thank you very much.[16]

Despite the fact that it seems that Almond is simply not that familiar with the comedy of *The Colbert Report* and *The Daily Show*, he feels justified in making the claim that moments of real satirical punch are few and far between on the shows. Moreover, he suggests that Colbert and Stewart actually take pleasure from the very things they mock: "The queasy irony here is that Stewart and Colbert are parasites of the dysfunction they mock. Without blowhards such as Carlson and shameless politicians, Stewart would be out of a job that pays him a reported $14 million per annum. Without the bigoted bluster of Bill O'Reilly and Rush Limbaugh, *The Colbert Report* would not exist. They aren't just invested in the status quo, but dependent on it."[17] Who does Almond champion? Bill Maher. Didn't we say Bill Maher was a great satirist at times, but mostly prone to derisive mockery? Ironically, Almond engages in derisive mockery himself as he uses smarm and sarcasm to attack the satire of Stewart and Colbert. This is all to show that even the experts, or especially the experts, can disagree about the specific contours of satire and who best exemplifies it.

George Test explains that satire combines "judgment, aggression, play, and laughter" (30). He argues that, "The playfulness of satire, especially when yoked with serious questions, may disconcert some" (32). This means that there is no way to guarantee audience reaction; and some audiences may feel mocked or confused. But, if the goal is to encourage a critical reaction, satire has to take such risks. It can't be bland or palatable or just plain fun; it needs to be provocative and uncomfortable. It can't offer simple distractions, easy answers, or innocuous jokes. Gray, Jones, and Thompson emphasize that satire requires a certain level of sophistication from the audience, since this is comedy that involves "work" and won't offer "clear-cut or easily digestible meanings" (15). This process asks the audience to question power, to use critical thinking to critique social processes, and to resist the status quo.

When satire is combined with *parody*, as is the case with *The Colbert Report, The Daily Show, The Onion*, and The Yes Men the combination is especially powerful. Parody ridicules an "original." While satire exposes public deception, political vice, and social abuses, parody takes it to another level since the comedian embodies that which is being lampooned. One of the best examples is the satire of Stephen Colbert who performed in-character as a Bill O'Reilly-esque pundit who thought the whole nation should agree with him no matter how outrageous his beliefs. When Colbert presented himself as a right-wing, bloviating, political pundit who thought with his gut, hated books, and believed that his fears should be those of the nation, his exaggerated performance of the exact thing he wanted his audience to critique added an additional layer to his satire. Colbert's parody of punditry layers his remarks against the object of his parody. Similarly, *The Onion*'s parody of journalism lampoons the news media at the same time that it satirizes the story covered. Such a technique teaches the audience to question the original; it exposes how the original works by offering the audience an exaggeration that reveals in extreme ways the flaws in the original. The Yes Men embody members of the power elite—corporate spokesmen, government officials, industry experts—allowing their audience to immediately perceive the rhetoric of deception at the heart of the official party line. The sheer physical presence of the comedians dressed in suits and appearing in-character on television news adds an additional layer of critical pleasure to their performance (see Figure 5.3). After witnessing The Yes Men in action, no other spokesman will be perceived in the same way.

As Gray, Jones, and Thompson point out, "parody aims to provoke reflection *and re-evaluation* of how the targeted texts or genre works" (18). This means that satirical parody has the potential to be an even more effective source of public education and community building, since it adds additional layers of critique and

Figure 5.3   The Yes Men pose as members of the Chamber of Commerce[18]

asks the audience to work even harder to make sense of the joke and of its connections to the future of our nation.

One final feature of satire that we want to describe here is *wordplay*, *puns*, and other fun and smart uses of *satirical language*. While some satire is purely visual, as in the case of political cartoons, language is commonly a central feature of satire. This is so because satirists want to point to the deceptive use of language by those in power. Obviously, since satire and irony are linked to using language in ways that are not literal, there is a lot of wordplay at the center of the practice. The wordplay is always aimed at calling attention to the ways that those in power use words to hide and deceive and distract the public. Even though a critique of the ways words are misused by those in power is key to satire, it is important to remember that the conditions for honest and meaningful communication after 9/11 were under serious threat. We had deceptions, lies, and the misuse of words from both the government and the press. Captured Afghans were called "enemy combatants" so the United States did not have to follow the Geneva Conventions in their treatment and could hold them indefinitely at Guantánamo Bay. Donald Rumsfeld visited the site of tortured detainees at Abu Ghraib and renamed the site "Camp Redemption." We heard about the "war on terror" as US citizens had a constant flow of fear pumped at them from the government and the press— leading it to seem that we were more aptly experiencing the "war of terror." The illegal transfer of suspects for interrogation to undisclosed black sites was dubbed "extraordinary rendition," which caused Salman Rushdie to remark: "Beyond any shadow of a doubt, the ugliest phrase to enter the English language last year was 'extraordinary rendition'. To those of us who love words, this phrase's brutalization of meaning is an infallible signal of its intent to deceive."[19] Rushdie compared the phrase to other terms like "final solution" and "ethnic cleansing," insisting that the turn of phrase not distract the public from the brutality masked by innocuous language: "Language, too, has laws, and those laws tell us this new American usage is improper—a crime against the word."[20] These were not word games; they were deliberate misuses of words for political gain.

Thus the satirists had the difficult job of trying to reveal these abuses of language in a way that was smart and entertaining and had the hope of helping the public reconnect with the truth behind the falsehoods. In a 2006 interview with *New York Magazine* Colbert explained how the role of language in the post-9/11 era had influenced his own work: "Language has always been important in politics, but language is incredibly important to the present political struggle . . . Because if you can establish an atmosphere in which information doesn't mean anything, then there is no objective reality. The first show we did, a year ago, was our thesis statement: What you wish to be true is all that matters, regardless of the facts. Of course, at the time, we thought we were being farcical."[21] Colbert makes a direct link between false notions of the truth and deliberate linguistic misrepresentation. And while all of the satirists we have profiled in this book use language in creative, smart, and fun ways, it would be fair to say that Colbert has been one of the masters of satirical language in the post-9/11 era. As Adam Sternbergh put it in his *New York Magazine* article, farce is a language "no one is speaking more fluently than Colbert."[22]

As McClennen points out in *Colbert's America* "each section of *The Colbert Report* showcases different forms of wordplay" (127). The opening rundown was driven by puns. Puns point to the multiple ways that words can signify. They can happen through play with homophones—words that sound similar—words with multiple meanings, or manipulating words and creating neologisms. Colbert began his show with a rundown that always included wordplay and often included puns like "It's not a recession, it's a correction. Correction, it's a recession. This Is *The Colbert Report!*"[23] Next Colbert had even more fun with words in the opening graphics that had an animated version of him swoop down holding an American flag while words swirled around him (see Figure 5.4).

Figure 5.4   Colbert leaps across the screen while punning[24]

Here are just a few examples of the puns and neologisms that circled around the screen as a computer-generated Colbert heroically entered:

Puns and neologisms:

- Factose Intolerant
- Colmes-free since 2009
- Lincolnish
- Libertease
- Fundit
- Überballed
- Heterosapien
- Grippy
- Megamerican
- Superstantial
- Freem
- Fearnix rising
- Originalist
- Flagaphile
- Eneagled
- Gutly
- Consubstantial?

Of course the most famous wordplay of *The Colbert Report* was the recurring segment entitled "The Wørd." This was the segment that introduced the neologism "truthiness" on the opening episode and we've described a few of these satirical wordplays throughout this book. Colbert explained the purpose of the segment in an out-of-character interview with Terry Gross, saying "The Wørd" segment is an essay based on a single word: "I'm speaking a completely self-sufficient, stand-alone essay, hopefully comedic. And on the left side of the screen it's giving bullet points that are excerpting parts of what I said, or commenting on what I just said. And the bullet points end up being their own character. Sometimes they're reinforcing my argument, sometimes they're sort of countermanding my argument. But it's sort of a textual addition of jokes or satire to the verbal essay I'm doing at the moment."[25] Geoffrey Baym argues that the bullet points functioned as a corrective to Colbert's spoken words: "the written text provides an unspoken voice, a second level of meaning that often contradicts, challenges, and undermines the spoken words" ("Stephen Colbert's Parody of the Postmodern," 130). But as McClennen argues the bullet points didn't offer a common, unified mode of communication: "Sometimes they add further exaggeration to what Colbert is saying, sometimes they critically contradict him, sometimes they just add a silly aside, and sometimes they express a sense of frustration and defeat with his use of rhetoric. The brilliance of the bullet points, then, is their varied discursive registers" (132). In each case, though, Colbert exemplifies how a playful use of language can pack a political punch.

Colbert's use of puns, neologisms, and silly words worked to draw attention to the powerful ways that satirical use of language can expose how words are manipulated by those in power. The satirical use of playful language has a serious intent. And its goal is to bring the audience together as it recognizes the need to reclaim words while also reclaiming our nation from those ruling us with deceit, deception, and for personal gain. During Colbert's interview with Gross he pointed out the pun that he felt was at the core of his show: the pronunciation of "report" with a silent "t" purposefully created a homophone with "rapport." Colbert explained that the rapport he hoped to build with his show is "a sense of understanding between the speaker and the listener. We're the same people you and me, we get it. The rest of the people out there they don't understand the things that we understand. The show is like an invitation to the audience to be part of the club."[26] This is how satire works: it reveals falsehoods for what they are, it does so with a smart and complex use of language, it creates a sense of community and engagement, it asks us to resist and question the status quo, and it helps us have fun while we do it.

What if I Still Don't Get it?

One of the thorny questions at the heart of satire is whether it tells the audience what to think. If satire uses humor to expose falsehoods or sheer stupidity, then isn't it actually telling the audience that they *must* agree with the satirist and reject the object of their satire? This was the line of questioning Christian Brady, Dean of the Schreyer Honors College at Penn State, used when he questioned both of us on our claim that satire encourages critical thinking. In a blog piece that thinly congratulated us on the book project we were launching, he went on to criticize our thesis: "In a previous Twitter exchange we discussed the role of satire and it was stated (and I paraphrase) that satire 'never tells anyone what to think.' That statement has bothered me because it is patently untrue."[27] Brady doesn't get it, just as many other satire skeptics don't get it. First of all, satire doesn't create the object of its ridicule. In order for there to be satire, there have to be powerful people deserving of it. As we explained above, satire is not put-down comedy aimed at a laugh at someone's expense. There is a serious distinction and it can't be forgotten. Pseudo-satire might be content with suggesting that the object of satire is ridiculous in some form or another, but true satire is committed to asking the audience to decipher meaning and draw conclusions. The point is that we are already being deceived and duped; satire just points out that fact. So, it is the object of satire that is trying to control how we think, not the satire. Brady goes on to write "Satire tells us, at the minimum, that the position being mocked is *not* worth maintaining."[28] If that were true, though, then everyone would always get the joke. But, as we point out in chapter eight, not everyone can decipher the layers of meaning in satire.

The reason for this is that satire never says what it means. As we explained above, irony and wordplay can be tricky to intellectually navigate, but that process has real critical payoff since it requires the audience to negotiate meaning and understand the figurative use of language. So if you "get" the joke, you had to work hard to do so; you had to recognize the relationship between the object of the satire and the satire. Satire can't make that process simple or transparent. And it can't tell you what to think or it isn't satire; it's pseudo-satire, cynical mockery, or outright comedic derision. Those modes can be fun, of course, but they are not actual satire. Critics like Brady, though, seem to not understand how figurative language actually works. They forget that there is a difference between saying what you mean and using satire to ask an audience to question meaning. And they forget that what makes satire work is largely a result of what is unsaid. Megan Boler and Stephen Turpin explain that satire not only stipulates "what is otherwise unsaid within a given political climate," it also states "the unsaid, and [says] it for the unheard populace" (393). Baym further explains that satire is both a "discourse of integration" and a "rhetoric of challenge" ("Discursive Integration" 276). Colebrook contends that "irony is the resistance to a single point of view" (80). Thus Brady fails to appreciate that satire is trying to undo authoritative discourse and provoke critical thinking. Ian Reilly explains that "the fruits of satiric inquiry and provocation produce healthy forms of democratic participation; in this capacity, satire can be seen to encourage resistance, promote dialogue, and enact positive change. In keeping with this mode of inquiry, scholars often position satire as a form of ideological opposition" (43). The point that Brady misses is that this means that satire cannot offer only one way to respond to its critique. It opens the door; the audience decides how or whether to go through it.

Ironically, just as critics like Brady will suggest that satire tells us what to think, others will worry that it doesn't tell us what to think enough. Because satire is a form of entertainment, because it is wrapped in comedy, it often is accused—as we saw above with Almond—of not hitting hard enough. Again, though, satire can't take out its object of critique. Instead, it has to point the audience in the right direction and hope that they will do it. Stephen Duncombe in an interview with Henry Jenkins makes this point when he wonders if the comedy of Colbert and Stewart is just negative ironic joking that will lead to apathy: "it's still unclear that ironic joking leads to the sort of popular response I'm hypothesizing . . . It can, just as easily, lead into a resigned acceptance that all politics are just a joke and the best we can hope for it to get a good laugh out of it all."[29] Even though Duncombe is ultimately enthusiastic about the comedy of Colbert and Stewart, confessing, in fact, that he "loves" the shows, it is just these sorts of musings that remind us that the nature of satire continues to be confusing for many. Duncombe ends his interview recognizing the true nature of satire: "It's really up to the rest of us to answer the questions he poses. Sometimes I think we ask too much of culture: we expect it to solve our political problems for us. I don't think it can do this. It can create openings, give us insight, provide us with tools, but the rest is a political process that counts on all of us."[30] That, of course, is the whole point. Satire does not prescribe outcomes. If it were that easy, it would quickly render itself obsolete and we would no longer live in a world of deceit, abuse of power, and deception.

Another reason it has become especially difficult to navigate the difference between real satire and pseudo-satire is a consequence of an additional post-9/11 turn in language use: the rise of *smarm* and *snark*. Smarm and snark recently took center stage in an internet battle that began with a piece by Tom Scocca on *Gawker* "On Smarm" that pits two different types of public intellectual discourse against each other. But let us begin by describing snark, since that term was highlighted in the debate first. Snark is a neologism that derives from a combination of snide and remark and it tends to refer to a mode of negative, cynical speech commonly found on the internet. David Denby's book *Snark* describes it as a form of nasty, abusive language (1). For Denby snark is an offensive "combination of snide and sarcasm that goes beyond irony and satire to just plain ugliness. Snark erupts from the mouths of politicians and pundits, from bloggers and newscasters, and from comedians too lazy to be truly funny. It's the cheap shot that hits below the belt. It's everywhere, and according to Denby, it's damaging to everyone it touches" (back matter).

What is interesting is that Denby goes out of his way to explain that snark is not satire. He specifically points out that Jon Stewart and Stephen Colbert "can be rough," "but the Stewart/Colbert claws are sharpened in a special way. Even when pecking at a victim's tender spots, they also manage to defend civic virtue four times a week" (1–2). Denby explains that what makes the sharpness of Stewart and Colbert unique is that they are "always trying to say, '*This is not the way a national government should behave* '" (2). "Snark," he explains by contrast, "has zero interest in civic virtue or anything else except the power to ridicule" (2). While we agree with Denby that Stewart and Colbert are in the business of using satire to buttress civic virtue, we disagree with his assessment of snark. For us it is smarm that lacks civic virtue and that uses a sickly sweet mode to actually advance a position of superiority.

At a basic level the exchange we had with Brady is a perfect example of smarm. As Eric Albertson explains, "Smarm is the effort to silence dissent through the disapproval and exclusion of dissenters."[31] Brady, who can't help dropping his Oxford credentials at every turn, uses a condescending tone toward us that discounts the object of our study. Albertson links that sort of behavior directly to smarm: "Smarm is often directed downward at anyone who lacks more traditional elite credentials, particularly younger and/or lesser known writers who are using the internet as a means to gain an audience."[32] Thus, at the heart of smarm is a generational gap between those that think that the internet is dumbing us all down and those that see the internet as simply a new form of communication that brings both benefits and risks to society. Denby proclaims that "[s]nark is the expression of the alienated, of the ambitious, of the dispossessed" (25). Albertson sees Denby's remarks as a battle between "smarmy incumbents against the snarky insurgents."[33]

A key feature of the debate is the idea that those that practice snark use a tone that is disrespectful. Smarm, though, is accused of using a false tone of respect to thinly conceal disdain. What bothers those often accused of snark is the way that smarm feels fake. In contrast, those accused of snark seem to be aggressive cynics out for blood. And that is why it helps explain a larger breakdown in public discourse today. Few folks proclaim to communicate in the modes of either smarm or snark—these are generally epithets hurled at offensive speech. But the breakdown is real: those on the side of snark are exhausted by the games, while enjoying playful language aimed at revealing abuses of power; and those on the side of smarm seek gentle critique and favor a sweet tone, while they self-congratulate for being bastions of virtue and good living. Scocca asks, "What is smarm, exactly? Smarm is a kind of performance—an assumption of the forms of seriousness, of virtue, of constructiveness, without the substance. Smarm is concerned with appropriateness and with tone. Smarm disapproves. . . . Smarm would rather talk about anything other than smarm."[34] For Scocca, snark exists as a reaction to smarm. It is a mode that emerges to express exhaustion and disgust at the performance of smarm.

To make it even more complicated both sides accuse the other of practicing cynicism: smarmy cynicism is sweet and snarky cynicism is bristly—but the differences are deeper. Scocca explains the breakdown this way: "Snark is often conflated with cynicism, which is a troublesome misreading. Snark may speak in cynical terms about a cynical world, but it is not cynicism itself. It is a theory of cynicism. The practice of cynicism is smarm."[35] That is the key difference—and it is one with which we agree—snark responds to an existing cynical world; smarm produces the cynical world that the snarkers hate. Snark will be accused of criticism for the sake of cynicism or apathy or malice; but that is not right. Snark uses a sharp tone to expose lies, deceptions, and illogical twists of rhetoric. Snark is a mode of critique that refuses to accept the duplicitously civilized tone of smarm and that is why satire often gets pulled into the debate. Denby states that real satire is not snark because real satire has civic virtue; yet Malcolm Gladwell equates snark with satire: "What defines our era, after all, is not really the insistence of those in authority that we all behave properly and politely. It is defined, instead, by the institutionalization of satire."[36]

Confused yet? We bet you are. What all of this has shown is that satire is an extremely slippery communicative mode and it is emerging in force at an especially complicated moment in our history. How can you tell if what you are witnessing is the sort of satire that will strengthen our democracy? If it asks you to think, if it calls attention to issues central to the health of our nation, if it refuses to replicate the party line, if it does all of this using figurative language that never means what it says, and if it entertains you, then you can be pretty sure that you have just had some fun with satire.

Satire in a Hyper-Ironic Era

Ok, so satire is meant to be a playful, critical, ironic mode of discourse that points to the pitfalls and failures of those in power. But what happens when those groups are already being ironic? Colebrook points to the directly political nature of irony: "The problem of irony is at one with the problem of politics: how do we know what others really mean, and on what basis can we secure the sincerity and authenticity of speech?" (2). She reminds us that Socrates resorted specifically to irony "to challenge received knowledge and wisdom at a historical moment when the comfort and security of small communities was being threatened" and he used it to point out that "it may be that what is being said is *not meant*" (2). As Colebrook unravels the differences in irony over time, she notes that in the postmodern era irony is the norm: "We live in a world of quotation. Pastiche, simulation, and cynicism: a general and all-encompassing irony" (1).

As we explained above, after 9/11, little political speech meant what it said and most coverage of that speech in the mainstream news failed to ask questions about that duplicity. In the immediate aftermath of 9/11 a lot of that deceptive use of language was bundled together with ideas of how the postmodern era had ushered in an era of irony and simulation where nothing being said was real. Many scholars considered the complex ways that words connected to meaning in those days when all of the structures of reference seemed to collapse. What was key then was that irony was under attack from all corners as an inappropriate mode, even though, as we explained, it served a crucial public role early on as a corrective to misinformation and double-speak. There was a real tension between the brazen satirists and those who found satire to be disrespectful or worse.

Much of that has changed, though, in the 21st century. While the satirists still enjoy plenty of derision from those in power, and while those in power still use plenty of double-speak, we now have a moment when both politicians and the mainstream news regularly adopt a tone that tries to emulate satire. Such was the case when Sarah Palin defended Rush Limbaugh's use of the word "retard" by saying that he used the word satirically: "Rush Limbaugh was using satire . . . I agree with Rush Limbaugh."[37] Palin, who has a child with special needs herself, stated that when Limbaugh used the word it was not an insult, because he didn't mean it (see Figure 5.5). Now, you don't have to have watched Limbaugh's show much to know that the use of "retard" by Rush was anything but satirical; he commonly hurls insults at those with whom he disagrees. What is noteworthy is that Palin defended him by saying that he was using satire. Now this is quite a turn of events and one that Colbert had to cover since Rush actually said: "Our politically correct society is acting like some giant insult has taken place by calling a bunch of people who are retards, retards."[38] Does that sound like satire? Nope. But Colbert uses irony to expose that by jokingly saying "It's so subtle, see. So many layers."[39]

Figure 5.5   Colbert feigns surprise at Palin's reference to satire[40]

To counter, Colbert said we should all support Palin by calling her a "fucking retard": "Sarah Palin knows that it's okay to call someone a retard if like Rush you clearly don't mean it which is why we should all come to her defense and say: Sarah Palin is a fucking retard."[41] Colbert responded to the way that Palin was trying to hijack satire, by using the ultimate sarcastic move of seeming to joke, while also being pretty serious. Colbert shows Limbaugh and Palin what it means to really speak in layers.

There are other examples of political speech edging directly into the realm of comedy and satire. Herman Cain, who sought the republican nomination for president in the 2012 election, constantly described himself as a comedian. When asked by CNN what he would bring to the White House that differentiated him from the other candidates running, Cain replied: "I would bring a sense of humor to the White House, because America's too uptight!"[42] Cain's jokes, however, were largely examples of outright derision and insult. There were numerous instances of him making jokes in poor taste, but what was really noteworthy was the way that he tried to pass off as humor comments that were outright offensive and spoken with no original irony of any kind. *The New York Times* reported in October 2011 that Cain backtracked out of an offensive comment about immigrants by trying to call it a joke:

> At two campaign rallies in Tennessee on Saturday night, the Republican presidential candidate Herman Cain said that part of his immigration policy would be to build an electrified fence on the country's border with Mexico that could kill people trying to enter the country illegally. But by Sunday morning, in a dramatic change of tone, Mr. Cain, a former restaurant executive, said he was only kidding. "That's a joke," Mr. Cain told the journalist David Gregory during an appearance on NBC's "Meet the Press," where he was asked about the electrified fence. "That's not a serious plan. I've also said America needs to get a sense of humor."[43]

Now we could go on about how such sorts of jokes would be frightening coming out of the White House. We could further point out that we don't really need our president to be funny; we need the president to be presidential. But the key takeaway here is the shift in tone from the post-9/11 era. Now politicians use the rhetoric of comedy and satire to hide their outrageous claims and to avoid accountability for the serious impact of what they say. Can you imagine Bush doing that? Indignation and self-righteousness have been replaced by claims of comedy, satire, and lightheartedness.

All this combines to make the work of true satire even harder since the public is understandably confused by the misuse of the term and by the use of the rhetoric of comedy to cover for offensive speech. One might imagine that Mitt Romney would have been happy to suggest that his statement about 47% of the population being moochers was actually satire, but he didn't. In fact, he simply tried to claim he had never said it all, even though we all saw a video of him saying those exact words. Dan Balz interviewed the presidential candidate about the snafu for his book, *Collision 2012*, which was excerpted in *The Washington Post*. Balz tried to press Romney to see why saying that 47% of the population doesn't take personal responsibility for themselves would logically hurt a campaign. But instead Romney replied to him: "Actually, I didn't say that . . . That's how it began to be perceived, and so I had to ultimately respond to the perception, because perception is reality."[44] Romney flatly refused to admit he had said the phrase, but what is of even greater interest is that he suggests that the perception became reality. Viveca Greene, riffing on Linda Hutcheon, explains that "Irony as a rhetorical strategy can be used by the dominant and the subaltern, racists and antiracists, progressives and conservatives" (120). It serves as a good reminder since Romney's twist on perception and reality was certainly ironic. Luckily for our nation, the voting public saw through Romney's spin and elected not to vote for a man that held almost half of our nation in contempt.

Romney wasn't just full of irony, though, in the 2012 campaign. He also served as a parody of himself, which occasionally made it difficult for the comedians to distinguish his antics from their own. In *Mitt*, the documentary that provides a behind-the-scenes look at the candidate, the viewer is exposed to many examples of Mitt comedy. In one scene he tries to iron his shirt while wearing it—a sign of his vanity and lack of common sense (see Figure 5.6a). The shot, though, is hugely reminiscent of the spoof video by CollegeHumor, "Mitt Romney Style" that parodied Romney's fancy lifestyle and disconnection from the population he wanted to elect him (see Figure 5.6b).

Between Palin's invocation of satire, Cain's recourse to comedy, and Romney's trouble with reality, we regularly see politicians who cross the line into comedy— even if only for rhetorical purposes. Similarly, we see more and more news media overtly or subtly dipping into comedy as well. Anderson Cooper now ends his program with the RidicuList, a series of silly, nonsensical news items. This, of course, is of some concern for those of us that think there is some advantage to having serious news coverage available to the public. Cooper was tied with Stewart in that famous Pew Research poll from 2007 where the comedian ranked fourth in the list of "most admired new figures."[45] What one has to wonder is whether Cooper thinks he will be more "admired" by adding some silliness to his show. Sadly, though, that is not likely to happen, nor will younger viewers necessarily tune in. The reason why this strategy won't work is because Cooper is just being silly and funny, not using satire to help raise public awareness of vital social issues. The comedy of Colbert and Stewart, for instance, is fun and insightful; whereas the Cooper humor is just silly. If anything, the RidicuList only makes viewers less likely to want to watch a show that seems confused about whether it is silly comedy or news. Cooper is not doing the ironic satirical news that young viewers have come to trust. Jones explains that, "Despite (or perhaps because of) its ironic tone, the language of satire therefore may seemingly maintain a degree of authenticity to younger citizens simply because it doesn't seem so closely aligned with the 'manufactured' realities that politicians, advertisers, and news media construct and would have them believe" (*Entertaining* 245). From 9/11 to today we have increasingly seen satire take on the role of the most trusted news source and the rise of silly news on mainstream channels is not likely to help. Nor is the increasing cry of "I was just kidding" going to help us trust our politicians. What we see today is greater public trust in those that practice true satire since they are not trying to either distract or deceive us.

Figure 5.6   A fine line between reality and parody[46]

Over a decade after irony was pronounced dead after 9/11, we have it alive and kicking both where we expect and in wholly new parts of public discourse. We hope that this chapter has helped break down the distinctions between true satire and watered-down or counterfeit versions. Moreover, we hope that it is now clear that satire doesn't tell you what to think; instead it encourages you to ask questions and refuse prescribed conclusions. In a world filled with media spectacle and political spiel, satire often seems like a voice of reason and a source of trust, but it is important not to forget the complicated art of how satire works and the fact that it never says what it means. Amber Day points out that it is a mistake to see irony and sincerity as "mutually exclusive," since they can work together to create productive political insight (33). That, of course, may well be true—but it's still ironic.

6

Mesmerized Millennials and BYTE-ing Satire: Or How Today's Young Generation Thinks

In July of 2008, baby boomer Nicholas Carr wrote a piece for *The Atlantic* for its annual "ideas issue." His contribution—"Is Google Making us Stupid?"—quickly came to summarize a lot of boomer notions about the ways that internet technology is changing how our nation thinks. In contrast to Bill O'Reilly's cavalier epithet that all of Jon Stewart's viewers were just "stoned slackers," Carr's article posed as reasoned, quasi-scientific proof that our brains are working differently.[1] According to Carr: "Thanks to the ubiquity of text on the internet, not to mention the popularity of text-messaging on cell phones, we may well be reading more today than we did in the 1970s or 1980s, when television was our medium of choice. But it's a different kind of reading, and behind it lies a different kind of thinking—perhaps even a new sense of the self."[2] Carr's central argument is that the way users consume information on the internet might have detrimental effects on cognition, and it mirrors much of the baby boomer rhetoric about the evils of a young networked society. He believes that since most of the material consumed on the internet comes in short snippets and brief flashes, it discourages more reflective and sustained patterns of reading, thereby diminishing our capacity for concentration and contemplation. Even worse, much of the material consumed is far removed from the sort of information useful to educating a citizenry. Certainly democratic deliberation requires thoughtful reflection and not simply media bytes. Carr claims that he sees "within us all . . . the replacement of complex inner density with a new kind of self—evolving under the pressure of information overload and the technology of the 'instantly available.'"[3] Carr identifies two problems with contemporary media culture: its short, easily digestible form, and its content, which too often is simply superficial and base.

But here is the problem with Carr. He misses the fact that his own views on this are generationally biased and he forgets that not all flash information is created equal. As we will explain further in this chapter, the millennial generation (young people born since the early 1980s) has been demonized as a "me generation" that has the attention span of a squirrel. Critiques of the internet, of Facebook, of what some call "slactivism" miss the reality that not all of the content that is short is stupid. And not all activism that is fast is ineffective. The millennial generation has often been described as consuming Facebook, twitter, snapchat, and other flash communication rather than reading lengthy articles from *The New York Times*. This generation has been critiqued for its inability to have deep thoughts and to be critically engaged. But, as we explained in our chapter on "fake" news, it isn't clear that our nation is strengthened by citizens reading *The New York Times* instead of watching clips of UpWorthy. The key is what information is offered and what consumers of the information do about it. And most satirists point out repeatedly that this difference is essential.

Stephen Colbert highlighted this distinction in-character when he riffed on blogging: "The vast majority of bloggers out there are responsible correspondents doing fine work in niche reporting fields like *Gilmore Girl* fan fiction, or cute things their cats do, or photoshopped images of the *Gilmore Girls* as cats. That's great. Where I draw the line is with these attack-bloggers. Just someone with a computer who gathers, collates, and publishes accurate information that is then read by the general public. They have no credibility. All they have is facts. Spare me."[4] In contrast to boomers like Carr, who see the internet as nothing more than a threat to critical thinking, Colbert identifies a key nuance: there is a huge difference between frivolous, silly blogs and ones that offer important alternatives to the information offered on mainstream news outlets. This chapter will give you a range of examples of ways that short bytes of satirical information can have potent political impact. Not all memes are about cat breading; some, as we will show, are about the hypocrisy of the power elite and many are designed to be shared or perhaps even manipulated to encourage viewer engagement. And as we have already explained, some of the most powerful satirical memes are both immensely entertaining and highly critical, producing pleasure and political engagement at the same time.

One of the key features of the internet is that it is a medium that allows users the ability to create content that can have a public impact. Of course, there is virtually no realm of communication that is free of corporate or governmental influence: corporate-sponsored sites pop up higher in Google searches and there is constant censorship of searches and sites. But, despite those limits, it is now possible for citizens to create media that challenge those sources of information. Internet sites like *Media Matters* or *Crooks and Liars* regularly offer alternatives to mainstream news sources. And beyond that we now have a young generation that is accustomed to creating its own citizen-journalism and citizen-satire. As Russell Dalton explains in *The Good Citizen,* and as we pointed out in the introduction, there is a huge distinction between the duty-bound idea of citizenship of the boomers and the engaged citizenship of generation X and the millennials. Engaged citizens are less trustful of politicians; they ask more questions and thus they interact with information in highly different ways than boomers do. Dalton explains that boomers stress citizenship as a duty and they are more inclined to trust authority, meaning that they are also more likely to believe news items than the younger generations. The point is that Carr's argument about Google is as much an argument about how generations think differently as it is an article about changing information consumption. And the difference is key since the generations understand civic commitment differently.

This chapter suggests that, while this new generation may consume media in quick sound bites, or media bytes, that does not translate into social apathy. In fact, we find that this generation engages in highly effective ways with political satire. Our argument is that satire has had tremendous success reaching millennials because of its ability to communicate in nimble forms that readily adapt to current media technology. Colbert pointed out the irony of some of the technology worries when he exclaimed, "From now on, 'TCR' is going to be the most millennial-ized, Gen-Y-ified, multi-screen, Snapchat, Twit vid ever broadcast on a box invented in 1927 by an Idaho potato farmer."[5] Can short, witty satirical interventions be powerful? Do they really have an impact? And if they do, should we worry? If millennials rarely read more than 140 characters, does that mean that they can't form complex thoughts? What if flash satire, in fact, teaches them how?

This chapter will help you find answers to these questions. We have divided it into four sections: "Kids These Days" helps explain specific features of the generational habits, attitudes, and ideas of *and* about millennials. It also gives special attention to how millennials think about civic commitment and democratic engagement. "Short and Sweet in Satire History" offers a longer, historical view on the idea that short satirical bursts are new and it helps explore the differences between today's short satire and that of the pre-digital age. "Twitter Age" then examines the range of digital media forms that are available today. It looks at the link between satire and these shortened media forms and wonders why so many of these media sources have a satirical, or sarcastic, or mocking tone. That section offers an overview of key sources for digital satire/irony/parody and closes by thinking about the limits and possibilities for an era where there is often too much information. How are citizens to make decisions when there may be too much short and distracting content to sift through? The last section "Is this a *memingful* revolution?" considers the deep question of the extent to which this sort of information can have a real political impact. Tracing key examples of politically important viral satire media, the chapter closes by offering specific cases where flash satire is making a difference for our democracy.

Kids These Days

Boy, do millennials get a bad rap. From *Time Magazine* covers calling them "The Me Me Me Generation" to Bill O'Reilly calling them "stoned slackers," millennials are decried as lazy narcissists who are sure to be the downfall of the great nation the baby boomers built. Millennials, if we are to believe the popular narrative, are yuppies' kids that were raised with a silver spoon in their mouths and a trophy in each hand, who enter the workforce and immediately stamp their feet and demand a corner office. If you Google "millennials," you get page after page of ominous musings like "Do Millennials Stand a Chance in the Real World?"[6] and "Why Generation Y Yuppies Are Unhappy,"[7] or scolding articles like "20 Job Rules for Millennials" (the first of which is "Keep working—at something")[8] which sternly tells millennials that "if you're lucky enough to have a parent who will pay your bills while you wait for the phone to ring with your dream job offer," it's important to do something because that looks better on a résumé than an unemployment gap. Of course this is all useful advice, or so it would seem if you actually believe the absolute worst about generation Y. Indeed, Assistant Professor Paul Harvey of the University of New Hampshire has a warning of his own for the people on the short end of that stick: Watch out for millennials and their attitudes. He worries over the unfortunate employer who may have inadvertently hired one of these sociopaths and reminds all employers to make sure to ask the key question: "Do you feel you are generally superior to your coworkers/classmates/etc., and if so, why?" He warns that employers should brace themselves for a crop of new employees who "feel entitled to undeserved preferential treatment, who are more prone to get into workplace conflicts and who are less likely to enjoy their job." He then instructs "older workers" to "combat" "younger coworkers who have a tendency to take credit for work they didn't do" by keeping detailed records of their performance, such as thank-you emails from clients. Harvey warns, however, that attempts to "correct entitlement perceptions through high feedback and communication" often "actually appeared to make the problem slightly worse."[9]

Can all of that be true? Writers like Joel Stein, author of that now-infamous *Time* article, "The ME Generation," certainly make a good case for it. Backed with numbers and studies, like one that found a significantly increased occurrence of narcissism in college students, baby boomers seem to hold the higher ground in the debate. But their ability to control public perception is due to the fact that they are the ones with the bully pulpits of mainstream media platforms. And they're getting support from all sides, too. According to Russell Dalton, Hillary Clinton

> [J]oined the assault on the young with the sound bite that "young people think 'work' is a four-letter word." She is like the old fogy who grumbles that when she was young, she did her chores before dawn and trudged ten miles to school (the law school at Yale?). Through the snow. Uphill. Both ways. (169)

From across the aisle, Glenn Beck criticized millennials with his usual aplomb, citing the fact that millennials were "brought up by parents who wouldn't spank them because it was 'too barbaric'" as a reason for their supposed entitlement and laziness (see Figure 6.1).

The thing is, though, that for every bit of information writers like Joel Stein cited, there were pieces of the puzzle they simply omitted. But they're not lost to us, because increasingly, as millennials get more and more tired of being told that they're entitled and lazy, they speak out. A Google search of "millennials" will reveal articles written on behalf of and occasionally by millennials themselves refuting the stigma that has been attached to their generation. Millennial Emily Crockett calls out the millennial bashing for what it is on *Generation Progress*:

> A "troll" is somebody who deliberately goads others on "internet message boards" (you might remember these from GeoCities) just to get a reaction. And you, Joel

Figure 6.1   Glenn Beck discussing Generation Y on his show in 2008[10]

Stein, are the perfect example of an offline troll: a journalist who riles up readers by smearing an entire generation as lazy—only to turn around and completely undermine his own half-baked shock-bait with the latter half of his article. I'm loath to feed a troll, but this particular troll, who admitted to "cozying up to the editor of the magazine" in his early career, has too wide and too credulous an audience.[11]

Crockett dismantles Joel Stein's argument step-by-step, noting that the National Institutes of Health survey that found such alarming rates of narcissism in millennials has been "called into serious question under peer review," with another paper arguing that narcissism is a developmental, not a generational trait. She also refutes Stein's claim that millennials don't vote and aren't civically engaged with sourced information that young voters actually turned out in record numbers in the 2012 election,[12] that millennials lead the nation in volunteerism,[13] that millennials value things like being a good parent, having a home, and having a religious life far more than becoming famous, which, the *Washington Post* notes, "to a large extent . . . mirror the things older generations value."[14] *The Wire* compiled a list of magazine coverage spanning over a century, called "Every Every Every Generation Has Been The Me Me Me generation," full of articles claiming that the kids these days are going to be the ruin of society because they are self-involved, interested in the wrong things, and don't consider marriage to be priority number one.[15]

There is another side of the story and it is a financial one. Millennials are constantly blamed for the financial mess they have inherited. While it is possible to glibly report on the apparent materialism and fixation with money that seem to characterize millennials, economists like Lisa Kahn put that information into useful context in *The New York Times*. She points out that graduates who earned less out of school because of higher unemployment rates after graduation may never make up the financial loss, even 15 or 20 years later. Neil Howe, author of "Generations" (1991) said that millennials focus on money because "They look at the house their parents live in and say, 'I could work for 100 years and I couldn't afford this place.'"[16] Lowry, writing for the *Times*, also draws an important connection to the motto of Occupy Wall Street—"We are the 99%"—and "the World War II ethos [which] was 'use it up, wear it out, make it do, or do without," arguing that the emphasis is not on living without as it was then, but on wondering why it is they should do without. When one considers that this is the first time in decades that a generation might not have it better than their parents, it is no small wonder that, as Morley Winograd and Michael D. Hais write in *Millennial Momentum: How a New Generation is Remaking America*, millennials want "greater and broader economic opportunity" (37). And the millennials' desire for equality doesn't stop at economic concerns: the most racially diverse generation in American history, they support equality and inclusion more than other generations (27), and, according to a 2007 Pew study, are far more likely to agree with the statement "we should make every possible effort to improve the position of blacks and other minorities, even if it means giving then preferential treatment" (31).

An example of millennials standing up to the baby boomers that is particularly relevant to our book is a satirical apology video made by Can Opener Studio called "We Suck and We're Sorry" (see Figure 6.2). In this video millennials ironically own up to being self-centered, narcissistic, and immature, and say "We're the worst!" They also sarcastically tell the baby boomers that they are great, and they did their best. The video includes important information about the outsourcing of factory jobs, starting of two disastrous wars, and soaring education costs, but they deliver these lines with a deadpan denial that those are the real reasons millennials are struggling, saying "Here we go again—making excuses!"[17]

This is a particularly illustrative example of millennials refuting the labels foisted upon them, because they are not just contesting the claim; they are doing it

Figure 6.2   A "We Suck and We're Sorry" millennial asks Siri how to fix a bicycle, then decides to call his dad[18]

in a way that is fun and satirical. They take the mainstream media's rhetoric and ironically accept it while providing their own evidence that the rhetoric is incorrect. What better proof exists that millennials are in fact paying attention and are willing to get involved? Far from being the death knell of citizenship that the baby boomers would have you believe, millennials are simply redefining the ways they participate in our democracy. In fact, according to Winograd and Hais,

> Millennials also exhibit a disproportionately high level of what political scientists label political efficacy, a sense that they can utilize and influence government and the political process. They are more likely than older generations to disagree that "it's not worth it to deal with the federal government" (55% to 48%) and that "people like me don't have any say in what government does" (52% to 46%). They are more inclined than older cohorts to agree that "voting gives people some say in what government does" (74% to 67%) and that "most elected officials really care what people like me think" (46% to 36%). (38)

Millennial citizenship may not look like the citizenship of their parents or grandparents, but it is citizenship all the same. Why, then, Dalton asks, all the negativity? He offers the simple fact that not acting like previous generations "challenges the duty-based sensibilities of their elders," leading researchers to focusing on negatives like "trusting Bono more than the president of the United States" (170). Nevertheless, as we will explore later in this chapter, the ways in which millennials do exercise citizenship are just as valid, if often more fun, than their grandparents' ways.

Short and Sweet in Satire History

Ok, so maybe things are a little different now than they were for the baby boomers, and maybe this has meant an evolving sense of what active citizenship looks like. If O'Reilly thinks that the millennial generation is the first and only generation of people to have short attention spans and be self-involved, then he is overdue for an *oh, really* from those of us with either memory of, or access to, books about past generations. It's probably safe to say that the habit of older generations complaining about younger ones is a historical constant. But our memories don't need to be long to find examples of hand-wringing about the future of the new generation that's coming of age in a time of crisis. According to Winograd and Hais,

> At the outset of World War II, army psychiatrists complained that their GI recruits had been "over-mothered" in the years before the war (Strauss and Howe 1991, 264). History will tell us if the Millennial Generation will ultimately be as successful in the decades ahead at overcoming its supposedly soft upbringing as was the Greatest Generation. To date, however, the results are positive. Juvenile crime, teen pregnancy, abortion, and substance abuse rates are lower and standardized academic test scores and community participation rates are higher among Millennials than they were among both Baby Boomers and Gen-Xers. (29)

So fearing for the future in the hands of the next generation isn't new. But is the fear more rational now, since our world has changed so much in the lifetime of the millennials? Well, to answer that question, we first need to challenge the assumption that life is really so different now, since the assumption has been that those differences have markedly influenced the possibilities for millennial citizenship.

Generally, the most dramatic change is, of course, digitalization. It is digital media that people point fingers at when they are claiming that kids these days have no attention spans, and can't or won't read more than 140 characters. But if short and sharp satire is an invention of the digital age, then we'd like to know what URL Mark Twain used to post his satirical pamphlets on Tumblr. Satire has a long history of communicating with a few choice words and, sometimes, powerful cartoons that need none. And when we say a long history, we mean a *long* history. The British Museum is home to a satirical papyrus from Thebes, Egypt that dates back to the Late New Kingdom (around 1100 BC). It depicts animals imitating human activities, with special emphasis on the reversal of the natural order[19]—one of satire's most effective tools for drawing attention to flawed systems and power dynamics.

So what does an Ancient Egyptian satirical papyrus have to do with modern America? Well—everything. Because if this kind of thing has always been popular, then there's hardly any reason to fret about the fact that people seem drawn to it now. Sure, you could argue that some issues require people to devote a great deal of time and thought to a scholarly article. But the reality is, for most people, that sort of attention is rare: We simply don't have enough time and energy to devote that kind of research to every single issue that's worthwhile. And there are many issues for which reading a textbook isn't really necessary, or isn't even the best way to learn about something. And, finally, sometimes a five-volume reference book isn't the best way to get information to the specific audience who most needs to hear it. So when online video producer Jay Diaz made a video series imagining what would happen if the stereotypical gender roles of men and women were reversed in bars, relationships, and at the gym, whether he knew it or not, he was walking like an Egyptian (see Figure 6.3).

While the medium has changed from papyrus and brushes to a camera and YouTube, The Flip Side's videos don't represent a new threat to critical thinking. Rather, these short, funny videos make profound points about gender roles and stereotyping while making the audience—who likely would not be thinking about issues of gender otherwise—laugh. They also enable the viewers to remember the message, which is made wittily, if not unsubtly, by associating real-life experiences, laughter, and vivid images with it, which we listed as reasons satire makes an effective educational tool in Comedy U. It's short, sweet, and funny. And that's nothing new.

Not only is flash satire not new, but young brains' attention being captured by it isn't either. Just as the National Institutes of Health study that found millennials to be extremely narcissistic is now thought to have captured a developmental rather than a generational trait, we find similar flaws in conclusions drawn about short digital communication. The idea that short and dynamic communication is a preferred mode of communication among the young probably also has more to do with age than cohort. A Nielsen NeuroFocus research study found that the aging baby boomer's brain has a broader

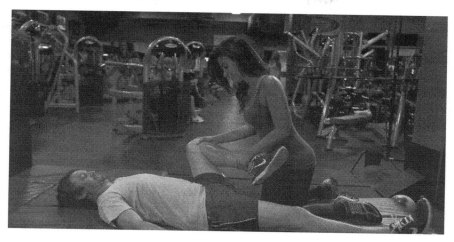

Figure 6.3 The Flip Side's video explores gender stereotypes at the gym through role reversal[20]

attention span and is open to more information than a millennial's, but also that the aging brain is more easily distracted. Young brains, the study found, have "better attention capture, engagement, and memorability with elements of dynamism such as rich media," and that they also can deal with "bleeding-over communication," as in internet ads, and don't need there to be a clear delineation between the communication and the ad to engage with the information. Millennial brains also handled intense colors and interactive sites better.[21] So perhaps when baby boomers are measuring the attention spans and skill sets of millennials against their own we are seeing more about age difference than generational difference. In all likelihood, had the technology been available, the Ancient Egyptians would have made satirical videos and graphic images instead of papyri, and the old folks and opinion leaders would have worried for the fate of the dynasty. The point is that the difference is not the length of time it takes to consume the cultural form; it is the technology and communicative options available that have shifted.

In the intervening years between the papyrus-filled days of our earliest recorded history and the videos of 2012 lie hundreds of other examples of satire's utility in short formats. Though it would be impossible to examine every noteworthy instance of flash satire making an impact, there are some standout examples we will look at in this section to further reassure the O'Reillys of the world that there's no reason to believe that the death of civilization is upon us. The question, of course, is how to determine which historical memes are worth looking at.

Fittingly, to help us narrow it down, there's a BuzzFeed list called "15 Historic Cartoons That Changed The World." According to BuzzFeed contributor Victor Navasky,

> Art critics, art historians, aestheticians, and others too often tend to dismiss cartoons and caricatures as silly—not serious—trivial, and irrelevant. Yet as the following list

of cartoons and caricatures that have wreaked havoc throughout history should make clear, cartoons can have a powerful psychological, emotional, and political impact.[22]

This criticism is not limited to cartoons, but they are a particularly good example of short and sweet analog bytes of satire that, as Navasky says, can be very powerful. Coming in at #3 on the list is a Thomas Nast cartoon in the *New York Times* which, according to BuzzFeed, was credited with bringing down Boss Tweed and his Tammany Hall cronies, which was acknowledged by Tweed himself, saying "I don't care a straw for your newspaper articles. My constituents can't read. But they can't help seeing them damn pictures." In this case, the short and sweet satirical cartoon was effective *because*, not in spite of, its brevity. There's only the name of the Tammany Ring—the cabal of powerful criminals under Boss Tweed—to read, but, as Boss Tweed knew when he expressed irritation that his illiterate constituents were seeing the cartoon, they could still access the message. Because they would not have otherwise keyed into the story, this razor sharp cartoon is a more effective political tool than any beautifully constructed editorial in the same paper detailing the crimes of Boss Tweed and his cronies could ever have been. The cartoon illustrates both the effectiveness of flash satire and the democratic nature of satire: it is an access point to critical thinking and citizenship that is open to everyone to both make and consume, without the exclusion and condescension of the traditional high-culture means of information.

Brilliant works like Nasts's Tammany Hall cartoon were not produced in a vacuum, of course. During the 18th and 19th centuries, there was a proliferation of satiric materials like pamphlets and cartoons in England, France, and beyond. Entire publications were created to collect and disseminate the works of various popular satirists like George Cruikshank and George du Maurier. The term "cartoon" as we understand it today was, in fact, introduced by the British humor and satire publication *The Punch*, which was founded in 1841. The magazine ironically titled a series of drawings contrasting the wealth of Parliament with the poverty of the population "cartoons," and the word then became associated with brilliant "pictorial satire and eventually with any humorous drawing."[23] The subtitle of *Punch's* first issue, *The London Charivari,* was a reference to the French "caricatural journal," founded in 1832, called *Le Charivari*. The French artists, having been seen as undermining authority for some of their earlier work in a satirical weekly called *La Caricature*, learned to avoid directing caricatures at powerful political individuals in favor of generalized social targets, and saw immense success at this effort, leading to emulation in other countries.[24] *Punch* was founded by the writer Henry Mayhew and wood engraver Ebenezer Landells, who wanted the magazine to be "less bitter than other British comic publications and of a higher literary standard." Still, in its early years, *Punch* was a radical publication, taking on hot-button issues of the 1840s like labor laws. *Punch* closed in 2002, leaving over 160 years' worth of short and sweet satire.[25] This tradition has not died, but it has evolved. Much like we have argued that citizenship is not dead at the hands of the millennials, the rich tradition of byte satire that packs a punch is alive and well despite looking a little different than it did in the days of pamphlet culture.

In the next section, we will explore how the internet and social networking sites in particular are functioning to spread short works of satire like *Punch* distributed satirical cartoons.

Twitter Age

It is true that there is a proliferation of shorter forms of social critique, with sites like Gawker repackaging the news in witty, brief, sarcastic ways. It's not new, but it does look a little different than it did when a proliferation of new satire meant a flood of pamphlets in the town square. According to Amber Day, the internet is

> a crucial component of the success of the majority of satirists examined here. At the most basic level, almost all of them are featured heavily on video-sharing sites such as YouTube and Google Video. There is no doubt that their popularity is at least partially due to their success as viral phenomena, with short clips from, say, *The Daily Show* forwarded widely among friends, transcending television schedules and national borders. (24–5)

Jones agrees, and adds that

> Furthermore, citizens themselves are now empowered to participate in the production of political video content—repurposing news interviews or other "serious" political content for their own political critiques and commentaries through video mash-ups and other remediated materials. It is in this convergence— between producer and consumer, politics and popular culture, and across once distinctive technologies—that Henry Jenkins foresees the potential for a reinvigoration of democratic citizenship. (12–13)

The internet isn't just important because it allows people to share satire produced by major performers like Stewart and Colbert. It is a place where the average citizen has a forum, and it is a place where millennials are especially comfortable.

In this section, we will provide an overview of the various forms of media and how people, and especially millennials, are using them to create and share satire. We will discuss each form in its own sub-section, and related media, like Twitter and Vine, will be grouped together. It's by no means an exhaustive list, but we will cover a wide range of sources of internet satire. We will also highlight examples of citizens using these forms to share satire they produced that either went viral or ended up having a major impact. A number of our examples come from media related to the 2012 election.

Facebook

Facebook's origin story is well-known, in part due to the popularity of the movie *The Social Network,* which revealed how Mark Zuckerberg founded the social media network with some fellow students while an undergraduate at

Harvard in 2004. The most important features of Facebook, for our purposes, are the ability to publicly "like" and "share" things. This makes Facebook a good place for millennials to post clips and images from *The Daily Show,* as Day suggests, but it is also a place where satire is created and shared by citizen-satirists. A page called Being Liberal is a prime example of this function. Because of Facebook's design, when someone subscribes to updates from the Being Liberal page, a line appears in the timelines of their friends that says "[so-and-so] likes Being Liberal." Now, say that to yourself out loud. It is a public declaration of allegiance to political ideology. As you might expect, the page creates and shares content that promotes liberal ideology. It is one of the most popular political pages on Facebook, and is run by a man named Wojtek Wacowski in Fair Haven, CT who went by [W] on the page before speaking to the *New Haven Register* in 2013. Wacowski told the *Register* that the page isn't about him, saying that "It doesn't matter who I am, it doesn't matter what I think. I have accidentally created a soapbox. It gives me the unique opportunity to interact with people in Tulsa, Okla., or St. Louis, Mo." He describes himself as "an information DJ, because in social media, you are a discotheque and you play music . . . People will only come if they like the music you play."[26] The page is indeed popular, boasting 957,764 "likes" and 616,609 "talking about this" at the time of this writing. Being Liberal identifies itself as a political organization, and its description reads "'Being Liberal'—What does it mean to YOU? Share here. Join the most active FB liberal community. Wear proudly the 'Liberal' label, as a badge of honor!" Being Liberal also maintains a presence on other websites we will discuss in this section, including Tumblr. Of interest is the fact that Being Liberal nods to the connections between satire and social media when they quote Colbert in their "about" section on Tumblr: "Why? Because Reality Has A Well Known Liberal Bias."[27] That last line comes straight from Colbert.

As we write this, the most recent post on Being Liberal is entitled "The monsters vs. The Munsters," and features black-and-white images of Republican politicians John Boehner, Paul Ryan, Ted Cruz, and Michelle Bachmann side-by-side with Herman Munster, Eddie Munster, Grandpa Munster, and Lily Munster, respectively. An individual Facebook user is tagged in the post as a way to credit him with submitting the photo. Top comments in the thread include "This is an insult to The Munsters" and "The Munsters were much nicer people." Clearly, subscribers are getting the message and finding it amusing, and are also engaging with it. Less than 15 minutes after it was posted, it was shared 169 times and liked by 671 people, and had 58 comments. As Jenkins writes in *Convergence Culture: Where Old and New Media Collide,* some of the forces in our new digital democracy "will look like old-style politics conducted in new ways," while other things, ranging from parodic news shows to Photoshopped images, "also have political effects, representing hybrid spaces where we can lower the political stakes (and change the language of politics) enough so that we can master skills we need to be participants in the democratic process" (220). This is the space Being Liberal occupies—sharing content that includes both clips from parody news and occasionally Photoshopped images, as Jenkins mentions, and allowing people to hone their skills as digital citizens.

Instagram

Instagram comes under the heading of Facebook because Facebook purchased it, somewhat infamously, for $1 billion in 2012. Instagram is not particularly notable for our purposes because of its built-in features, including the ability to edit photos, apply filters, and share them with other Instagram users, but it is worth mentioning for the same reason the *New York Times* believes Facebook bought it: it gives Facebook "a formidable mobile player—an area that is seen as a weakness for the sprawling social network."[28] Instagram users can share their images from their mobile apps to Facebook, as well as to Twitter and Tumblr, but the integration with Facebook is smoother than with Twitter, where the image will appear as a link and open in a separate tab rather than being viewable in the Twitter timeline. Instagram and the trend of millennials taking "selfies"—photos taken of and by themselves, using either their smartphone's forward-facing camera or a mirror— have been decried as examples and enablers of millennial narcissism. NPR's Geoff Nunberg chose "selfie" as his 2013 Word of the Year, and wrote that

> The connection to young girls isn't lost in all this—phrases like "the selfie society" are meant to evoke a flighty puerile narcissism. It may seem a stretch to pin down the state of the culture by pathologizing what adolescents are doing on Instagram. But we have a penchant for diagnosing narcissism where other ages would have seen nothing more than old-fashioned vanity.[29]

This is a great point, which has been increasingly made by millennials and the older generations who defend them, including psychologist Pamela Rutledge on *Psychology Today*, who writes that

> It's not a big leap to go from a pursuit of self-exploration to the desire for self-portrait. As far back as Ancient Egypt, people of wealth and power have commissioned self-portraits, although less for self-exploration than glorification. Nevertheless, a number of technological breakthroughs throughout history have continued to lower the barriers to the creation and display of self-portraits.[30]

There's our connection with Ancient Egypt again! It's good to get some historical perspective, though, in an era that imagines that the future is bleak and the past was rosy. While an Instagram filter on a selfie in a poorly lit school bathroom looks very different from a medieval monarch's commissioned oil portrait, Instagram selfies are simply an example of a new medium for an old phenomenon.

Twitter

Twitter, which was founded slightly later than Facebook but peaked in popularity much more recently, has one main feature that sets it apart from the rest of the social media networking sites: brevity. Messages sent on Twitter, which are generally publicly available rather than being limited to a circle of friends like Facebook status updates, are constrained to 140 characters. Theoretically, this means that

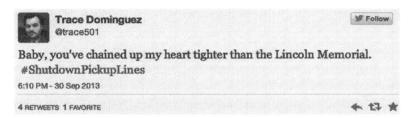

Figure 6.4   An example of viral Twitter satire by Trace Dominguez (@trace501)[31]

you have to make every word and punctuation mark count. Twitter is used by most public figures today, from actors to politicians, and is almost uniquely interactive, because any user can contact another by tagging their handle (username), and have their message be seen. Not every celebrity or politician responds to tweets from the general public, and there is a private messaging feature that you can only use if the person you are trying to contact follows you, but there is greater potential for public dialogue between citizens and public figures here than anywhere else. If a politician is understood to be avoiding the press, they may find themselves inundated with queries on Twitter. Journalists and politicians have used Twitter to make important announcements, and also to apologize or make corrections. Ill-considered tweets have brought down long careers, most notably Representative Anthony Weiner's. And for a fine example of Twitter satire, we may turn again to the government shutdown, which produced countless examples of citizen-satire like the one from Trace Dominguez, whose Twitter bio says he works for Discovery News (see Figure 6.4).

During the shutdown, there were viral hashtags like #ShutdownPickupLines. Hashtags—words or phrases following the pound sign—are aggregated by Twitter, so that users can see what others are saying about the topic. Hashtags are also often launched by comedians, journalists, actors, and politicians who want to start a conversation or solicit questions about something. Colbert launched the hashtag #IGotTheTweetsLikeGrassley to parody Republican Senator Chuck Grassley of Iowa's Twitter feed, which the *Huffington Post* described as "a confusing mess of Republican messages composed of abbreviations, internet shorthand, and just plain weirdness" (see Figure 6.5).[32]

It's unlikely that too many young people were paying attention to Grassley's Twitter feed before Colbert invited them to play this game with him, and it's important that they started paying attention afterward, because it's not insignificant that Grassley was calling Obama "stupid" and accusing the "x prof of con law" of not knowing the law. How could he be so certain? He told his followers that he was confident that the Supreme Court would overturn the Affordable Care Act. Looks like maybe he underestimated our president. But what makes this story even more fun, is that the Senator exposed his logical fallacies for all to see on Twitter, and Colbert used his access to a large fan base

Figure 6.5   Colbert invites viewers to parody Sen. Grassley on Twitter using this hashtag[33]

to encourage his viewers to engage in citizen-satire to mock the Senator via a medium they enjoy.

Vine

Vine comes under the Twitter heading because Twitter owns it. Vine is a mobile app that allows users to make and post videos. What gives it such great synergy with Twitter, of course, is the fact that the videos have to be short—really short. They can be 6 seconds long at the most. Vine, like other social media networks, has recently become an important tool for journalism in addition to its use as a social network. Indeed, Turkish journalist Tulin Dalogu, a *New York Times* contributor, captured the aftermath of a terrorist attack on the US Embassy in Ankara on February 1, 2013 using Vine and posted 6 vines to her Twitter account, @TurkeyPulse.[34] Funny vines tend to be especially popular, and end up in compilations posted by blogs and even news organizations. And yes, some of those funny vines are satirical, or contain social commentary. For example, user @ SpecialK posted a vine[35] juxtaposing the way President Obama shook hands with a white Oklahoma City Thunder basketball team staffer versus the black basketball player Kevin Durant, playing piano music while Obama gave the white guy a professional and distant handshake, and then changing the background music to a song called "My Nigga" by YG when Obama warmly clasped hands with and then slapped Durant on the back. We might compare this funny social commentary about code switching to Fox News calling Barack and Michelle Obama bumping fists on stage during the campaign for the 2008 presidential election a "terrorist fist jab."[36]

Snapchat

Like Vine, Snapchat allows users to take short videos, and like Instagram, pictures. However, the major difference between Snapchat and either of those services is that the images or short videos are directly sent to people rather than publicly or semi-publicly posted, and last for up to ten seconds before disappearing. It's possible to circumvent this by taking a screenshot of the image using your phone's innate ability to do so, but it's discouraged, and Snapchat alerts the sender if you do this. That's primarily an issue in the case of people who fear that teenagers are using Snapchat to send illicit photos to each other, in which case there are privacy concerns, among others, but it's far from the intended or primary use of Snapchat. In fact, one recent viral Snapchat, which was captured via screenshot and circulated to every major social media site, satirizes racial profiling in airport security. A young Sikh man in a turban, standing in line to show his ID and boarding pass to a Transportation Security Administration (TSA) agent and then go through security screenings, sent a Snapchat of himself with the TSA in the background and a surprised expression, captioned "Bout to get randomly selected" with three little icons of a smiley-face-like cartoon in a turban. This is the epitome of flash satire—after all, it wasn't even intended to last more than ten seconds or be publicly viewed—and it's the kind of funny that only happens when a joke packs a weighty punch.

Tumblr

Tumblr, a blogging/social media site, allows users to register a unique URL and create their own webpage, with content that is either original, shared from other Tumblr users, or a combination of the two. Often, viral images like the TSA Snapchat mentioned above get circulated on Tumblr as well. Users can interact with each other in a somewhat limited capacity—it clearly wasn't designed for chatting—and promote their own art and writing. Book deals have been known to result from popular Tumblrs. And, of course—you guessed it—Tumblr is full of satire! Tumblr has a reputation for having an active social justice community and for being fairly liberal on the whole, and posts about legislation, women's rights, discrimination, and racism are often widely shared and commented upon. Many Tumblr users actively encouraged their followers to vote, and as of this writing, a post with over 26,000 notes is going around that demands that people go to the "We the People" government petition website and sign one that calls for the restoration of Net Neutrality. On a lighter note, around Valentine's Day, users create topical valentines that often include intentionally poor Photoshop work and ironic use of Comic Sans font. These include references to popular TV shows and pop celebrities, of course, but there are also posts like this especially amusing one that features Mitt Romney (see Figure 6.6).

"Binders full of women," of course, is a reference to one of the biggest Romney gaffes of the 2012 presidential election. In the town-hall presidential debate at Hofstra, "undecided voter" Katherine Fenton asked how the candidates would work to rectify gender inequality in the workplace, and Obama cited his signing of

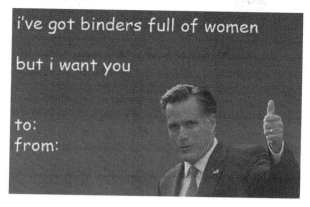

Figure 6.6   A satirical valentine made by Cassandra Seltzer and posted on her Tumblr[37]

the Lily Ledbetter Fair Pay Act. Romney, however, said that he and his staff made a "concerted effort to go out and find women who had backgrounds that could be qualified to become members of our cabinet" and asked women's groups for help, and was brought "whole binders full of women."[38] The gaffe instantly went viral, trending on Twitter at #bindersfullofwomen. There is also a Facebook page called "Binders Full Of Women," with a cover photo featuring colorful binders arranged into a rainbow, that has over 318,000 likes. In an example of how satire is not just short these days, it is fast: the Facebook page was created and the hashtag was viral before the debate had even finished. Jenkins writes that Photoshopped images might be seen as "the grassroots equivalent of political cartoons—they attempt to encapsulate topical concerns in a powerful image" (231–32). Tumblr, then, becomes an ideal medium for such efforts—exemplified perfectly by user-developed content like satirical valentines.

YouTube

Everyone knows by now that YouTube is a video sharing website, and we know that when YouTube is mentioned it's usually in the same breath with "copyright concerns." But YouTube isn't just for pirated movies and cat videos. It's a source of satire and citizenship. In fact, in 2010, Liesbet van Zoonen, Farida Vis, and Sabina Mihelj did a study called "Performing citizenship on YouTube: activism, satire, and online debate around the anti-Islam video *Fitna*." The researchers wanted to know "whether and how the participatory opportunities of the digital technologies invite performances of citizenship," looking specifically at reactions to the Dutch anti-Islam video *Fitna* (249). They found, unsurprisingly, that one of the popular responses to the video, along with culture-jamming videos (many made by Muslims expressing their view of Islam as peaceful) and vlogs (video blogs) that were mostly made by regular vloggers, there were also cut-and-mix style videos that "appeared to be especially welcome means for satire and parody" (259). As van Zoonen, Vis, and Mihelj write, "video upload channels have become important arenas for political activity and communication" (250). YouTube, where anyone with any skill level and any equipment can perform citizenship, is yet another example of the many ways that the internet has democratized information and participation. And of course, as Day and Jones argue, YouTube is also a place where people share and view content from satirists like Colbert and Stewart. Baym writes that *The Daily Show* and *The Colbert Report* are "a convenient fit for the multi-platform strategy of repurposing" because most of the clips are relatively short—between 30 seconds and seven minutes—and are self-contained, as well as archived on their websites and tagged with keywords like the names and topics featured in a segment. As Baym contends, this turns a satirical television show into "an unlikely database of political humor, criticism, and conversation, a collection of rhetorical artifacts that extends and expands the show's discursive research" (*From Cronkite* 148).

Reddit

Reddit is a website where users submit content as links or text, and other users vote content they like up and content they dislike down. It is organized into communities called subreddits, identified by the end of the URL at which they can be found. The political humor subreddit, thus, is/r/PoliticalHumor. On Reddit, like on other sites, users can either create their own content or share content made by others. On the political humor subreddit, user-generated content—like an image entitled "Bumper stickers we won't see in 2016," which is a bumper sticker-sized photo of the American flag with the text "SAVE OUR BENEFITS, PENSIONS, AND HEALTHCARE . . . THROW A REPUBLICAN OUT OF OFFICE"—is ranked on the page according to the number of upvotes and downvotes it receives.

A particularly interesting feature of Reddit, however, is Ask Me Anything (AMA). AMAs can be hosted by any person who believes the Reddit community is interested in them or their career, and they traditionally declare "I Am [name], Ask Me Anything." Users may request celebrity AMAs by providing the Reddit moderators with contact information for their publicist, or a celebrity may contact the Reddit moderators to arrange an AMA. AMAs require proof, usually including a picture of the participant at the computer, which can be privately sent to the moderators or included in the AMA.[39] Some of the top 100 Reddit AMAs of all time (as of the time of this writing) include astrophysicist Neil deGrasse Tyson, longest-held Iraq hostage Peter Moore, novelist Stephen King, actor Benedict Cumberbatch, skateboarder Tony Hawk, and musician "Weird Al" Yankovic—but the number one AMA of all time, by a wide margin, is "I am Barack Obama, President of the United States—AMA."[40] President Obama's AMA crashed Reddit temporarily because of immense web traffic.[41] Reddit is a community, with its own standards and mores, and understanding that is vital to writing popular questions, which are the ones that tend to get answered. And celebrities who don't adhere to the "anything" part of "Ask Me Anything" and attempt to stick to promoting their latest work, or people who shy away from controversial questions, are met with great disapproval. The AMA is a fascinating example of an entirely new kind of town hall—a virtual forum for performances of citizenship.

CollegeHumor

CollegeHumor is a website that produces daily original comedy content made by in-house writers and producers, as well as user-submitted content. While not all of the material featured on this website is political or even satirical, a particular example from CollegeHumor bears mentioning in any discussion of viral satire related to the 2012 presidential election. Referencing a number of specific Romney gaffes, including the 47% comment he made when he believed he was off-the-record, as well as parodying the general perception that Romney was out-of-touch because of his immense wealth, CollegeHumor produced a parody music video called "Mitt Romney Style," referencing the extremely popular Korean song "Gangnam Style" by Psy (see Figure 6.7). "Gangnam Style," as it turns out, was already critical of class, referring to the materialistic culture of the Gangnam District of Seoul. That line of social critique and its wild popularity made it ripe for a Romney parody.

The video has over 51 *million* views on YouTube, and overwhelmingly received thumbs-up rather than thumbs-down from viewers. It is a smart bit of satire, and it is very well made, featuring horses, golf courses, actors in black tie, and a convincing

Figure 6.7   A scene from the "Mitt Romney Style" music video[42]

Mitt Romney, but what makes this video so funny is the fact that it stayed so true to the original video and song while tailoring the lyrics to the Romney campaign.

BuzzFeed

As Baym writes, "To increasing numbers of people, corporate media products are resources to be reappropriated: reedited, recontextualized, and recirculated among an emergent public sphere" (*From Cronkite* 153). This is the guiding philosophy that has made sites like BuzzFeed, a major creator and aggregator of viral content, so wildly popular. If it's going viral, or about to, BuzzFeed has an article about it. BuzzFeed's articles mostly take the form of lists of Graphics Interchange Format (GIFs)—graphic images, or pictures that move on a loop, from popular TV shows and movies, but there is some long-form content, and there is a page dedicated to politics, as well as one dedicated to LGBT news and entertainment. It asks users to label content with badges like "WIN" and "TRASHY," and if enough users select the same badge it is added to the post's thumbnail image so other users know what to expect from the content. Though BuzzFeed is notorious for cute animals and time-wasting, and can and has been used as shorthand for "everything that's wrong with this generation," we beg to differ that everything on BuzzFeed can be dismissed as meaningless. While it's true that long lists of GIFs will never be the equivalent of an in-depth *New York Times* investigative piece, we think there's something to be said for the way BuzzFeed approaches certain issues. If you would, think back once again to our discussion of the government shutdown in the introduction. It was a complex disaster. A lot of factors and forces played into it. Many people didn't understand what was happening and were too frustrated to want to give it much consideration. Enter BuzzFeed, with a list called "Ferris Bueller Explains The Government Shutdown," by BuzzFeed staff member Benny Johnson. Viewed almost 400,000 times, this list, subtitled "I am not going to sit on my ass as the events that affect me unfold to determine the course of my life," explains the setup, players, and current outlook for the government shutdown using only GIFs from *Ferris Bueller's Day Off* and one or two sentences to go along with each GIF explaining which real politician each character represents, or what the analogy is. For example, John Boehner is represented by Cameron Frye. In the 37th GIF in this article, Ferris says "Here's where Cameron goes berserk" under the heading "And now the bill goes back to the House with the government shutdown only a few short days away." Is it brief? If you count the time spent scrolling through over 40 GIFs—yes. But is it meaningless? No, not even if we consider the fact that they want us to react with a heart, "OMG," "WTF," or "LOL." Even if all we are asked to do is respond with a click of our mouse, it doesn't invalidate the clear and accessible information on this list—information that undoubtedly reached people it wouldn't have otherwise, some of whom needed the situation laid out in its simplest terms to truly understand it. These seemingly silly responses aside, the point is that the BuzzFeed is sometimes used to explain an important part of our democratic process in a way that is easy and fun to understand, while also giving us a simple and concrete way to respond.

Gawker

Gawker is the main blog of Gawker Media, which also includes Jezebel, Deadspin, and Defamer. Gawker is self-described as a news and gossip site, and contains a mixture of content based on anonymous tips, mistakes, and errors in judgment made by other news outlets, and some original reporting. Essentially, what Gawker does is repackage the news, with its identifiable brand of snark. Gawker often accomplishes something similar to what the BuzzFeed article about the government shutdown did—it makes a complex, possibly dry story appealing and easy to understand—but occasionally Gawker posts material other outlets choose not to, which makes for an interesting debate about what should and should not be published. One such instance was their publication of screenshots of emails, photos, and contacts in Sarah Palin's personal email account after it was hacked by people associated with the online community 4Chan. Gawker also reported on the response it got from readers after publishing the emails, and discussed the fact that their legal advisors said they were in the clear. Gawker traditionally has been very transparent in such situations, including when it came under attack by 4Chan after Gawker criticized 4Chan's decision to share the real identity and contact information of an 11-year-old girl who was the star of a viral video, resulting in the girl being placed under police protection over death threats.[43] Gawker responded by publishing more articles about the denial of service attack 4Chan launched against the website, linking back to the article that had upset 4Chan users to begin with. It is a source that breaks the fourth wall of journalism and dispenses with the veneer of objectivity and gravitas mainstream news media still cling to. Gawker, though it mainly repackages material from other sources, has a unique style which draws its audience back in to read their coverage again and again.

UpWorthy

UpWorthy, like many of the other sites we've looked at, aggregates content rather than creating it. However, UpWorthy has a unique mission statement that makes it relevant to our interest in how millennials form communities online. Co-founder Eli Pariser told *New York Times* reporter David Carr that UpWorthy's mission is "giving people the information and tools to help make them better, more aware citizens."[44] According to UpWorthy's "About" page:

> At best, things online are usually either awesome *or* meaningful, but everything on Upworthy.com has a little of both. Sensational and substantial. Entertaining and enlightening. Shocking and significant. That's what you can expect here: no empty calories. No pageview-juking slideshows. No right-column sleaze. Just a steady stream of the most irresistibly shareable stuff you can click on without feeling bad about yourself afterwards.

And, even more importantly—UpWorthy says its audience is "Basically, *The Daily Show* generation. People who care about what's going on in the world but don't want to be boring about it."[45] That sentence articulates one of the fundamental beliefs behind this book. Millennials care—they just also like to laugh, which, it turns out, is often pretty beneficial to engaging with the world. And, according to David Carr, UpWorthy's mission is working. He writes, "By putting tasty headlines on nutritious subjects—chocolate sauce on brussels sprouts, as it were—Upworthy can make the sharing impulse work on topics beyond LOLCats and fashion disasters." UpWorthy works a lot like satire; it allows us to process and reflect on intense topics with a bit more gravitas than slipping on banana peels and a bit more fun than an article in *The Nation*.

Quick and Powerful

It isn't just that our information is put in smaller packages, but it is also true that there's a lot more of it. So what sticks, and why is it so effective with millennials? Well, Winograd and Hais write that millennials are strong believers in community and collective action, and that millennials are adept at using social networks to stay connected and create communities that are larger and more diverse than any previous generation (26). According to Dalton, the Obama campaign was able to harness this ability by creating the Obama site MyBO, as well as using established social networking sites and blogs, to create a powerful online community that had real impact on the ground. A Democratic strategist claimed that it was unlike anything American politics had ever seen before (185). We've seen that Obama's successful Reddit AMA had a huge impact and drew an audience big enough to crash Reddit's servers. All of the examples we've covered—and those are just a small part of everything that's out there—demonstrate that millennials have repackaged and rebranded citizenship, not abandoned it completely.

Is This a Memingful Revolution?

Information and meaning are not the antitheses of comedy and entertainment. Millennials recognize this, and so do people like the founders of UpWorthy, who had amazing success sharing the same information by packaging it in a more humorous, click-friendly way. But it's not just the media who are slowly catching on to the benefits of integrating the kind of media millennials like into their information delivery systems. There has also been rise in academic uses of satire to reach out to students, with universities offering courses in topics like philosophy viewed through the lens of popular satirical media like *The Colbert Report*. We think that this demonstrates the fact that universities are beginning to recognize that satire is meaningful to millennials, in addition to the educative potential we discussed in chapter 2. The most famous example of this is, of course, the Boston University course "The Colbert Report: American Satire" taught by Michael Rodriguez, who told Boston's NPR station, WBUR, that the literary qualities of *The Colbert Report* help students to learn to write stronger essays and make more effective arguments. Rodriguez also explicitly connects Stephen Colbert to some of the greatest thinkers in history, saying that, like Socrates, Colbert uses "the opponent's own assumptions and presuppositions to then deconstruct them and show that they are, in fact, invalid." Rodriguez told WBUR that the class fills up instantly and has a long waiting list, and that the other classes he teaches are empty. Testimony from students who take the class makes it clear why it's so popular: they're learning and having a good time. Like we discussed in Comedy U, there are a lot of benefits to using humor as a teaching aid. One student said that it became easier for her to identify uses of techniques like burlesque and vaudeville after taking the class. Another student said that the course made him "a savvier consumer of media," and that he can interact with arguments more skilfully.[46] Satire isn't just a spoonful of sugar to help ideas that are too complex, too boring, or too disheartening go down—it's a nutritional supplement to the knowledge diet.

At Penn State, too, many professors use satire as a teaching aid. Dr. Jessica O'Hara, our Assistant Course Director for Rhetoric and Civic Life, teaches an honors composition course, and the Director of the Excellence in Communication Certificate, says she has been using Colbert clips to teach for years, but began to incorporate the study of satire into her freshman English class more formally in the fall of 2013:

> I teach rhetoric, argument, and critical thinking, and studying satire in the classroom is the best—and most amusing—way to expose the inner workings of all three. Watching these clips also helps students stay current with the news and the latest political discourse. It's incredibly efficient and effective for reinforcing course content and driving class discussion.[47]

This is what the people who work to educate millennials are seeing—that satire clicks for them, and makes the information resonate in a way that it might not have otherwise.

But millennials aren't just consuming and studying satire, they're also interacting with original satirical texts and producing their own and sending that out into the internet, where they, too, have a voice. Whether they're responding to a prompt from a professional satirist like Colbert, who has a particular penchant for getting his audience to improvise with him (it must be all of his training at *Second City* paying off) or joining in on a popular satirical hashtag like #MockTheVote on Twitter, millennials are doing citizenship. As we've discussed, citizenship norms have changed, and can't be measured along the same parameters as in the past. In fact, today's millennials see citizenship along a far broader continuum of community commitment that includes, but is not limited to, voting. And if we recognize that the measures of citizenship have changed and expanded, then we must also be willing to recognize that practicing citizenship is going to look different. It's too easy to point to the images of young Vietnam War protestors and civil rights activists in the 1960s and say that millennials are too busy taking selfies to participate in activism like that. Millennials are called "slacktivists" for doing things, like supporting causes on Facebook, that are perceived as meaningless, empty gestures that do nothing but make the slacktivist feel good. But first of all, online and offline activism are not mutually exclusive, and second of all, according to Geoff Livingston, author of the book *Now is Gone* about new media and Mashable contributions: "[t]here are some important social media strategies for

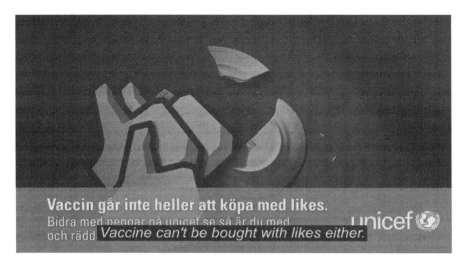

Figure 6.8   UNICEF's "Likes don't save lives" campaign[48]

transforming those one click 'slacktivists' into fully engaged activists."[49] Livingston writes that the first step is to stop using the term slacktivism because "labeling this previously untapped crop of casual contributors 'slacktivists' punishes them out of the gate for doing good" when "the new era of online cause action should excite non-profits."

Katya Andresen, Chief Operating Officer of Network for Good, told Livingston that it irritates her that the term slacktivism is used "as a pejorative way to describe what should be viewed as the first steps to being involved in a cause" and that it is "okay if someone's initial commitment is modest—and truly an opportunity that it's easier than ever to spread information, create new initiatives for social good, and take action."[50] For the millennials, a group that cares deeply about their fellow citizen and uses social media like it's one of their own appendages, what some people have derogatorily called slacktivism seems more like a gateway to meaningful engagement than a self-congratulatory waste of time to us, much like "fake" news has served as a palatable way to access politics and the news for an increasingly disillusioned segment of the population. Likes and shares are certainly not meaningless—at the very least, it is an indisputable truth that they help spread awareness—but, as Livingston argues, they are also "a new first step on the engagement ladder."[51] Carie Lewis, the Director of Emerging Media at The Humane Society of the United States, told Livingston that The Humane Society is successful because of individual engagement, and that slacktivists "need to be cultivated and feel appreciated for their contributions, as small as they may seem."[52] It's true that a "like" has no direct monetary value, as the United Nations Children's Fund (UNICEF) campaign showing people trying to pay for goods and services with "likes" crudely illustrates (see Figure 6.8), but, as Citizen Effect CEO and Founder Dan Morrison points out, if you focus on asking people to retweet, share, and email, you can build a relationship with the "slacktivists" and then some of them will "naturally graduate up the value chain." That approach is far more likely to be effective than UNICEF's tactic of insulting, belittling, and challenging casual supporters.

We've talked about the maligned millennials and discussed some of the most noteworthy bytes with bite. Because satirical news and politics have both the style and the substance, they are an ideal way to engage a generation that has been left with a hollow shell of the reliable news media and dependable societal structures that their forebears had. As we discussed in chapters 2 and 3 on satire and education and on satire and news media, satire plays a role that we can no longer count on the news media to play. But what makes this different in terms of the millennial generation is not just the way that users consume information, but also the way that they engage with it—by sharing, interacting, and by creating their own. Certainly members of the boomer generation did not have the degree of access to information and impact that millennials working the internet do today. Sure millennials go online, space out, and consume stupid stuff, but that isn't all they do. The social media and media-aggregating sites we've covered in this chapter, along with the specific examples of significant byte satire we analyzed demonstrate that, even if millennial citizenship in the digital age looks different, it's just as valid as ever. In fact, the structure of this new form of communication allows for even more citizen-produced content than ever before in our nation's history. Certainly one way to measure the health of a democracy is by citizen participation, and, if that is the measure we use, then there seems little doubt that we are witnessing a historic moment in our democracy.

7

Savin' Franklin: Satire Defends Our National Values

While baseball may be the favored "American" sport, there is little doubt that the Super Bowl is a quintessential American sporting event that draws the nation together around our televisions. In 2011, the Super Bowl became the most watched television program in US history, drawing 111 million viewers.[1] Why do we all tune in? For the ads, of course. Or, at least those of us who aren't football fans do. Each year there are a few ads that spark buzz, occasionally controversy, and 2014 was no exception. In 2014 the buzz was over an ad for Coca Cola that played "America the Beautiful" amidst images of the United States as a multicultural nation. The ad featured scenes representing a wide range of diverse people (including the first male same-sex couple to ever appear in a Super Bowl ad). The outrage was sparked by the fact that the patriotic song was sung in a variety of languages. Before the ad had finished airing, viewers had taken to Twitter using the hashtag #SpeakAmerican to rant. And it should come as no surprise that some viewers found the multicultural, multilingual view of the United States to border on treason. Michael Smerconish of the *Philadelphia Inquirer* reported that shortly after the ad was released a Minnesota-based church announced that it was throwing away all of its Coke products because "Mexicans singing the National Anthem is an abomination."[2] He quoted another angered viewer who exclaimed, "it's not bigotry to demand that we have a unified language," and if we don't, "we are no better than the 3rd world cesspool dwellers that refuse to lift themselves."[3] *Time Magazine* reported that another blogger wrote, "@CocaCola has America the Beautiful being sung in different languages in a #SuperBowl commercial? We speak ENGLISH here, IDIOTS."[4] Actually, the United States does not have an official language, but that didn't stop the hate mail.

The pundits quickly jumped into the fray, too, with Glenn Beck saying that clearly the purpose of the ad was to "divide people."[5] Rather than consider the ad a complex view of a nation with an increasingly changing demographic, most conservative pundits saw the ad as divisive and inflammatory. And they found it to provide an unsatisfactory view of the immigration debate. Michael Patrick Leahy of Breitbart.com wrote: "Executives at Coca Cola thought it was a good idea to run a 60 second Super Bowl ad featuring children singing 'America the Beautiful'—a deeply Christian patriotic anthem whose theme is unity—in several foreign languages. The ad also prominently features a gay couple."[6] Most mainstream news media coverage of the controversy simply reiterated the main talking points coming out of the debate, rarely providing a corrective to the inaccuracies that framed much of the outrage. CNN contributor Benn Ferguson stated that the commercial inspired resentment because it showed US immigrants "not assimilating."[7] Former GOP Rep. Allen West, also a Fox News contributor, worried that having an ad like this from a "company as American as they come" is a sign that "we are on the road to perdition."[8]

Luckily we had satire to save our sanity and our national values. Both Jon Stewart and Stephen Colbert responded to the attacks on the ad by offering much-needed perspective and balance. Stewart began by reminding his viewers that "America the Beautiful" is not actually the national anthem: "You know, the only thing more delicious than a tall, cool glass of 'Co-cola' is the irony that the self-appointed patriotic American watchdogs seem unaware that our national anthem is in fact not 'America the Beautiful'" (see Figure 7.1). He then went after the idea that having immigrants sing "America the Beautiful"—a song about the beauty of the nation after all—was not, in fact, representative of a melting pot of immigrants in love with this country: "They're singing 'America the Beautiful' while drinking Coca-Cola," Stewart exclaimed. "How much more American assimilation can they have? Maybe if they were open-carrying a gun shaped like Jesus while using a bald eagle strap-on to fuck an apple pie."[9] He then reminded viewers that if anything was wrong with the ad, it was that it was too schmaltzy, playing on our heartstrings perhaps a tad too much.

Colbert added his own geeky take on the debate by pointing out the hypocrisy of conservative pro-English pundits like Leahy forgetting that *E Pluribus Unum* is not in English either. He quoted Leahy: "When the company used such an iconic

Figure 7.1   Stewart points out that the ad's only major flaw is its schmaltzy sappiness[10]

song, one often sung in churches on the 4th of July that represents the old 'E Pluribus Unum' view of how American society is integrated, to push multiculturalism down our throats, it's no wonder conservatives were outraged." "Yes, the old' *E Pluribus Unum*," Colbert retorted. "That's Latin for 'Speaka da English.'"[11] Then continuing his habit of undercutting homophobia he keyed into the outrage over the representation of a gay couple: "For Pete's sake! Since when are gays allowed to gay up 'America the Beautiful'? If the woman who wrote this song, Katharine Lee Bates, saw this ad, she would be disgusted. And so would her life partner, Katharine Coman, with whom she lived for 25 years in what was then referred to as a 'Boston marriage.'"[12] Both Colbert and Stewart helped offer the US public a different view of our nation. One where we are able to pay attention to changing demographics without being afraid, and one where we are able to remember the immigrant past that is the real story of our nation's roots.

In fact, as this chapter will show, satire is not only saving our nation today; it always has. Satire emerges in full force in moments of crisis, when the public is often being barraged with misinformation and political spin. It serves as a corrective to falsehoods, deceptions, and ideological frames that offer imbalanced and impartial views as fact. We begin by describing the history of US satire and demonstrating its central role in the shaping of our nation's history and core values. We then look specifically at the connection between satire and national crisis over the course of US history with particular attention to satire's role after 9/11. The last section of this chapter dives into the debate over the meaning of America that was exemplified in the Super Bowl ad controversy we just described. We look back over recent decades that saw Republicans claim that they alone define core American values and we analyze the ways that satirists have attempted to dislodge those claims. As evidence, we compare the rise of America-defining pundit books against their satirical counterparts by Stewart and Colbert.

Satire is as American as Apple Pie

America: land of the free, home of the anti-intellectual populists. As Terrance MacMullan writes, "We Americans distrust smart people. Decent Americans know, deep in their guts, that in order to be tricky, you must first be smart . . . Americans don't like smart people because we suspect they might trick us" (58). It is a suspicion rooted in the circumstances of our founding, when the colonists first began to suspect that they were being taken advantage of by the hoity-toity King George. It makes sense that this kind of populism would develop in a mixed group of tradespeople, farmers, and the adventurous—devoid of aristocrats— who found themselves united against difficult living conditions and then the crown. You need only look at the "In America" section of Wikipedia's "Anti-intellectualism" page[13] to find a collection of arguments tracing American anti-intellectualism to colonial roots. There's Richard Hofstadter, in his book *Anti-intellectualism in American Life*,[14] quoting the Puritan John Cotton writing that "the more learned and witty you bee, the more fit to act for Satan you will bee" in 1642. There's the economist Thomas Sowell explaining that many of the people who built America, of course, had been persecuted by the educated upper classes in the homeland they had fled. And besides—few of those intellectuals would have had the skill to survive—or, as the colonists might have said, the ability to do "good, honest hard work." As Sowell puts it, "The rise of American society to preeminence as an economic, political and military power was thus the triumph of the common man and a slap across the face to the presumptions of the arrogant, whether an elite of blood or books"—America was built not by the European elites, but the "beaten men of beaten races." [15] And finally, there's the Reverend Bayard R. Hall saying that in frontier Indiana, "We always preferred an ignorant bad man to a talented one, and, hence, attempts were usually made to ruin the moral character of a smart candidate; since, unhappily, smartness and wickedness were supposed to be generally coupled, and [like-wise] incompetence and goodness." [16] Like a herd of mustangs, fear and mistrust of intellectuals came across the pond with the colonists and trampled its way westward. And so the American appreciation for honest hard work and being self-made and self-taught combined to create an idea of a model American.

A close relative of anti-intellectualism is anti-politics. Anti-politics refers to a negative reaction to politics, which is fine unless you are a politician or a citizen who needs political literacy in order to elect politicians. Needless to say, anti-politics is more about a negative posturing than sustaining an actual critical position. Russell Peterson argues that anti-political humor is everywhere, saying:

> Even our politicians disdain politics. A candidate can't go wrong by running against Washington, DC and all that it supposedly stands for. George W. "I'm from Texas" Bush successfully campaigned as an anti-establishment "outsider"—and his dad was the president! Ronald Reagan got applause when he proclaimed that the government was not the solution, but the problem—though he himself had just campaigned for, and achieved, the government's top job. (13)

It is a paradox that makes sense only if you understand that America's devotion to the two most important principles it was founded upon—liberty and egalitarianism—makes it impossible for us to believe in government, since it fundamentally contradicts our convictions that no one can tell us what to do and no one of us is superior to anyone else (17). The government, by nature, is comprised of people who think they are better suited to tell the rest of America what to do; they are leaders. This means that we have a contradictory urge to elect leaders who disparage leadership. At a certain level, these contradictions are a central feature of American identity. From the days of slave owners proclaiming that all men are created equal to the days of dropping bombs from an unmanned aircraft on anyone in the vicinity of a terrorist, there has been a gap between theory and practice in this country. At certain times, the peace between American ideals and everyday reality has been uneasier than others. Today that anxiety is most evident when we watch GOP politicians verbally contort themselves trying to assert that America is both a politically correct, wealth-redistributing liberal nightmare (made so by Barack *Hussein* Obama), and the greatest nation on earth, with so much freedom that everyone else on the planet hates us for it.

Whether anti-intellectualism is good or bad is almost beside the point. In America, it simply *is*, and it appears that that's unlikely to change soon. It does mean, however, that we have to grapple with some of the other truths that result from this part of the American psyche. Terrance MacMullan writes:

> The fact that most Americans think smart people are tricky and dumb people are honest makes it difficult to be a public intellectual in America. Luckily, Americans also enjoy a good laugh, which is why people who want to be public intellectuals need to learn from Jon Stewart. (59)

Public intellectuals perform a key role for invigorating democracy, since they call attention to major social issues and offer points of debate in ways that allow citizens to think about the central issues facing our nation. This means that our proclivity to distrust public intellectuals has a very clear downside to the health of our democracy. But as MacMullan points out, it's not that Americans are entirely incapable of embracing a public intellectual—rather, they just need to come in a palatable package, ideally one that does not appear threatening. And this is where the satirists come in. Satirists give us the information and perspective that keeps our democracy healthy without the perception of intellectual elitism. While, as we've mentioned, satire and irony can invoke similar accusations of elitism, it is generally true that satirists can reach a broader audience. More of the public tunes in to Stewart than listens to radio interviews with Noam Chomsky. There is no question that our nation would benefit from a more vigorous public sphere, inhabited by public intellectuals representing a range of viewpoints that worked alongside the satirists. But, as MacMullan writes, whereas intellectuals used to speak to the public in accessible ways, today they mostly just speak to each other, and make little effort to make what they have to say accessible to the public (60).

But it's not just the lack of alternatives that makes satire an appealing source of information and opinion. While we might have a hearty tradition of anti-intellectualism, we also have a longstanding love for satire since it holds the promise of mocking the stupidity, hubris, and folly of those who hold power over us. Freud said that "we count any rebellion against authority as a merit,"[17] and how true of America, which, according to Peterson, was, "born in rebellion and celebrates anti-Authoritarianism in any form, from the Boston patriots' dumping tea in the harbor to Elvis' hip-swiveling impudence" (17). Impudence, iconoclasm, irony, sarcasm, mockery, satire, contrarianism—these are all our birthright. After all, we are the descendants of John Hancock, whose mocking signature on the Declaration of Independence loomed so gigantic that it overshadowed those of all of his colleagues and sent a strong sign of his disfavor across an ocean. We are the heirs of Abraham Lincoln, who loved to tell this story about the Revolutionary War hero Ethan Allen:

> One of Lincoln's favorite anecdotes sprang from the early days just after the Revolution. Shortly after the peace was signed, the story began, the Revolutionary War hero Ethan Allen "had occasion to visit England," where he was subject to considerable teasing banter. The British would make "fun of the Americans and General

Washington in particular and one day they got a picture of General Washington" and displayed it prominently in the outhouse so Mr. Allen could not miss it. When he made no mention of it, they finally asked him if he had seen the Washington picture. Mr. Allen said, "He thought that it was a very appropriate [place] for an Englishman to Keep it. Why they asked, for, said Mr. Allen, there is Nothing that Will Make an Englishman Shit So quick as the Sight of Genl Washington."[18]

We, the brash young upstart nation, with just enough foolishness and heart not to know that we were doomed, we who thumbed our noses at the mightiest empire on earth and won—we, the people, have earned the right to mock our own government and elected representatives.

Peterson points out that—just as James Madison said "If men were angels, no government would be necessary"—if politicians were angels, no satire would be necessary (quoted in Peterson 207).[19] Politicians have never been angels, and an America without satire has never existed. Even when America was but a twinkle in the eye of a few revolutionaries, satire was there to set the mood. As Colin Wells writes, during the Revolutionary period, satire was "the most popular and politically important literary form in American political life—it emerged during this time as a crucial means for shaping American social and political discourse, intervening in virtually every major controversy from the Stamp Act crisis to the War of 1812" (158). The Founders didn't just enjoy humor—they believed it was politically important. And so they employed the pen *and* the sword, using satirical works as "weapons in a literary and ideological war to decide the future of the new Republic" (159). And their satire often took a form we would recognize today: portrayals of King George as a buffoon—a move that reminds us of the website that allowed you to dress up an animated George Bush and click your mouse to have him choke on a pretzel. While Bush really *did* choke on a pretzel, the incident was great fun for the satirists. *The Spoof* wrote a satirical piece on the incident claiming it was centrally featured in Bush's memoir:

> "The pretzel-choking decision was by far my most critical," wrote Bush, "Because it taught me the important lesson of chewing before attempting to swallow food." Bush also ranked the pretzel-choking incident as his fourth most embarrassing after (1) Cheney shooting a guy, (2) Dodging a flying shoe, and (3) Getting caught on tape sarcastically searching for WMDs under his office desk. Bush concluded by saying he regrets not getting to serve a third term because he's pretty sure he could have bankrupted the US and broke the entire world.[20]

King George offered the satirists plenty of opportunities to mock him as well and there were a number of satirical cartoons that scoffed at his pomposity. Pre-revolutionary American satirists used subtler forms too: "During the war, broadsides proclaiming martial law or demanding the arrest of rebels were frequently answered by anonymous verse parodies . . . ridiculing not only the colonial official who issued the proclamation but the language of political authority itself" (159).

Other familiar methods include the uses of situational masks/personae. Two of Benjamin Franklin's most biting and most famous works, "An Edict by the King of Prussia" and "The Sale of the Hessians," are, according to Bruce Granger, "illustrative of the situational mask, wherein personae are created 'who embody and illustrate the ironic contradictions between what *seems* to them and what, as the reader knows, actually *is*'" (28). Linda Morris, too, writes, "American satire of the eighteenth, and especially of the nineteenth century, often relies upon the creation of a naïve persona who inadvertently, and in an understated manner, reveals social truths. Yet, American satire also frequently relies on comic exaggeration" (377).

These techniques are familiar to us because they're the same ones used by today's political satirists. While it is indeed likely that many would scoff at the notion that Stewart has taken up the mantle of the Founding Fathers, as Rachel Sotos explains,

> The fake news, Comedy Central style, certainly is true to Franklin's blend of journalism and comedy. And while I can't predict the future, I wouldn't be at all surprised if we soon see doctoral dissertations and books comparing the "journalists" of *The Daily Show* with Franklin's pseudonymous characters. Samantha Bee is perhaps today's Silence Dogood and Polly Baker, Stephen Colbert our Poor Richard. (32)

Sotos also quotes the journalist and historian Eric Burns, who drew a connection between early and present-day America in his book, *Infamous Scribblers*. Although Benjamin Franklin is remembered today for being a great inventor, he was also "the first American humorist" and "as ethical a journalist as America produced in the eighteenth century"—contrasted with Samuel Adams, who, it turns out, was not just a brewer, but was also a muckraking journalist "so committed to the American Revolution that his journalism turned yellow fighting for the red, white, and blue" (quoted in Sotos 31). The contrast of Sam Adams' plain-and-simple fabrications of quotes intended to inflame the colonists against the British soldiers with the biting satire of Franklin also serves as an example of the Peterson's distinction between satire and pseudo-satire. Adams was just outright mocking; Franklin was satirizing in the hopes of producing critical engagement and enlightened reason.

Sotos isn't alone in seeing a connection to the late greats. Robert Miller, the publisher of *HarperStudio,* notes "Twain is the grandfather of Stephen Colbert, Jon Stewart and Steve Martin. He has such a dry, subversive wit that you feel like he's invented modern humor."[21] But today's satirists are not only just as funny and clever as our historical humorists; they are also a key part of encouraging civic engagement and entertaining citizenship. Importantly, the link between Franklin and Colbert highlights the way that satire has always played an important role in public discourse in the United States, especially in response to political trends and crises—a connection we will look at in the next section of this chapter. Steven Michels and Michael Ventimiglia note that "*The Daily Show* disregards majorities—and minorities, too, for that matter—of all kinds, therefore strengthening the kind of pluralism through dissent that classic liberals such as James Madison and John Stuart Mill so deliberately encouraged" (89). And the evidence suggests that, even if their critics don't always understand that they're following the proud tradition that was a part of this country's inception, the satirists know exactly what they're doing.

Colbert was certainly aware of the connection since he frequently called attention to the long, proud lineage of British and American satire on *The Colbert Report*. In homage to one of his satirical predecessors, Jonathan Swift, he did a segment on December 13, 2010 that served as a shout out to one of history's most famous satirists and a link between the two.[22] Swift, known by many as the author of *Gulliver's Travels*, was an Anglo-Irish satirist. One of his most famous satirical texts was *A Modest Proposal for Preventing the Children of Poor People in Ireland From Being a Burden to Their Parents or Country, and for Making Them Beneficial to the Public*, commonly referred to as *A Modest Proposal*. Written and published anonymously by Swift in 1729, *A Modest Proposal* is considered by many to be one of the best examples of satirical writing in history. Swift's titular proposal is that the impoverished Irish might ease their economic troubles by selling their children as food for the rich. This is an argument that is heightened by its satirical form—Swift slowly draws you in with a deadpan description of the ills of the poor before he delivers the stinging hyperbole of his suggested solution.

Colbert also referenced *Poor Richard's Almanack*, one of Franklin's masterpieces, in his "Better Know a Founder" segment.[23] *Poor Richard's Almanack* appeared yearly from 1732 to 1758 under the pseudonym of "Poor Richard" or "Richard Saunders." The almanac was a bestseller, with print runs that reached ten thousand per year. Like Colbert's satire, especially "The Wørd" segment, the almanac was known for its wordplay and aphorisms, many of which we still use today (see Figure 7.2). Even when Colbert doesn't overtly link his comedy to over two hundred years' worth of American satire, there are still links there to be made, such as when he appeared before the House Judiciary Committee to testify about migrant labor, a move reminiscent of Mark Twain's appearance before Congress in-character. In response to worries that Colbert's appearance was a mockery of

Figure 7.2   Stephen Colbert explicitly connects himself to Jonathan Swift[25]

our system, Don Bliss reminded readers of *The Washington Post* of Twain's own similar moves: "Loosen up, Republicans. Stephen Colbert's testimony on migrant labor before the House Judiciary Committee was in a great American tradition."[24]

Every time Colbert's character proudly declared his distrust of books and disdain of facts, he sounded more American than Reagan hitting a homerun while consuming a hot dog, an apple pie, and an entire liter of Coca-Cola. Colbert's persona combined two great, intertwined American traditions: anti-intellectualism and satire. What Colbert did was exemplify the best and the worst of the democratic process, since, on the one hand, his feigned anti-intellectualism pointed to a dangerous feature of our mass psyche, and, on the other hand, his satirical portrayal of anti-intellectualism helped remind us of how important critical thinking is to the health of our democracy. It is easy to forget the details of our history when we are constantly being told that everything we stand for is under attack. But it turns out that the satirists may well be one of the best signs that our nation's core values are alive and kicking. Satire helped found our nation and it has helped defend it ever since. As we discussed in our chapter about millennials and satire, the medium through which people today make and receive satire—primarily the internet and television—may be new. But the message isn't. It's the same good, American humor it was when Franklin wrote it with a fountain pen. So the question, perhaps, isn't why satire *now*, or why satire *then*, but why satire *when*? To better understand the connection between satire then and satire now, we will explore the connection between satire and national crisis.

Satire and America's Identity Crisis

The connection we've just drawn between historical satirists like Franklin and modern ones like Colbert highlights the fact that satire has always played an important role in public discourse in the United States. But the colonial satirists and modern day ones are also connected because their satire was created during a moment of war, military conflict, and social crisis. Wells emphasizes satire's use as a weapon of war:

> Befitting the political turbulence and fervor that characterized the era, early American satirists envisioned their works as weapons in a literary and ideological war to decide the future of the new Republic. During the Revolution, anti-British satires appeared regularly in newspapers or as broadsides, responding to specific events and depicting King George III and his supporters as villains or buffoons. (158)

Jonathan Swift may have been writing his pamphlets in 17th- and 18th-century England and Ireland, but the issues he tackled are essentially the same as those faced by the American colonists in the early days and they are pretty similar to the issues we face today. Swift was especially keen to expose when the rich and privileged used illogical arguments to attempt to explain why their privilege was just. Thus his work influenced many of the founders of America and American satire, and continues to influence today's satirists. In moments of crisis those in power often turn to hyperbole and fallacy to attempt to publicly justify why they should remain in power—and their misrepresentations of reality then become key ingredients in satirical critique. According to Morris, satire emerged in the colonies as a way to correct abuses of power and failures of reason:

> From the beginning, conditions were ripe for political, social, and religious satire. Satirists poked fun at the Puritans, rude country people, and people who aspired to lives of fashion, as well as at the British, who fought to keep the colonies under their legal and economic control, and at the democratic institutions that arose after the Revolution. Political abuses were frequently the targets of satire, whether in the eighteenth or nineteenth century, no matter the party in power. Writers used their biting humor to attack the institution of slavery as early as 1797 and as late as 1865. (377)

If one understands satire as a response to national crisis, it becomes easier to see why it emerges in what might seem to be radically different contexts. The key criterion is conflict since conflict often brings abuses of power. Rebellion depends on the idea that one should not accept the status quo and satire is an especially good tool for encouraging the masses to challenge the system.

While the history of our nation's tradition of satire in the literary arts is long and complex, the history of satire TV is significantly easier to trace. It is worth remembering that television was not a common feature in American homes until the mid 1960s, which is exactly about the same time that satire emerged as a powerful critical tool on the medium. According to David Marc, the first entirely satirical piece of television programming was *That Was the Week that Was*, which aired on NBC from 1964–65 and had a comic review of the week's news a decade before *Saturday Night Live* introduced the "Weekend Update" segment (Gray, Jones, and Thompson 10). The next major satirical show, *The Smothers Brothers Comedy Hour* (CBS, 1967–70), introduced jokes about recreational drug use and US foreign policy in Southeast Asia to primetime television (Gray, Jones, and Thompson xiii). Though it had begun as a comedy-variety show typical of its era, soon, the satire on *The Smothers Brothers* grew too sharp and critical for TV in that period and the show was canceled. *The Smothers Brothers'* legacy lived on, though, in the form of Pat Paulsen's political ambitions. Paulsen was a cast member on *The Smothers Brothers,* and he stepped through the silver screen and into the material world of politics by staging a fake run for president—a stunt that may remind you of Colbert. Colbert ran twice—sort of—but Paulsen ran six times between 1968 and 1996, and got more votes each time. When Paulsen first ran, it was an extremely volatile moment in US history—student protests, civil rights clashes, and anti-war demonstrations were common as the nation clashed over Nixon's presidency, conservative values, and the Vietnam War. Paulsen's campaign slogan was "Just a common, ordinary, simple savior of America's destiny," and one can imagine Colbert using something almost identical. He responded to all criticism with his catchphrase "Picky, picky, picky." Paulsen channeled the hypocrisy of the power elite and the failures of politicians to serve the interests of the electorate. Similarly, when Colbert ran in 2007 it was the deadliest year in Iraq since the start of the war.[26] Thus, both Colbert and Paulsen used their campaigns to challenge the prevailing political rhetoric of their time.

A year after *The Smothers Brothers* premiered, NBC launched the smash hit *Rowan and Martin's Laugh-In*. The show ran for five seasons, holding the number one slot in the Nielsen ratings for two of them. Performing a nearly impossible feat given the conservative nature of the time, *Laugh-In* managed to mostly avoid jokes that a network censor would deem "political." Instead, their humor was largely based on irreverent and funny topical jokes. The weekly audience, averaging 26–32 million viewers, proved that jokes about the news were more popular than the news itself (Gray, Jones, Thompson xiii–xiv). The power of *Laugh-In* is noteworthy, since it shows that the draw of satire over "real" news has a longer history in our nation than the current moment.

What is interesting to note is that effectively from the advent of television as a medium commonly available to our citizens, there have been comedic and satirical shows available for the public to consume. These shows have often been more popular than serious programming. They prove that humor is a key feature of our nation and they reveal the fact that the public often makes sense of their world through the prism of comedy. Each show might have its own comedic spin, but the ongoing presence of this form of entertainment certainly suggests that the turn to comedy today is not an un-American trend. One of the most innovative programs in our history was *Saturday Night Live*, which burst onto the scene in the 1970s. In its early days it was highly irreverent humor, but its satire diluted as ratings grew, and production decisions become more conservative. The show has often bumped back to prominence, though, especially with performances like that of Tina Fey impersonating Sarah Palin, which gave the comedy show its highest ratings in decades. The key historical turning point for the purposes of this book, though, is the 1990s, which ushered in the true era of satirical television with cable networks like Comedy Central (then Comedy TV) and shows like *The Simpsons* and *Politically Incorrect*. Since then, political satire has been a mainstay of Comedy Central, which introduced *The Daily Show*, and was hosted by Jon Stewart beginning in 1999 (Gray, Jones, and Thompson 24–6).

So why is it that satire and crisis go hand in hand? In moments of crisis there is an overall breakdown in perceptions of reality. Think about the 2009 economic crisis, for instance. Some argued that blame should be on the banks, others on government for deregulating the banks, and others still on people who had foolishly trusted the banks and taken out mortgages they couldn't afford. Then there were those that blamed the media for making it almost impossible to learn what the real facts were in the crisis. Which version is right? And how can you tell? Satire helps you understand the crisis because it exposes flaws in rhetoric, logical fallacies, and rhetorical spin. Most importantly, it is irreverent and enjoys attacking those in power who are protecting their privilege at the expense of the people. It spares no one. All it seeks is to help its audience see the truth and have fun doing it.

Thus we agree with Peterson that satirical humor functions as democracy's feedback loop, and hopes to encourage solutions to crises rather than mockery of them. Though Peterson offers the caveat that comedy is "not exactly" a holy quest, and acknowledges that "Mark Twain may have overestimated its lethality" (206), he is right to say that "laughter is necessary, even if it serves—as it did for President

Lincoln—no higher purpose than to keep us from crying" (205). Laughter also brings us together, creating a community of people who get the joke. This then strengthens our sense of the public sphere, which is often weak in times of uncertainty or crisis, and which has certainly been eroded by the struggles of the new millennium. Henry Louis Gates, Jr. said that the dissenter insists "critique can also be a form of commitment, a means of laying a claim. It's the ultimate gesture of citizenship. A way of saying: I'm not just passing through here, I *live* here."[27] When the public sphere has been undermined and our democracy feels at risk, satire offers a perfect and perfectly American way to meet the challenges of the time. It offers a way to be a dissenter and a critic while strengthening communities, instead of contributing to the splintering apart of an angry and fearful citizenry. It offers us the respite of laughter from the troubling times, while beginning to work to raise us up out of them. And, best of all, it is our constitutional right—one of the constitutional rights over which we seem to have unanimous agreement. We know for certain that it's what the Founders would have wanted.

One of the challenges, though, is wading though the various types of humor on offer during moments of crisis. Peterson notes that though satire is often an effective tool for handling national crises, war is uniquely challenging to mainstream "equal-opportunity offender" comedians because the only way to remain neutral on the subject is to ignore it, as Johnny Carson did the Vietnam War (200). Peterson quotes Jay Leno saying that "It's not the time to pick on the president or the government or the military," and Lorne Michaels, creator/producer of *Saturday Night Live*, saying, "We won't do anything that attempts to undermine President Bush's authority."[28] Paul Lewis writes that, when he chaired a panel on terrorism and humor at an international humor studies conference in June of 2002, he learned that

> jokes about the suffering of 9/11 victims and mourners began to circulate in Europe and elsewhere shortly after the attacks, but my searches of U.S.-based joke Web pages during the days, weeks and months following the attacks suggested that American humor after 9/11 was remarkable for its avoidance of these targets. In a culture defined by its transgressive audacity particularly in the area of violence-based humor, this restraint in itself was unusual enough to suggest questions. (176)

One of the questions this raised was whether there is a link between the perceived severity of a crisis and how long it takes for jokes to circulate. Ideas about humor after 9/11, clearly, were mixed. Soon after the attacks, some suggested that humor could help heal a wounded nation. But once again, it is impossible to assess humor as a whole. What the post-9/11 audiences needed was humor that could foster an audience's interest in seeking accountability for public actions, in a time when the president was openly acting on gut impulses and heightened emotion. American society was increasingly losing access to and interest in a public sphere for democratic deliberation.

According to Wendy Brown, "The patriot idealizes the country, which is indistinguishable from an abstract idea (e.g. of what America stands for) and devotes her- or himself to this ideal" (quoted in Sarat 35). Indeed they do, and in doing so, they attack any dissenters as being unpatriotic at best or traitors at worst. As William Saletan wrote for *Slate* in response to the 2004 Republican National Convention speeches by Dick Cheney and Zell Miller,

> In a democracy, the commander in chief works for you. You hire him when you elect him. You watch him do the job. If he makes good decisions and serves your interests, you rehire him. If he doesn't, you fire him by voting for his opponent in the next election. Not every country works this way. In some countries, the commander in chief builds a propaganda apparatus that equates him with the military and the nation. If you object that he's making bad decisions and disserving the national interest, you're accused of weakening the nation, undermining its security, sabotaging the commander in chief, and serving a foreign power—the very charges Miller levelled tonight against Bush's critics. Are you prepared to become one of those countries?[29]

As Saletan explains, when you criticized President Bush's policies and leadership in the wake of 9/11, you were accused of "refusing to support American troops in combat." It was as if democracy were to be put temporarily on hold, until we had "won" the war, whatever that would look like. In fact, if you disagreed with the president, you could not even participate in our democracy in what is perhaps the most basic and obvious way—by running for office yourself. As Marc Racicot, chairman of the RNC, said in 2003, "Senator Kerry crossed a grave line when he dared suggest the replacement of America's commander in chief at a time when America is at war," implying that somehow running for office because you believe that you could serve the country well as a leader is treasonous rather than the highest possible expression of faith and love for America.[30]

The problem is that just as 9/11 sent our nation into crisis, much of the crisis revolved around exactly what it meant to be American. Any dissent of any kind of the administration was cast as treason. But, again, the true satirists were able to overcome the desire to sport flag pins and stick to safe joke territory. According to Joanne Morreale, *The Daily Show* became more political after 9/11 (in Gray, Jones, and Thompson 117), and on the first show after the attacks, Jon Stewart demonstrated his understanding of his position as a satirist as being both a privilege and a right that is not to be taken for granted:

> [This is] a country that allows for open satire, and I know that sounds basic and it sounds as though it goes without saying—but that's really what this whole situation is about. It's the difference between closed and open. It's the difference between free and burdened and we don't take that for granted here by any stretch of the imagination and our show has changed. I don't doubt that. What it's become, I don't know.[31]

Simply because they were the only ones who would criticize, laugh at, and reflect upon the barrage of crises and changes US citizens were suddenly faced with, the satirists became the source of a very particular form of public pedagogy after 9/11. Lewis writes that "Whether the 9/11 attacks 'changed everything' as people have been wont to suggest, they certainly scrambled American humor, first by sucking the oxygen out of public joking, then by reshuffling the order of butts: whom we joked about and how" (174). Pundits and journalists fell over themselves pronouncing the death of irony in the immediate aftermath of the attacks. However, as Peterson writes, it was soon clear that "the reports of irony's death had been greatly exaggerated" (195). Lewis credits Malcolm Kushner of *USA Today* with calling upon the country to exercise our "freedom to laugh at each other and ourselves,"[32] and "to enjoy inner-directed and, perhaps, self-critical humor, rather than hostile and outward-targeted joking" (178).

Unfortunately, many comedians failed to rise to this challenge, and instead retreated into silliness due to the sensitivity of the administration and television networks. Bill Maher, then the host of *Politically Incorrect* on ABC, was fired for commenting that the United States lobbing cruise missiles at targets from far away might be called "cowardly," but that flying airplanes into buildings surely isn't. What Peterson terms his "reckless truth-telling" cost him his job, and earned a warning from White House Press Secretary Ari Fleischer, who said that Maher's firing should be taken as a reminder "to all Americans that they need to watch what they say, watch what they do."[33] It was a warning that many heeded, if the Center for Media and Public Affairs' data showing that 80 jokes about Clinton were made between 9/11 and the end of 2001, compared to just 25 jokes about Bush, is anything to go on (199). So while Letterman, Leno, and *SNL* waved flags and applauded firefighters, *The Daily Show* voiced the concerns the public had about the imminent war that inspired the largest peace protests since Vietnam, declining to reprise Johnny Carson's total avoidance of the topic of a controversial war along with his late-night compatriots.

As Peterson writes, even if *The Daily Show*'s "Mess O'Potamia" segment on the war didn't explicitly advocate an anti-war position, "Jon Stewart and company at least refused to join the Patriot Parade in which their competitors—in both the mainstream comedy and "real" news realms—seemed to be marching" (203). Satire, once again, was the nation's last defense against the total erosion of the society we like to think that we have (see Figure 7.3).

Figure 7.3   Mess O'Potamia coverage from 2005[34]

No, *I* Am America

There is a great battle underway, right now, in America. No, it's not iPhone vs. Android—it's a battle over who is a better American, and who gets to define what it means to be American. This battle is fought on several fronts, including left wing vs. right wing and politicians vs. citizens, and, most importantly to us, pundits vs. satirists. It is a battle between pundits who identify with the nation so strongly that they blur the lines of where the self ends and the country begins, and the satirists who are scrambling for ways to parody something that is already massively overblown and dramatic. This is a natural progression for the pundits who, since 9/11, have been slowly escalating their patriotism to the point of having American flag lapel pins so huge they threaten to tear their suits. In this section, we will look at some of the fundamental characteristics of these hyper-American identities, the ways the right wing pundits have defined America, and the ways satirists are countering their definitions.

Whether America is exceptional in the ways we believe it is or not (spoiler alert: it isn't), there is at least one thing Americans do better than the rest. Americans are by far the most invested in the idea that their country is the best. In *Talking Right*, Geoffrey Nunberg says that US patriotism seems extreme to many of our fellow developed nations. Perhaps it is because World War II taught Europe some hard lessons about nationalistic pride, or perhaps it is more about what makes us different from the Europeans than what makes the Europeans different from us, but the unassailable fact remains that Americans are exceptionally patriotic. Nunberg cites British journalists John Micklethwait and Adrian Wooldridge, who say that "American Patriotism runs deep. No other developed country displays its flags more obsessively or sings its national anthem more frequently" (190), and points to polls done before and after 9/11 in which 83–90% of US citizens described themselves as "extremely proud" or "very proud" to be an American (189). As you may have guessed, Republicans are slightly more likely than Democrats to say that they are "extremely proud," but, for the most part, patriotism doesn't discriminate based on party affiliation. And yet, to hear the right-wing talk, you'd think that the Republicans are the patriots and that Democrats actually hate their country and are trying to destroy it.

Somehow, Republicans have cornered the market on patriotism. Supposedly they and they alone know what it means to be a real American. Nunberg notes that on the web the phrase "patriotic liberal" is outnumbered 40–1 by the phrase "patriotic conservative" (189). The right's message is clear: you love America as-is, or you get the hell out. Love it or leave it. Criticizing America doesn't make us stronger, in their view. Neither does fighting for the rights of any underprivileged or minority group. That tears us apart. America is what it is—and that is a nation of white Christian males, by white Christian males, and for white Christian males. If you don't like it, don't let the Atlantic Ocean hit you on your way over to France. We'll be over here eating Freedom Fries.

But, according to Nunberg, most liberals are patriotic. "If they have reservations about past and present policies, it's most often because they believe that those policies fail to live up to the best American ideals, usually a sign of patriotism and optimism itself" (190). Wariness about entering into a war with a country that had nothing to do with 9/11 hardly constitutes rooting for the terrorists to win. So how is it that the right has been able to monopolize what it means to be a patriot and an American? Well, because the battle over defining patriotism has never been grounded in the facts, no more than the Iraq War was. The poster boy of both of those efforts is President Bush, a man who championed legislation that would actually curtail a great deal of civil liberties for American citizens and called it the Patriot Act, and then opened the Department of Homeland Security to protect our way of life while severely altering it. Republicans were in charge during and after the attacks of 9/11, when people were made pliant by their fear, and their version of patriotism gained so much ground that even a decade later, when almost everyone agrees the wars in Iraq and Afghanistan were disastrous, Democrats have not been able to reclaim or reframe what it means to be a patriot.

Enter the satirists. *The Daily Show* takes a fun approach to defining America in *America (The Book): A Citizen's Guide to Democracy Inaction*. The book presents its satire of American politics in the form of a parody of a high school textbook, including study guides and exercises. It includes a foreword by 'Thomas Jefferson,' which ends with a takedown of American exceptionalism, saying of the Founders and the Constitution: "We were imperfect. It was imperfect. And we expect our descendants to work as hard as we did on keeping what we think is a profoundly excellent form of government supple, evolving, and relevant. After reading this book, you should be better prepared to do just that" (Foreword xi).

Contrary to the hype, America is *not* exceptional in most ways that matter. According to *Business Insider*, we are not the best in literacy, math, life expectancy, press freedom, international trade, economic freedom, happiness, income equality, infant survival, GDP, infrastructure, employment, oil exports, industrial production growth rate, net trade of goods and services, or women holding public office. We do have the most incarcerated citizens, adults who believe angels are real, and national defense spending.[35] And yet, most Americans would tell you that we are lucky to live here, and point to countries that clearly have it worse to justify that feeling—something CollegeHumor tapped into with their "America Sucks Less" music video that satirized American exceptionalism by turning the sentiment on its head and saying that it's not that America is better, but that other countries are worse.

So why do Americans believe we are exceptional, in the face of all the evidence to the contrary? The reasons are far too numerous to get into in this book, but it boils down to a (possibly delusional) belief that we have unparalleled might, and that we are justified in using that might because we have superior values. The term "values," of course, has gone the way of patriotism. Perhaps in large part because of the undue influence of the religious right, the conservatives have a near monopoly on American values. They define what those values are, and are the arbiters of who is upholding them and who isn't. Guess which people usually aren't? That's right—it's the left wing, and the marginalized. So what are our shared American values, according to the right wing gatekeepers? Well, thankfully, there's ouramericanvalues.org to tell us. Apparently, our American values are "Family, Faith, and Freedom."

To help us keep track of how we're doing on those fronts, ouramericanvalues. org helpfully breaks down the news into three categories: "Pro-Life News," "Traditional Marriage News," and "Pro-Israel News." On life, "American Values is deeply committed to the defense of all human life against the assaults of the culture of death." On marriage, "American Values works for the protection of families against the many forces trying to break down these fundamental social institutions and re-build them in the name of freedom and multi-culturalism." On Israel, "American Values believes America's relationship with Israel needs to be the cornerstone of U.S. foreign policy." So there you have it. Americans are anti-choice, anti-gay, and pro-Israel. They're good Christians, and they believe in family. Canadian satirist Rick Mercer said it best in November 2004 when he exclaimed, "Thanks to family values, when it comes to freedom and personal choice, the wheels are off the bus in America. And let's face it—it was a pretty short bus to begin with" (162).

Who, then, was in a better position to take on America's identity and values crisis than Stephen Colbert, whose satirizing of the religious right's values and patriotism has been informed by his own real patriotism and faith? In 2007, Colbert wrote his first of two books about America, called *I Am America (And So Can You!)*. With the title alone, he outdoes the pundits, ensuring that not only does he define America, he embodies it. He *is* America. If that sounds ridiculous, well, it's not. Because that is the only way he could one-up the right wing pundits, who are churning out books defining America, the problems it faces, and the value-based solutions to those problems at an alarming rate. There are Bill O'Reilly's *Culture Warrior*, or *Pinheads and Patriots* (or his murder-themed series of books, including *Killing Lincoln*), Glenn Beck's *Glenn Beck's Common Sense*, Joe Scarborough's *The Last Best Hope: Restoring Conservatism and America's Promise*, and Ann Coulter's *Guilty: Liberal "Victims" and Their Assault on America*. If this is all sounding very Us vs. Them, that's because it is. Fundamentally so. Because if only some of us are patriots, then some of us are not patriots. If some of us get to decide what patriotism is, then some of us don't. In Bill O'Reilly's book *Culture Warrior*, the Us vs. Them is a "culture war" between "traditionalists" and "secular-progressives." Fittingly, O'Reilly promoted his book on *The Colbert Report*, where, when O'Reilly asked if Colbert had read the book, Colbert said "*Read* your book? I've read your book in more ways than one, sir. Now—I'm living your book, okay? This is a fantastic book."[36]

Colbert asks O'Reilly "What's destroying our country more: activist judges, illegal immigrants, gay marriage, or NBC News?" O'Reilly tells him that it's NBC News, "no question," because "NBC News incorporates all of the others." O'Reilly then jokes about Brian Williams being a Venezuelan illegal immigrant, but the rest of what he said is not to be taken lightly. O'Reilly sees himself as a soldier engaged in hand-to-hand combat in the culture war against the secular progressives, and he thinks the media is on the side of the "S-Ps." And, famously, in this interview, Colbert mentions O'Reilly's toughness, to which O'Reilly responds that's "an act." Colbert's response? "If you're an act, then what am I?"

So while right-wingers from Sarah Palin to Rush Limbaugh tie up all the airwaves defining who the patriots are and are not, the left wing sits on the sidelines refusing to make a play. The satirists then are left to save America—or, at least, our notions about what America is and who gets to say so. By way of example, Day offers an episode of *The Daily Show* from the 2008 presidential campaign:

> *The Daily Show* devoted an entire episode to responding to comments being made by members of the McCain campaign (including vice presidential candidate Sarah Palin) about the patriotic "real America," in reference to the small towns in which they supposedly had strong support. Stewart responds first by concluding that the big cities like Washington, D.C. and New York must then be the capitals of fake America, "the ground zero [of fake America], if you will,"[37] meaning, he muses that Osama bin Laden must feel pretty stupid knowing that he bombed the wrong America and that, if you were from fake America and signed up to fight in Iraq and died, then it doesn't count. (Day 62)

What, then, of all of the Americans who are pro-choice, or gay, or a little wary about the phrase "a strong and viable Israel in concert with a powerful and resolute United States"? Well, obviously, they're not real Americans. So what are they, fake Americans? Well . . . yes. Of course. Mocking the idea that there was a litmus test for "real" and "fake" Americans, Jon Stewart created a quiz we could use to help us determine if we are the real deal (see Figure 7.4).

Suggesting that dissenters—particularly liberals—are not real Americans is not, of course, new. It was kind of Joseph McCarthy's whole shtick in the 1950s. But it is alarming and disappointing that in the intervening 60 years, America has not been able to separate simple traits like atheism (or, as O'Reilly would probably have us call it, secularism) or liberalness from a hatred or disdain of America.

Figure 7.4   Jon Stewart's "Are You a Real American?" quiz[38]

Stewart doesn't hate America, even though he criticizes it soundly almost every Monday-Thursday night at 11pm. In fact, as Morreale writes,

> Interviews both on and off the show make clear that, despite Stewart's critique of politics and media, he aims to edify rather than destroy and to praise as well as to blame. His mock history textbook, *America: The Book,* ends with a chapter that reminds readers that the American system, despite its flaws, is still the finest in the world. (quoted in Gray, Jones, and Thompson 117)

That's the patriotism we lost during the McCarthy era, and misplaced again after 9/11. But until the right wing can see that the rhetoric of American exceptionalism and the exclusive and reductive defining of American patriotism and values makes us just as bad as the people we call enemies, or until the left reclaims their stakes in defining America, it's down to the satirists to keep on savin' Franklin.

8

Laughing So Hard I Could Cry: Analyzing the Satire Scare

According to us, satire is saving our nation. It is correcting the misinformation of the news, holding politicians accountable, and helping reframe citizenship in ways that productively combine entertainment and engagement. It is also opening up through new media to allow citizens to be not just consumers, but also creators of content and political information. What's the downside? There *has* to be a downside, right? This can't possibly be good. Given that we have shown a radical shift in the role of satire in affecting public thinking, should we be afraid? Does this mean democracy is doomed? Worry from all sides of the political spectrum frets that satire is mocking the nation and undermining the core values of our country. What are the real concerns here? Are any of them valid?

As with any major shift, change can mean the loss of valuable qualities. In this case, the loss of serious news reporting consumed by a large sector of our nation is generally considered in all quarters to be a bad outcome. But, as we've explained, satire did not create that loss, if anything, it has come to occupy such a central role in informing our nation as a reaction to that loss. So one key and ongoing dilemma is that satire is often blamed for the conditions that it ridicules. True, today satire does exert influence over the news, but it got that power precisely because the public lost faith in the news process and because the news itself was doing such a lousy job. So blaming satire for its public role seems to make little sense. That hasn't stopped the skeptics though: you can find essays and articles and opinion pieces that criticize and condemn satire.

But the worry doesn't stop there. The satire scare is much deeper than the issue of its role in news reporting and in shaping the public's knowledge base. Skeptics worry that satire is (1) too cynical (2) too persuasive (3) not persuasive enough (4) too confusing (5) too pedantic (6) too popular (7) too subtle (8) too brash (9) too close to news (10) not newsy enough (11) too fun, and (12) not funny enough. P. J. O'Rourke tells us "Satire doesn't effect change."[1] Arnold Zwicky claims that "Satire in general is dangerous."[2] They can't both be right, right? What is fascinating for us is the fact that researchers come at the issue from opposing sides, suggesting, at least anecdotally, that satire might be getting it just right. In fact, as we explained in our chapter on the art of satire and irony, it is precisely the ambiguous, open nature of satire that makes its impact an open door. That openness, though, leads to lots of worries that satire shames people into agreeing with it, that it alienates people who don't get the joke, and that it can be offensive. Satire doesn't have a clear expected outcome, even if its hope is to spark critical thinking. That vagueness is at the heart of much of the worry about the dangers of the comedic mode. We argue, though, that that vagueness is exactly why satire shouldn't scare us. What *is* scary is the reality that satire mocks and the possibility that the audience for the joke can't apprehend that reality even with the help of satire.

While most of the concerns about satire are framed speculatively, there is a significant body of research that attempts to quantify data on these issues. In the first section of this chapter, we cover the research that puts satire alongside news as a source of public information. Not only is it noteworthy that satire always scores higher on these polls and surveys, but we also find it significant that satire holds a place alongside traditional news in these studies. As we explained in chapter 3, such a shift is a remarkable change in the way we understand news media today. One odd outcome is that because satire is often considered alongside news, it is then held up to the same standards for reporting. That logic is completely flawed. It is clearly true that we often learn more from satire than the news—especially if we are younger—but it makes no sense to then conclude that satire is the same as news. The next two sections of the chapter look at the scholarly research beginning with the skeptics and concluding with the optimists. While we hope to point out the various findings of these studies, we also hope to show how hard it is to get conclusive evidence of impact from a comedic genre that specifically avoids prescribed outcomes and that is meant to provoke a process of critical reflection that takes place over time. In a certain sense the mere idea of empirical, data-driven research on satire defies logic. How can one craft a controlled study in the context of satire? We understand the urge to have hard answers to these questions; we are, after all, living in an era where having facts is especially comforting. And we would love to be able to prove without a shadow of a doubt that satire is, indeed, saving us. But, as it turns out, we are the ones responsible for that. Satire's job is to motivate us to try.

Satire Hits the Big (News) Leagues

If you've seen Jon Stewart on any show other than his own, you've probably heard him denounce the idea that his show is a source of news, probably by making reference to "puppets making crank calls" preceding his show on Comedy Central. You've also probably heard people say—critically—that young people are turning on *The Daily Show* instead of the news. And yet, much of the way satire is criticized and studied today seems to be based on the premise that it is enough like news that it is okay to treat it as such. One of the ways in which this happens is that satire gets lumped into the mainstream media in research into the effects of news programming. In this section, we will take a look at how satire is getting a seat at the real news table, even as its loudest critics denounce it for failing to do what news should—sufficiently inform and educate the public.

In 2010, Brian Williams of NBC News told *New York Magazine* that Jon Stewart "has chronicled the death of shame in politics and journalism."[3] Williams, a frequent guest on *The Daily Show*, also said "Many of us on this side of the journalism tracks often wish we were on Jon's side. I envy his platform to shout from the mountaintop. He's a necessary branch of government."[4] This was far more than a statement of admiration of a friend—this was Brian Williams commending someone he identifies as a journalism colleague, albeit one from "the other side of the journalism tracks." Journalist is a title that Jon Stewart himself would reject—and has rejected—outright, with increasing frequency and vehemence since he tied with Brian Williams, Tom Brokaw, Dan Rather, and Anderson Cooper in a 2007 Pew Research Center for the People and the Press survey that asked respondents to name the journalist they most admired.[5] "To call him a journalist—I think he'll be the first to laugh that one off," standup comedian Pete Dominick, who has worked for Stewart as a warm-up comedian, told CNN's Deborah Feyerick[6] after the *New York Times* published an article comparing Stewart to Edward R. Murrow for his work toward getting the 9/11 First Responders Health Care Bill passed.[7]

In 2012, Ted Koppel told *The Republican* that Stewart and Colbert "don't pretend to be journalists," but that "they are doing a better job than the real journalists."[8] Weeks later, Colbert confirmed that he has no intention of being a newsman by telling David Gregory on *Meet the Press* "I don't imagine that I'm a newsman. I really admire newsmen, I really enjoy good news."[9] So if we can all agree that *The Daily Show* and *The Colbert Report* are not news, why are we evaluating them as if they are?

This fundamental question of whether we can and should evaluate satire news alongside traditional, mainstream news has been building for years, particularly as the popularity of first *The Daily Show* and then its spinoff *The Colbert Report* grew. Jones writes that the myth that young Americans are getting more of their news from late-night comedy than from the news media originated with a statistic from a Pew Research poll in 2000 which reported that 47% of people under the age of thirty were "informed at least occasionally" about the presidential campaign by late-night talk shows. Jones questions the accuracy of that statistic, but says that regardless, it is appealing because it "seemingly verifies fears of public ignorance of the political process, youth disengagement from politics, a declining reading culture, couch potato kids, the entertainmentization of politics, and the cynicism that supposedly grips our society" (167). The statistic fanned the flame of journalistic concern about audiences' attraction to entertainment and difficulty distinguishing between entertainment and serious news until it grew into a roaring, fiery myth about where young people get their news. But, luckily for the late-night comedians, although they were hardly rushing to offer a *mea culpa* and resign to save the public from the scourge of politics-themed entertainment, there was yet more light to be shed on the topic of satire news. In 2004, a National Annenberg Election Survey found that "Viewers of late-night comedy programs, especially *The Daily Show* with Jon Stewart on Comedy Central, are more likely to know the issue positions and backgrounds of presidential candidates than people who do not watch late-night comedy." Senior analyst Dannagal Goldthwaite Young of the Annenberg Public Policy Center identified some of the characteristics that set

The Daily Show viewers apart: "People who watch *The Daily Show* are more interested in the presidential campaign, more educated, younger, and more liberal than the average American or than Leno or Letterman viewers,"[10] he said, noting that the findings didn't demonstrate that the show is responsible for its viewers' knowledge, but adding that *The Daily Show* "assumes a fairly high level of political knowledge on the part of its audience—more so than Leno or Letterman." At the same time, because *The Daily Show* does deal with campaign events and issues, "viewers might certainly pick up information while watching. It is probably a bit of both." Of course,

> Empirical analyses of news consumption among young political humor viewers indicate young viewers of The Daily Show and Colbert Report consuming more (not less) political information from traditional sources, particularly online, and through talk radio (Young & Tisinger, 2006). (Young 2012, 155)

The fact that these effects were not observed for viewers of Letterman or Leno makes it clear that there is something unique about satirical news like *The Daily Show* that allows viewers to learn more, "even when education, following politics, party identification, gender, viewing network news, reading the newspaper, watching cable news, and getting campaign information on-line are taken into account."[11] Thus it seems less strange that satirical news is increasingly popping up alongside the mainstream news media in research into the ways audiences consume and are affected by news.

As we've said, the lines between entertainment and news have blurred because entertainment is looking a lot more like news, but also because the news is looking a lot more like entertainment. If you think this has escaped the notice of young people, you're not giving them enough credit. Jones cites the media researcher Kevin Barnhurst, who has done several studies on the news consumption habits of college-aged students. Barnhurst finds that "they generally disdain the displays of political opinion on television news programs, considering them little more than 'reality-based variety shows' and something not to be taken seriously. Similarly, he finds that young people largely find newspapers irrelevant to their lives, because newspapers' version of 'news' has little meaning within the localities where these young citizens live" (Jones 28). Indeed, it seems both audiences and news researchers are beginning to view satire news as being on par with "real news." On a *Huffington Post Media* article entitled "CNN Is Terrible. Here's Why," one of the top 3 comments, by Steven S., reads

> Funny article. What I don't like about CNN, and why I rarely watch it, is that it has a distinct right-wing bent. Kind of like Fox News lite. Except that it's [sic] more dangerous than Fox because it hides its right wing agenda in the cloak of "objectivity." What nonsense. I thought the "main stream media," of which CNN is a part, is supposed to be liberal. Well, it isn't. If I want my dose of liberal media, I tune in to Jon Stewart and MSNBC.[12]

It is unclear whether the researchers or the audiences began thinking of fake news in this way first, but what is becoming clearer and clearer is that this view of political satire is becoming part of the public wisdom that informs much of the criticism of satire today. Any criticism that satire is not informative enough, or that it is too biased, or that it doesn't foster citizenship rests on the premise that it *ought* to—and those are things we have traditionally expected of our media and our classrooms.

For better or worse, Jon Stewart, Stephen Colbert, and other political satirists have expanded their niche until they found themselves next to the (alleged) Real Journalists. As we discussed in "Savin' Franklin," satire is not new, and nor is its mass appeal, especially not in times of national crisis. And, to be sure, shoddy journalism is not a new phenomenon. But this is the first time we are seeing satire news receive the same treatment as traditional news media, and having it included alongside the former bastions of Real News, like CNN, in research. Perhaps if audiences and researchers are able to accept the reality of our new and evolving media landscape, what we should do is simply reconceptualize the fourth estate so that it can include satire, rather than fretting that it is hastening the demise of our democracy. In this chapter, we will review some studies compiled by researchers who take a decidedly less optimistic approach as well as the more optimistic approaches, and contextualize the data that informs our own optimistic outlook on satire.

The Satire Scare

There is no doubt that there has been a radical shift in the role of satire and its place in affecting public thinking. And as a result, there is worry from all sides of the political spectrum that satire is mocking our nation and undermining our core values (see Table 8.1). But as Robert McChesney says, "If we had a legitimate or decent media you wouldn't have to put on a clown suit to get noticed" (quoted in Boler 34). So should we be worrying about the state of the news, or worrying about the effects of satire news taking its place?

Well, some of the fear is based on the very nature of satire, because, as Gray, Jones, and Thompson write, it is "ultimately a negative form (albeit with positive intentions) and therefore runs the risk of alienating the audience through its negative properties" (14). Some worry that because satire is negative and must function by highlighting the faults of the political system, it will heighten cynicism in its audiences and cause viewers to disengage from the process entirely, to the detriment of our democracy as a whole. Jonathan Morris and Jody Baumgartner (2008) found a causal connection between young people from the ages of 18–30 watching *The Daily Show* and cynicism toward the news media, which is consistent with their earlier research (Baumgartner and Morris, 2006). Political satire makes people cynical, whereas other kinds of political humor that we don't count as satire—such as *The Tonight Show*—do the opposite (Baumgartner and Morris, 2008). Baumgartner and Morris also suggest that people who turn to *The Daily Show* for news regularly may suffer more from cynicism because Stewart goes beyond "highlighting the shortcomings of elected officials, candidates, and political institutions" and focuses exclusively on the negative, which "may lead viewers to believe that the system comprises only of bad apples and that it is poisoned beyond repair" (in Amarasingam 64).

Table 8.1 Satire Scares

Satire makes people cynical and unengaged	People don't really understand satire	Satire is too reductive and uninformative
Baumgartner and Morris (2008) "Finally, we will use experimental and survey evidence to demonstrate that exposure to *The Daily Show* negatively impacts trust and support for the mass media among its primary audience — young adults" (316).	**LaMarre, Landreville, and Beam (2009)** " . . . there was no significant difference between the groups in thinking Colbert was funny, but conservatives were more likely to report that Colbert only pretends to be joking and genuinely meant what he said while liberals were more likely to report that Colbert used satire and was not serious when offering political statements" (212).	**Moy, Xenos, and Hess (2005)** "There was a main effect of watching late-night comedy on evaluations of candidates; more importantly, viewers were more likely than nonviewers to base their evaluations of George W. Bush on character traits after he appeared on *The Late Show with David Letterman*" (198).
Baumgartner and Morris (2006) "Although research indicates that soft news contributes to democratic citizenship in America by reaching out to the inattentive public, our findings indicate that *The Daily Show* may have more detrimental effects, driving down support for political institutions and leaders among those already inclined toward nonparticipation" (341).		**Young (2006)** "The results suggest that viewing late-night comedy was not directly associated with the salience of the candidates' most caricatured traits, but among less politically knowledgeable individuals, the salience of certain caricatured traits did increase at higher levels of late-night comedy exposure" (339).
		Young (2008) "This manuscript posits that humor suspends argument scrutiny of the premise of a given text through various cognitive mechanisms involving processing ability and motivation" (119). **Kim and Vishak (2008)** "The results indicate that compared to news media, entertainment media are less effective in acquiring factual information, particularly in retaining issue and procedure knowledge. The study, for the first time, reveals that entertainment media facilitate online-based political information processing, whereas news media promote memory-based political information processing" (338).

The thing is, if you turn to media coverage of studies like that of Baumgartner and Morris that found watching *The Daily Show* made viewers more cynical about politics, you'll see only the glass-half-empty interpretation of the findings. As was pointed out by HuffPost Media blogger and USC Annenberg School professor Marty Kaplan in 2006, there's more than one angle of approach to the study's findings. While the *Washington Post*'s Richard Morin focused on the scary news that "Young people who watch Stewart's faux news program . . . develop cynical views about politics and politicians that could lead them to just say no to voting," Kaplan highlights the fact that people who watch *The Daily Show* are more confident about their political knowledge than those who rely on network news, and that the researchers put forth the idea that people who are more confident that they understand politics are more likely to participate in politics than those who don't trust their own understanding. Or, put more simply—people who watch *The Daily Show*, despite supposedly becoming more cynical about politics by virtue of watching the show, might actually become more active voters and citizens. We think of cynicism as a paralytic, believing that feeling cynical about the political process would make most of us throw our hands in the air and say, "What's the point?" But it's not so clear cut as that. We certainly understand why watching Stewart express his colorful exasperation with the seemingly endless failures and follies of our political system might make it appear as though he were a cynic, and might make viewers cynical. But we also think that Stewart's frustration and disappointment come from an optimistic belief that we really have the potential to be better. It's the difference between a parent being frustrated that their son did poorly on an exam because he's simply not good at math, or being frustrated that their son did poorly on the exam because they believe he had the potential to do better but was too lazy to study. Stewart believes that we have it in us to ace the test of democracy, and his frustration stems, not from a cynical belief that we are not capable of having a healthy democracy, but his belief that we collectively could— and can still—do better, with a nudge in the right direction from We the People (see Figure 8.1).

But there is an even more sinister fear than the fear that people who watch *The Daily Show* and *The Colbert Report* are becoming cynical. Essentially, the fear that viewers of these shows are becoming cynics is the fear that they understand the shows all too well, and see the patterns of deceit and failure that inform the shows as patterns that permeate politics. But what if the reverse were true, and people are watching fake news without getting it at all? Some research into the effects of *The Colbert Report* in particular suggests that it might be possible that some viewers of satire news are just clueless. On the one hand, this is a plausible problem. Satire, after all, requires some decoding on the part of the consumer. Because of the layer of irony that all satire must include, it "tends to require a level of sophistication that network television infrequently demands of audiences" (Gray, Jones, and Thompson 15). What if there were people out there who just didn't get the satire, and were taking all the absurdity at face value? If people are not interpreting it as satire, then not only can it not have the positive effects of satire we've described, but it could have unforeseen negative effects as well.

Figure 8.1   Jon Stewart's Rally to Restore Sanity was the polar opposite of cynicism[13]

Heather LaMarre, Kristen Landreville, and Michael Beam (2009) seemed to confirm the worst of those fears when they demonstrated that "conservatives were more likely to report that Colbert only pretends to be joking and genuinely meant what he said while liberals were more likely to report that Colbert used satire and was not serious when offering political statements" (212). Even stranger, they found that there was no significant difference between conservatives and liberals in finding *The Colbert Report* funny. With all due respect to the researchers, that strikes us as incredibly bizarre. LaMarre, Landreville, and Beam conducted this study using an online survey, showing participants a 2006 video clip of Stephen Colbert interviewing Amy Goodman and asking questions about their percep- tions about Colbert's opinions, ideology, and seriousness. We find it difficult to believe that these findings hold true for the population of viewers who have watched *The Colbert Report* regularly. While it is possible to imagine that people with passing familiarity with the show or none at all would selectively interpret Colbert's ideology through the lens of their own political beliefs, it is hard for us to imagine that any long-term exposure to *The Colbert Report* would allow for that possibility. Simply put, one would have to be pretty unobservant to fail to notice the cues Colbert gave on his show as to what he truly believes. Although Colbert's persona on the show and deadpan delivery added a layer of complexity to discerning the true intent behind the satire, his facade was never flawless. Stephen Colbert, the persona, did break character on the show. And Stephen Colbert, the person, has given interviews in which he has candidly talked about his positions on some issues. He also regularly lends his out-of-character support to causes he deems worthy.

Yet LaMarre, Landreville, and Beam were not the only ones to find that some people who watched Colbert in character just weren't getting it. Baumgartner and

Morris also researched the effects of *The Colbert Report* on the political attitudes of young viewers, and found that Colbert has had an unexpected influence:

> Instead of giving viewers pause to ponder the legitimacy of Colbert's implicit criticisms of the far right, this experiment found that exposure to Colbert increases support for President Bush, Republicans in Congress, and Republican policies on the economy and the War on Terror. Instead of honing in on the implicit arguments of The Colbert Report, some viewers seemed to take the satire at face value. Quite simply, they didn't get the joke. ("Stoned slackers or Super Citizens?" 16)

Michael Xenos, Patricia Moy, and Amy Becker also found that political comedy can help viewers form opinions that are consistent with their ideology (2011). So is it possible that there are legions of Colbert and Stewart viewers who have been regularly and dramatically misunderstanding the shows? We doubt it. Again, we believe that the kind of viewing that fosters citizenship and creates communities around satire like that of *The Colbert Report* precludes the notion of people utterly failing to understand the show watching it regularly. The key is that most of these studies test only clips of the shows; they are not a sampling of regular or frequent viewers.

And finally, our favorite skeptics, Baumgartner and Morris, suggest that we may be giving satire news an undeserved amount of thought. They argue that the recent interest in *The Daily Show*, for example, has been related to the belief that satire news has the ability to engage apathetic millennials in the political process. But, using survey data from the 2008 election, Baumgartner and Morris show that watching *The Daily Show* does not correlate with more political knowledge or engagement (2011). This is fairly consistent with findings that satirical news shows can make viewers more cynical about the political process—as we've said, cynicism is often considered to be a paralytic. So does this mean that we have an entire generation of lazy, cynical, apathetic, and disengaged youths poised to take the reins of America and steer it right off a cliff? Well, there are a few problems with this interpretation of the facts. For one thing, they don't square with the picture of millennials we painted in chapter 6. Simply put: it cannot be possible that millennials are eschewing traditional news sources in favor of satire, being turned cynical and disenfranchised by that very satire, *and* that they also vote in record numbers (as in the 2012 election),[14] lead the nation in volunteerism,[15] and "exhibit a disproportionately high level of what political scientists label political efficacy" (Winograd and Hais 38).

We are inclined to believe that the reason for all the apparently conflicting data is that the effects of satire are simply not designed to be measured this way. As we've explained, satire doesn't set out to tell people what to think or do. If that were its goal, it would be easy to measure its effects: we'd just plop a few (randomly selected and assigned) volunteers in front of a clip of Jon Stewart telling them to go out and canvass for Hillary Clinton (that's right—we're throwing our hats into the university's 2016 pool), and see if they go do it more than people who didn't see the clip. But that is not the goal of satire. If it were, we'd tell you ourselves that it doesn't work. Much of the criticism of satire, and fake news in particular, rests on faulty premises. To say that what young people should be watching instead is "real news" rests on the premise that there exists some objectively real, reliable, and effective news source out there to be watched—an assumption we've cast some serious doubts on in this book. To say that satire isn't doing enough to cultivate citizenship in young people suggests that there is some measure of "enough" that isn't being met, and that, again, there are viable alternatives that would accomplish this goal. But if you're a numbers person who's still reading our assertion that satire is saving our nation with a Colbert-style raised brow, have no fear—quantifiable support for the beneficial qualities of satire follows.

Have No Fear; Satire Is Here

As Juvenal is famously quoted, "It's difficult not to write satire." The research we presented in the previous section certainly painted quite a bleak picture of satire's impact as a part of the changing news landscape. For all the research that finds that satire is not informative or that it creates apathetic, cynical, and disengaged youth voters, there is research to suggest the opposite (see Table 8.2). Of course, as we know, it is rare for a piece of media to have a universal impact—so it is possible that satire could be detrimental to some people and beneficial to others. However, we believe that the research showing that satire is both informative and engaging holds true for the majority of its viewers, and that that partially explains the fact that young people are both watching a great deal more satire and performing more citizenship than their older counterparts who watch CNN but then stay at home on Election Day.

Is it possible that there were people watching *The Colbert Report* and utterly missing the irony? Can people watching *The Daily Show* be growing more and more cynical with every bitter laugh Jon Stewart wrings out of them? Are lazy millennials turning off Comedy Central at midnight with a smug chuckle, feeling convinced they are experts on foreign and domestic policy and that just by tuning in to laugh for an hour, they've done their part? Sure, it's possible. Likely in some cases, even. But it is unlikely that fake news is having these effects across the board. So, yes—when you are studying how well satire measures up to goals that are generally imposed by people other than its creators, and doing research on a subject with effects that are not universal, and generally hard to trace—some disquieting conclusions are bound to surface. But, as it turns out, it is equally likely that some bright spots will emerge.

For some such examples, we may turn again to *The Stewart/Colbert Effect*. Josh Compton writes, "*The Daily Show* may be teaching, influencing, and motivating political information and political participation—effects that move beyond individuals' political attitudes (13). But wait—aren't some scholars worrying that satire news is creating a bunch of apathetic cynics? Well, not everyone agrees. Richard van Heertum doesn't believe that, as Baumgarten and Morris argue, *The Daily Show* and *The Colbert Report* foster cynicism in their viewers, he argues instead that "their popularity relates to an underlying irony and cynicism that resonate with those youth drawn to the show" (117). Young and Esralew, drawing

Table 8.2   Satire Saves

Satire complements real news	Satire creates engaged citizens
Young and Tisinger (2006) ". . . young people are tuning in to late-night comedy in addition to—rather than in the place of—news and that the audiences of various late-night comedy programs have distinct sociodemographic and political profiles" (113).	**Cao and Brewer (2008)** "In this study, we challenge the notion that political comedy programs undermine political participation by showing that exposure to such programs is positively associated with some forms of political participation" (90).
Xenos and Becker (2009) "Our findings provide general support for the gateway hypothesis ['exposure to such programs facilitates the acquisition of political information from hard news sources, particularly among less politically sophisticated comedy viewers'] but raise important questions concerning the causal structure of gateway effects" (317).	**Hoffman and Thompson (2009)** "Results demonstrate that viewing late-night TV and local TV news had a positive, significant effect on civic participation, and this relationship was mediated by political efficacy" (3).
Cao (2010) "I found that watching the show was positively related to following the issues that were covered with relative frequency by the program . . . among politically inattentive viewers. As viewers' political attentiveness increased, however, the magnitude of the positive relationship decreased" (144).	**Hoffman and Young (2011)** "Results suggest that viewing satire or parody has positive and significant effects on political participation through the mediator of political efficacy, as does viewing traditional TV news. However, this relationship is not borne out for viewers of traditional late-night comedy" (1).
Feldman, Leiserwitz, and Maibach (2011) "Findings suggest that just as exposure to late-night comedy correlates with increased audience attention to politics, so too does exposure to *The Daily Show* and *The Colbert Report* go hand-in-hand with attention paid to science and the environment" (27).	
Young and Esralew (2011) "*The Daily Show* and late-night comedy in general are part of a diet of healthy political characteristics and behaviors, all of which correlate positively with political participation, discussion, and debate viewing" (113).	

on 2004 National Annenberg Election Survey data, found that "late-night comedy viewers, particularly of TDS, are more likely to engage in these behaviors than non-viewers" (6). Perhaps the particular influence of *The Daily Show* and shows like it may be related to the fact that people who watch late-night comedy process the information they gather from the shows differently than they process information from standard news shows (Kim and Vishak, 2008).

The fact that people process information from comedy shows differently says something about how they perceive the act of watching satirical news versus how they perceive watching mainstream news. According to Young, "not only do people report viewing TDS/CR for many different reasons (including fun/entertainment, learning, to make news fun, and for context/background), but certain TDS/CR viewing motivations operate together (like humor and learning)—while others appear to be mutually exclusive (like humor and context)" ("Laughter, Learning, or Enlightenment," 165). Although Young was not surprised to learn that people report choosing to watch *The Daily Show* and *The Colbert Report* because they're funny shows or seen as sources of information,

> the additional responses, such as viewing TDS/CR because the respondent perceives these shows as "truthful, accurate, and unbiased" or because they provide important "context, background, or perspective" offer important insight to our study of political humor audiences and effects. In addition, the hybridity of political satire's form and function is illustrated by the fact that viewers who see the show predominantly as entertainment also cite it as a source of information—suggesting that viewers perceive this genre as satisfying multiple needs or gratifications simultaneously. (165)

Young also notes that, in 2004, many of the respondents in his study who said that the satirical shows "make news fun" don't necessarily mean that they are getting the information from fake news, but that they are turning to *The Daily Show* and *The Colbert Report* "to bring another level of enjoyment to information that viewers *already have*" (165–66). Such research is in harmony with statements Stewart has made in the past, like when he told C-Span that "If [kids] came to our show without knowledge our show wouldn't make any sense to them . . . We assume so much knowledge on our show . . . We assume a knowledge base . . . They're not getting their news from us. They're coming to us to find out what the funny is on it." One of the respondents echoed our own claims from chapter 2 about how humor helps people learn, saying "Mainly [shows like TDS/CR] take the information I read daily in the newspaper or in the news and make them easier to remember . . . being able to recall things in quick and witty ways makes them more entertaining." Other respondents emphasized Jon Stewart's belief that people turn to his show after they already gathered information to help them "find the funny," writing that "[TDS/CR] touch on topics I already know about from reading the newspaper, but expound on them in hilarious ways," and that "After watching the news and catching up on the latest stories, I like to see the way that Stewart and Colbert make them humorous because the news can be very depressing" (2012, 163).

So what exactly are people learning from *The Daily Show*, if it isn't their initial source of information? McBeth and Clemons used data from the 2008 presidential election and found "that the fake news of Jon Stewart and Stephen Colbert may be more real than today's real news programs," with participants believing that *The Daily Show* and *The Colbert Report* were more neutral than ABC News issues such as the Jeremiah Wright controversy (5–6). As Young writes, even if they would not cite fake news as the source of their information,

> Those viewers who report watching TDS/CR for context or background clearly perceive that they are deriving some form of enhanced meaning or understanding through these shows—even if they don't cite TDS/CR as a source of information per se. The fact that the individuals who watch TDS/CR for "context or background"

are significantly higher in "need for cognition" points to a unique educational function that TDS/CR may play beyond merely transmitting information about the occurrence of current events. (2012, 166)

Even more encouraging, Young and Esralew found that "*The Daily Show* and late-night comedy in general are part of a diet of healthy political characteristics and behaviors, all of which correlate positively with political participation, discussion, and debate viewing," which suggests that the people who watch political satire are ones who are likely to participate in and discuss politics, and therefore are not the kinds of people who will become cynical, apathetic, and disengaged by it (113). Xenos and Becker's finding that people who watched *The Daily Show* sought more information after watching it, too, suggests that we need not fear that people are relying exclusively on fake news for their information (2009).

There is some research to suggest, however, that even viewers who report that they only watch *The Daily Show* are better off than those who stick to the alleged "real news." Following a 2007 Pew Research study that found viewers of *The Daily Show* and *The Colbert Report* had the highest knowledge of national and international affairs (Fox News viewers were near the bottom, below "online news discussion blogs" and above only "Local TV news" and "Network morning shows").[16] A 2012 Pew study found that people who watched only *The Daily Show* fared about as well as those who only watched Sunday shows, beaten only by NPR listeners. Fox News viewers fared significantly worse than those with no news exposure at all, although those who just watched CNN or MSNBC fared only slightly better than those with no exposure to news.[17]

Taken together, this body of research suggests that the basic arguments offered by the glass-half-empty crowd's worry over the pernicious effects of satire are unfounded. Firstly, it seems that young people are not abandoning newspapers and network news en masse to watch late-night comedy. Secondly, fake news can indeed function as a source of information. Thirdly, there are benefits exclusively provided by fake news, that, in addition to the information people are consuming from mainstream sources, contributes to informed and engaged citizenship. And finally, despite the fact that Stewart and Colbert certainly highlight the abundance of negativity, ineptitude, and corruption in the political system, satirical news is not creating a huge bloc of apathetic cynics who are so turned off by the process that they no longer wish to participate in democracy at all. Although the body of research will continue to expand, and the news landscape will continue to change, it's worth questioning why these myths, especially the particularly stubborn one that young people are relying solely upon late-night comedy for their news, or that young people are lazy and apathetic, persist. We're willing to bet it has something to do with the fact that the news media are undoubtedly changing, and that we can't yet know for certain how our democracy will be affected in the long term by the satirical fifth estate. But we think there's reason to be optimistic about how satire will factor into the equation. It's possible to read the fact that Stewart is one of the most trusted names in news as a sign of disaster. We think, though, that where there is trust, there is hope—and there is every reason to believe that satire is the response to our SOS signal and not the iceberg.

9

I'm Not Laughing at You, I'm Laughing With You: How to Stop Worrying and Love the Laughter

One of our nation's most significant stories of patriotic pride and political protest is the tale of the Boston Tea Party of 1773 that resonated with the slogan "no taxation without representation" and sparked the flame of rebellion that led to the American Revolution. The event is a watershed in our history, not only for the way that it led the colonies to independence, but also for how the story is understood today. Of interest is the fact that the event was originally referred to as "The Destruction of the Tea in Boston"—a name that apparently was referred to infrequently since it seemed negative. Alfred Young explains that writers in our newly independent nation were "reluctant to celebrate the destruction of property, and so the event was usually ignored in histories of the American Revolution."[1] That would all change, though, with proper branding. Once the event was referred to as "The Tea Party," it not only shed the negativity of "destruction," but it also added a fun twist of irony that made the event symbolic of the swashbuckling, yet witty, nature of many of our nation's early leaders.

The event has been invoked as inspiration by various groups of differing political persuasion, but it is the current resuscitation of The Boston Tea Party—The Tea Party Movement—that runs the greatest risk of destroying our nation's core values and damaging the prospects for our democracy. Founded in 2006 and linked to Ron Paul and the Koch Brothers, the Tea Party Movement runs on a platform that focuses on the reduction of debt, taxes, and government spending. While liberals and progressives, too, want the reduction of needless spending, one key point of conflict is over how to treat those in our nation who are less privileged. The Tea Party channels the free market neoliberal mentality that suggests that, if someone is in need, it is their fault; whereas liberals and progressives have a far more complex understanding of the various social factors that influence one's class status and social privilege. At heart, they believe we should work to give those that are disadvantaged a leg up and they think our government should play a role in helping our citizens in need.

This is clearly a major political disagreement, but as we've explained throughout this book, the disagreement has often become an impossible stalemate framed in the logic of blue states versus red states, government shutdowns, and political brinkmanship. Part of the reason for this is that among our elected officials, especially those affiliated with groups like the Tea Party Movement, there has been a significant retreat from critical thinking, from seeking complex solutions to complex problems, and from offering compassion to those less fortunate. The democratically essential habits of debate, dialogue, deliberation, and mediation have given way to a chorus of shrill, aggressive, partisan rhetoric that often has no ability and no desire to seek any sort of compromise. When our politicians can't model democratic deliberation, and our mainstream news media can't cover the issues in a way that is accurate and reasoned, it makes it especially challenging for our citizens to find a way to think through the crisis themselves.

And that is where satire steps in to help us wade through the rhetoric. Night after night, day after day, there is a veritable satire movement in place that is helping to restore the democratic values that are under threat in our nation today. Satire speaks truth to power and it does so in a way that demands critical thinking and creates community, while entertaining and inspiring us. Its wit allows us to avoid falling into cynical apathy or downright depression; its exposure of social flaws helps us open our eyes and become more aware; and its style can coax a broad audience to question the status quo. On television, in move theaters, on social media, in print, and on the street, satire is literally everywhere you look today. Most of us can't go an hour, let alone a day, without being exposed to satire. And that's not even counting those of us that create it daily as well.

In its ongoing critique of our nation's power elite, satire helps to reveal the fact that there are other ways to resolve political disagreements, that corporations are not actually people, and that there are other models for informing the public about the news. It also serves as a corrective to misinformation and lies—reminding us, for instance, that the Boston Tea Party was not a movement to end all taxes; rather, it was a movement in favor of democracy. It demanded that taxes be determined by representatives of the people and not by an elite set of Englishmen disconnected from American colonists. The rebellion demanded that those who decide on taxes do so representing the very same people that will later pay them. Sadly, those that started the Tea Party Movement are not that clear on their US history. Dangerously, they have attempted to weave their false narrative into the fabric of contemporary politics. Luckily, satire helps makes sense of all of this, and gives us a tool to correct the undemocratic narratives at the heart of Tea Party politics.

In one recent example, Tea Party politician, Paul Ryan, a former candidate for vice president, spoke at the Conservative Political Action Conference in March of 2014 (see Figure 9.1). Portraying our nation as wholly divided between the right and the left he assured his audience that Republicans understand the American people, in stark contrast to how little "the left" understands the needs of the poor.[2] Channeling Jonathan Swift's disdain for the plight of the poor, but lacking the satirical edge and missing the obvious irony, Ryan suggested that offering children in need a school lunch showed how the left offers the poor "a full stomach and an empty soul."[3] Ryan told an anecdote about a boy that wanted to have his lunch in

Figure 9.1   Paul Ryan tells us that kids that eat free school lunches aren't loved while surrounded by a lavish stage set[4]

a brown paper bag like the other kids: "He wanted one, he said, because he knew a kid with a brown paper bag had someone who cared for him. This is what the left does not understand."[5] Wow. Really?

Let's unpack this rhetoric for a moment. First, watch how Ryan turns the social support platform of the Democratic Party on its head by suggesting that it is really the right that cares about the poor. Then, notice that, according to Ryan's version of the story, a boy that needs a school lunch does not have parents that love him. And then note the link that Ryan makes between having a soul and having a full stomach, as though there was a fundamental incompatibility between receiving help and being human. But Ryan's spin is even worse than that and we can thank Jon Stewart for reporting on it. It turns out that the woman Ryan took the story from never met the boy mentioned in the anecdote. And then to top it off, the story's original author and the boy she wrote about regularly make public appearances *advocating* for free school lunches.[6] So Ryan demonized the left, ridiculed poor parents, stripped those receiving aid of their humanity, and fabricated the facts of his story all in order to suggest that it is conservatives who have our nation's best interests at heart. As Stewart points out, Ryan is not just mocking our national values; he is also mocking the Christian values that ostensibly guide his political platform. Illustrating Ryan's anti-Christian values, Stewart commented: "Point taken. People on food assistance have empty souls. As Jesus once said, if you give a man a fish, don't. Period. End of bible."[7]

So who is involved with negatively mocking our national values, our democracy, and the citizens our government serves? As this brief anecdote shows, the evidence suggests that it is actually the Tea Party that is mocking us, not the satirists that are exposing the lies, deceptions, cruelty, and false logic of the Tea Party. And while the Tea Party is the most egregious example of these tactics it certainly is not alone. Divisive, contentious, hysterical rhetoric has become so dominant in politics and the media today that we increasingly need to turn to satire for a dose of reality and sanity. As this book has shown, satire is a unique form of comedy that is not about mockery, but rather about productive critique. It is not a form of humor meant to distance the subject from democracy; it is meant to distance the subject from those usurping our democratic values while claiming that they have our nation's best interests at heart. Of course not all of the funny bits we see making jokes about our society are that sort of satire. But once that distinction is made clear, it is then possible to see that our democracy depends on satire. In the words of Bill Moyers, "You simply can't understand American politics in the new millennium without *The Daily Show*."[8] As we conclude our book we explain why satire shouldn't worry you, why it is important in new definitions of citizenship and activism, and why it may be our nation's best hope.

It's Not Satire that Should Worry You

If you care about this country, there is plenty to worry about, but we can guarantee that satire shouldn't be on the list. The worriers fret that satire will undermine our values, will distract us from real politics, will radically reshape the nature of political activity, and will leave us all disaffected cynics. While we confess to our own fair share of disaffected cynicism, we can assure you that those feelings emanate from the sad state of political rhetoric that has come to dominate much of the everyday functioning of our democracy, and not from satire. The point is this—and it has to be emphasized again and again—satire only reminds us of the sad state of affairs; it doesn't create it. It can't mock what doesn't exist. But, as we've explained, satire's goal is not demoralizing mockery; its goal is to invigorate public debate, encourage critical thinking, and call on citizens to question the status quo. It doesn't tell you what to think; it just asks you to do it.

As Amber Day explains, "Ultimately the realm of the satiric is one of the most vibrant arenas of public debate in operation today" (23). Satire calls attention to folly in ways that get noticed. When campaign finance was becoming more corporate-controlled than ever, Colbert's satirical stunt of opening his own super PAC was the most effective tool our nation had in drawing attention to the dangers of these new laws. If a millennial knows about super PACs, then the credit goes to Colbert. Similarly, we can credit Michael Moore's *Fahrenheit 9/11* for offering viewers indelible images of George Bush Jr. on vacation during his first days as president, and then looking confused and stiff as he sat in an elementary school classroom when our nation was under attack. Sure some of those images had appeared on the mainstream news, but Moore's voiceover and music track added just the right amount of wit and irony to help pop those images in ways the traditional news could not.

Satire does more, though, than package key political information in memorable forms; its fundamental structure requires critical thinking and analysis.

When those practices are combined with the mass public appeal of satire, we have excellent conditions for democratic deliberation. Satire is an active form of comedy; it requires active consumption and encourages discussion, debate, and critique. It can't ruin our country; it can only strengthen it. If it's not asking the right questions and uncovering the right social problems, we will stop paying attention to it. And, if there is no hubris, deception, or corruption to reveal, then it will lose its material. But as long as it manages to continue to draw public attention to the most pressing issues facing our nation in a way that is both pleasurable and productive, we can only be thankful for the public role it's playing.

The New Citizen-Satirist

For some time scholars have been rethinking contemporary notions of citizenship. Citizenship has changed generationally, as Russell Dalton explains, with millennials and generation Xers understanding their role as citizens in vastly different ways from the baby boomer generation. In addition, Liesbet van Zoonen points to the role entertainment has played in changing citizenship across generations and national contexts. Jeffrey Jones argues that it is time to no longer separate entertainment from politics, asking us to recognize that the information that citizens use to make political decisions often comes from a range of entertaining media. Theories of corporate citizenship, cultural citizenship, and more grapple with the various formative notions that structure the way that communities connect with the democratic process.

We believe it is time to take the citizen-satirist more seriously as a key part of the story. The citizen-satirist combines many of the features of entertainment and politics that both Van Zoonen and Jones describe as a major part of contemporary political activity. Today's active citizens do not choose between serious politics and silly play: they seamlessly combine them and that combination increasingly features satire. In fact, we argue that that combination is at its most productive when satire is at the center.

According to van Zoonen, it makes no sense to separate citizenship from other parts of life (3). We don't have political selves distinct from apolitical selves, which is why social media like Facebook that combine silliness with serious political information conform naturally to the way we engage with the world. Van Zoonen suggests that, in fact, the blending of political information with entertainment is likely to mean *more* people pay attention to politics, not less: "Politics has to be connected to the everyday culture of its citizens; otherwise it becomes an alien sphere, occupied by strangers no one cares or bothers about" (3). Of course not all entertainment has an equally positive role to play, which is why we need to look closely at the form of entertainment and the impact it has on the way we support our democracy. Van Zoonen outlines three key questions to ask when weighing the intersections of entertainment and citizenship: "does entertainment provide a context to contemplate the concept of citizenship, does it provide an environment in which citizenship can flourish, and does it make citizenship pleasurable?" (4).

And, as we have detailed throughout this book, much news media does not meet the standard required to help nourish citizenship, rather it is satire that does. What we don't want is "a citizenry that is uninformed, misguided, and manipulated, but nevertheless completely confident about its own judgment and choices" (van Zoonen 11). Yes, as we've shown, that is exactly the sort of citizen produced by news channels like Fox News and embodied in the rhetoric of the Tea Party. Instead, in contrast, the educated and engaged citizen watches satire TV, shares the latest Yes Men hoax on Facebook, signs a moveon.org petition, and tweets ironic political commentary while giggling at a silly Vine. That is the new citizen-satirist our nation so desperately needs.

These shifts in the ability to engage with media have changed since the days when Neil Postman worried over the negative political effects of television in *Amusing Ourselves to Death*. And while Postman was right to worry about the political impact of a passive audience consuming media, most media consumers are not passive like they were when Postman wrote his seminal work in the mid 1980s. Back when Postman was working on these issues, television had a simplicity to it that is completely different from the medium today. The worry, at the time, was that television was incapable of communicating complex thought and that it would engender a passive, uncritical populace. And the worry linked directly to the notion that television would become a medium for rigid conservative thinking, since, as van Zoonen points out "conservatism has a simpler message than liberalism" (12). The idea was that the right would dominate not only because of its control of stations, but also because of the immediate, superficial, narcissistic nature of the material on television.

Much of that is, of course, true, which is why the emergence of the citizen-satirist is so novel for our era. As Jones explains,

> What we must first recognize is the state of contemporary citizenship that so frustrates Putnam and others—that daily citizen engagement with politics is more frequently textual than organizational or "participatory" in any traditional sense. For better or worse, the most common and frequent form of political activity—its actual practice—comes, for most people, through their choosing, attending to, processing, and engaging a myriad of media texts about the formal political process of government and political institutions as they conduct their daily routines. (23)

Jones points out that media are more often the space where politics happens. Henry Jenkins reinforces this point by claiming that "social networking sites and massively multiplayer video games provide an important means through which media users now obtain the skills necessary to engage in cultural and political participation" (quoted in Jones 23). What we are witnessing now is not only the layering of experience van Zoonen describes, where citizenship is not cordoned off from other parts of daily life, but we also are seeing the increasing interaction with and production of content by citizens. Today's citizen-satirist is not just learning about politics by actively consuming satire; they are learning about it by doing it.

These changes in the potential for media to encourage active citizenship are mediated then by the fact that most politically productive entertainment media comes in the form of satire. Satire is the critical mode that makes these forms of media accessible to an audience that can interact with key information through the creation of a critical community. It is time, then, to move on from the worries about television and social media. It is time to stop being afraid of the ways that the millennial generation gets its information. Instead, what we need to worry about is the degree of accuracy of the information that millennials consume and the extent to which it fosters critical thinking or asks for dogmatic blind faith. As Jones makes clear, "Satire is a biting attack, and as such, automatically thwarts any charges that young people are overly idealistic and naïve (as opposed to their baby-boomer parents . . .) Satire may indeed be a new generational language simply by its existence and usage in opposition to that" (251).

Most importantly, citizen-satirists provide a model for political action. Stephen Duncombe reminds us that "Jokes are active, social things. More than any other form of communication they demand participation from the audience" (131). That participation, as we've pointed out, is very specific in the case of satire. The layering of meaning, the intent to cause the audience to question received truths, the community created over a shared laugh, and the inherent commitment to democracy and social justice all combine to make the citizen-satirist a model for a new version of political participation.

From Slactivism to Satiractivism

Satire has done more than invigorate our nation's potential for citizen engagement; it has also created a new model for activism. Hand in hand with the way that millennials consume media critically, they are participating in a new version of political activism. Bolstered by collaboration with the members of generation X, we can find a whole host of examples of political activism from the generation demonized in the mainstream media as "stoned slackers."[9] Think, for example, of the productive collaboration between Adbusters and the Occupy Wall Street Movement or between The Yes Men and the various projects they have supported through the Yes Lab. Then there are the green screen challenges and the Twitter activism practiced by the Colbert Nation. In one example, Colbert encouraged viewers to tweet round-the-clock non-facts about Senator Jon Kyl after he lied about Planned Parenthood on the Senate floor and dismissed criticism by saying that what he had said was "not intended to be a factual statement."[10] Mediabistro's Lauren Dugan reported that first night, "#NotIndendedToBeAFactualStatement was 0.13% of all tweets on Wednesday at 12AM Eastern, which means about 18,571,428 tweets and retweets containing that hashtag were sent out that hour alone."[11] We think that over 18 million tweets in one hour shows that millennials are doing a little more than sitting on their couches slouching, smoking weed, and watching television. At least they are tweeting too.

All silliness aside, though, as we explained in our chapter on millennials, this generation votes at a higher percentage than either baby boomers or generation Xers, and they do more community service too. They have inherited a brutal economy and graduated college with more debt than any previous generation ever.

But still they are demonized in the press as "slactivists," whose Facebook likes, virtual petitions, and support for causes like Kony 2012 add up to a bunch of useless "feel good" fake political engagement. Despite the fact that there is absolutely no data to support the way they are trashed publicly, they are still taking hits.

One common form of critique is the idea that the sort of activism practiced by young people today is not serious enough, that it is not a true measure of "real" political protest. But, what exactly is "real" political protest anyway? Surely we aren't talking about events like Woodstock? Because we are pretty sure not everyone there was intent on promoting peace, unless they confused peace with a peace pipe. The point is that just as citizenship needs a reformed definition that is adjusted to the political realities of our time, so too activism, since clearly we are faced with a generation that is redefining what it means to be politically active. What we can learn from labeling millennial activism "slactivism," though, is the ongoing disdain for this young generation—disdain that has absolutely no basis in reality.

Instead, we would like to call for a positive spin on this new activism, one that recognizes both the power of social media as a key feature of contemporary activism as well as the central role that satire now plays in activism today. As Angelique Haugerud writes in her study of the public satirical activism of the group Billionaires for Bush, this new version of activism is just as politically motivated as ever: "A moral vision of a more just future, not a romanticized vision of the past, inspires progressive ironic activism" (13). Today's activism is increasingly tied to satire as a fundamental part of the way that it reaches a broad audience and inspires progressive political action: we call it *satiractivism*.

One excellent example of the increased presence of satiractivism is Occupy Wall Street (OWS), with its links to the ironic Adbusters, and with its production of satirical stunts and content. The Yes Men worked closely on a number of stunts to bolster the public impact of OWS through their Yes Lab. In one of them two clowns attacked the Wall Street bull to enrage it (and to distract the police into arresting them) while a Matador leapt onto the roof of a patrol car in order to boldly prepare to present his blood-red cape to the bull (see Figure 9.2). "I wondered whether I, neophyte matador, could bring down this behemoth, world-famous for charging towards profit while trampling underfoot the average worker," said the Occupy Wall Street/Yes Lab activist. "Come what may, I knew I must try."[12] One of the arrested clowns wailed: "This bull has ruined millions of lives!" as he lay on the ground face-down. "Yet he and his accomplices have been rewarded with billions of our tax dollars—and we, here to put a stop to it all, are thrown to the ground. ¡Un escándalo!"[13]

While the OWS movement was critiqued in the media and discounted as ineffective, it is worth remembering that their phrase "We are the 99%" succinctly demonstrated the increasing class gap that is destroying our democracy and allowing our nation to be run by the wealthy and corporations. It highlighted the extent to which average citizens have been completely disenfranchised by a system that protects banks over the people who take out mortgages. And it became an instant part of the public lexicon. Politicians did indeed pick up on the issues central to OWS, whether to take up the mantle or disdain the cause. As Frederick Gillmore

Figure 9.2   Maybe a matador can tame the bull and spare our nation from its wrath
Photo Credit: Bess Adler[14]

points out, despite the fact that the movement was a "leaderless, directionless movement of unsophisticated anticapitalists and anarchists, journalists of all stripes who aren't unsophisticated or anticapitalist have incorporated the vocabulary of OWS—'income inequality,' '99%' and '1%'—into their articles, and this vocabulary is now part of the national dialogue. Quite an achievement for the occupiers, when you think about it."[15]

And despite the media double-speak, which incorporates ideas from OWS while trashing them at the same time, OWS still continues to inspire public engagement. In a push to call attention to the lack of government support for public housing they launched the "We need homes, not jails" campaign.[16] With one simple tweet, OWS effectively sends its message to almost 200,000 followers (see Figure 9.3). But, most importantly, it does so through the use of irony, wit, and hard facts.

Today's activism constantly uses satire and irony as a way to spread its message—and it is effective. More young adults support causes today than in the previous generations with 71% involved in at least one form of social activism in 2011.[17] These young people are taking real action and having a real impact—with

Figure 9.3   Occupy Wall Street uses Twitter and irony to spread its message[18]

71% going beyond mouse clicks—and yet they have to deal with being called "slackers." Satiractivists like The Yes Men, Billionaires for Bush, and members of OWS show our citizens that political engagement and public protest can take many forms. In addition to public demonstrations that include impersonations, parody, culture jamming, and other forms of satirical stunts, satire activism includes producing memes, tweeting with specific hashtags, creating fake websites, false news stories, and more. Satiractivism combines all of the political punch of previous forms of activism but adds the additional fun of public joking—a feature that makes it even more appealing to millennials.

We can think of no better example of the way that satire today is aimed at inspiring citizens to engage with society and work positively for change than Colbert's commencement address at Knox College in Galesburg, Illinois, 2006. Colbert specifically called on his young audience to reject cynicism and work to build a better world:

> Cynicism masquerades as wisdom, but it is the farthest thing from it. Because cynics don't learn anything. Because cynicism is a self-imposed blindness, a

rejection of the world because we are afraid it will hurt us or disappoint us. Cynics always say no. But saying "yes" begins things. Saying "yes" is how things grow. Saying "yes" leads to knowledge. "Yes" is for young people. So for as long as you have the strength to, say "yes."[19]

Satire and Hope

Taken together these developments give us great hope. As Haugerud explains, "hope, not despair, is irony's gift" (13). She reminds us that Billionaires for Bush cofounder Andrew Boyd considered their work satirizing the 1999 World Trade Organization meeting in Seattle as a project that was ultimately about hope and inspiration: "Irony was no longer an expression of our lack of confidence. . . . We were neither nostalgic nor snide. We had achieved a new attitude—sly and mischievous, yet full of hope for the future" (quoted in Haugerud 13). The hope behind satire is what Henry Giroux would call "educated hope." Giroux explains that "hope is more than a politics—it is also a pedagogical and performative practice that provides the foundation for enabling human beings to learn about their potential as moral and civic agents."[20]

Thus the hope of satire is not a naïve hope, nor is it one that is overly optimistic about its abilities to effect change. It is, however, deeply tied to the notion that a better world is possible and that it begins when we refuse to passively consume the party line and start to demand more. Haugerud emphasizes that fact that the hope of satire activists is tied to the way that they "wholeheartedly embrace the moral vision of a fairer economy, a more just social order, and a vibrant democracy— values in sync with those of many ordinary citizens but somehow marginalized in official discourse and political practice and in mainstream news media" (13).

The Yes Men specifically describe their quest to reveal the truth as a project aimed at inspiring hope and change. In their latest movie they explain their project this way:

On their journey, the Yes Men act as gonzo journalists, delving deep into the question of why we have given the market more power than any other institution to determine our direction as a society. They visit the twisted (and accidentally hilarious) underworld of the free-market think tanks, where they figure out a way to defeat the logic that's destroying our planet. And as they appear on the BBC before 300 million viewers, or before 1000 New Orleans contractors alongside Mayor Ray Nagin, the layers of lies are peeled back to reveal the raw heart of truth—a truth that brings with it hope.

Hope explodes at the end of this film with a power that may take audiences straight out of the theater and into the barricades. A word of warning to theater owners: make sure your seats are securely screwed down. [21]

What we love about this quote is that even the hope of The Yes Men is filled with fun irony. Satirical hope, then, is powerful and progressive and a bit unruly. Its deep commitment to question authority makes it fun and unpredictable. Its open call to encourage the active involvement of the audience reveals its rebellious instincts and its desire for collective action.

Media and culture scholar and activist Stephen Duncombe, who is also a member of the Billionaires for Bush governing board, refers to the inspirational potential of satiractivism as "ethical spectacles." He points out that satirical humor is an especially powerful political tool since it creates a shared community. As Duncombe explains, "Good humor confers an instant intimacy between the comic and the audience, both of whom share in the meaning-making" (132). This is especially important since the dreams we need to make our nation better require a sense of shared commitment and popular appeal. He explains that one of the weaknesses of left politics has been its inability to reach out and communicate with the very same people that it's hoping to serve and he explains that the future of progressive politics depends on politics with popular appeal: "Progressive dreams, to have any real political impact, need to become popular dreams" (174). Satire is an extremely successful version of Duncombe's ethical spectacle, since satire can create spectacles that are fun, popular, and progressive. It asks the audience to come together and think critically and creatively about our future: "The ethical spectacle is a dream put on display. It is a dream that we can watch, think about, act within, try on for size, yet necessarily never realize. The ethical spectacle is a means, like the dreams it performs, to imagine new ends" (174).

The hope of satire is not just found among political activists like Duncombe and satiractivists like The Yes Men. Satire also breathes hope into the work of scholars who focus on media and democracy. For example, Megan Boler explains that, in contrast to other scholars that work on media and democracy, her own work is filled with optimism "because I focus my research on satire as a form of salvation from the bitter realities of what we call media and democracy" (63). Satire brings hope to the depressing state of our news media and its negative role in fostering productive debate and democratic deliberation. Boler quotes Robert McChesney who reminds us that, "If we had a legitimate or decent media, you wouldn't have to put on a clown suit to get noticed," and she confesses that "the court jesters and satirists speaking truth to power give me hope" (63).

This book has shown how satire has responded to a series of crises in our nation. With humor, with insight, with a collaborative wink, satire has repeatedly helped to expose the way that existing power structures have threatened the health of our nation's democracy. Satire has exposed lies, deception, logical fallacies, and abuses of power. But it has done more than that; it has given us hope in the face of what can seem like insurmountable odds. Against corporate media, corporate politics, and a culture of fear, satire has reminded us that we do indeed have the ability to change the narratives that govern this nation, that we can speak truth to power, and that—most of all—we can have fun while we do it. Satire has given us icons to look up to, peers to cheer on, and simple, yet effective, ways to express our outrage, spread the word, and ask for change. It has become a common feature of our daily life and a powerful weapon of information and educated hope in an age of deceit and distraction. In an era where power and privilege often seem to control every aspect of our lives, satire still offers a space for rebellious critical thinking and collective enjoyment. Amy Goodman reminds us that "Free speech is democracy's last line of defense. We must demand it. Defend it. And most of all, use it—now" (14). When we combine free speech and satire, though, we do more than stake out democracy's last line of defense; we use wit to expose its enemies and we energize its citizens to join the fight. So now you have to ask yourself, do you want to laugh with us or do you want to laugh at us? The decision is up to you.

Notes

Prelims

1. Farhi, Paul. "Truthinessology: the Stephen Colbert effect becomes an obsession in academia." The Washington Post. 9 Jul. 2012. Web. http://www.washington-post.com/lifestyle/style/truthinessology-the-stephen-colbert-effect-becomes-an-obsession-in-academia/2012/07/09/gJQAYgiHZW_story.html
2. McClennen, Sophia A., and Remy M. Maisel. "Is it Stupid to Study Colbert?" HuffPost Media. 11 Jul. 2012. Web. http://www.huffingtonpost.com/sophia-a-mcclennen/stephen-colbert-studies_b_1665768.html

1   The Politics of Seriously Joking

3. "O'Reilly Hits Obamacare 'Hysteria,' Warns Against Gov't Shutdown." *YouTube.* 28 Sept. 2013. Web. http://www.youtube.com/watch?v=kasRvSt8jnE
4. "March of Dumbs." *The Daily Show.* 1 Oct. 2013. Web. http://www.thedaily-show.com/watch/tue-october-1-2013/march-of-dumbs
5. Allon, Janet. "10 Most Appalling Comments from the Right—Just this Week." *Salon.* 9 Oct. 2013. Web. http://www.salon.com/2013/10/09/10_most_appalling_comments_from_the_right_just_this_week_partner/
6. Leber, Rebecca. "Six Headlines about the Government Shutdown that will Destroy your Faith in Journalism." *ThinkProgress.* 1 Oct. 2013. Web. http://thinkprogress.org/media/2013/10/01/2706821/media-government-shutdown-blame/
7. Gettys, Travis. "Laura Ingraham on Shutdown: 'I'm Just Beginning to Enjoy it.'" *The Raw Story.* 8 Oct. 2013. Web. http://www.rawstory.com/rs/2013/10/08/laura-ingraham-on-shutdown-im-just-beginning-to-enjoy-it/
8. Legum, Judd. Twitter post. 2 Oct. 2013. Web. https://twitter.com/JuddLegum
9. "Remarks at a Press Availability with United States Trade Representative Ambassador Froman." *U.S. Department of State.* 5 Oct. 2013. Web. http://www.state.gov/secretary/remarks/2013/10/215148.htm
10. Tau, Byron. "Obama: Big Money Helps Cause Washington Gridlock." *Politico.* 8 Oct. 2013. Web. http://www.politico.com/story/2013/10/obama-big-money-politics-washington-gridlock-97999.html

11. "Psychiatrists Deeply Concerned for 5% of Americans Who Approve of Congress." *The Onion.* 9 Oct. 2013. Web. http://www.theonion.com/articles/psychiatrists-deeply-concerned-for-5-of-americans,34163/

12. "The Shutdown Blame Game." *The Daily Show.* 8 Oct. 2013. Web. http://www.thedailyshow.com/watch/tue-october-8–2013/the-shutdown-blame-game

13. Ibid.

14. "Government Shutdown's One-Week Anniversary." *Colbert Nation.* 7 Oct. 2013. Web. http://www.colbertnation.com/the-colbert-report-videos/429570/october-07-–2013/government-shutdown-s-one-week-anniversary

15. Binder, Matt. "Public Shaming: Tweets of Privilege." Tumblr. Web. http://publicshaming.tumblr.com/about

16. "Today's Journalists Less Prominent." *Pew Research Center for the People & the Press.* 8 Mar. 2007. Web. http://www.people-press.org/2007/03/08/todays-journalists-less-prominent/

17. Kurtzman, Daniel. "Stephen Colbert at the White House Correspondents' Dinner." *About.com.* Web.

18. Ibid.

19. Weisenthal, Joe. "WHOOPS: AP Falls for Hoax Press Release Saying that GE will Repay Government $3.8 Billion Tax Break." *Business Insider.* 13 Apr. 2011. Web.

20. "Today's Journalists Less Prominent."

21. Ibid.

22. Young, Dannagal Goldthwaite. "Daily Show Viewers Knowledgeable about Presidential Campaign, National Annenberg Election Survey Shows." *NAES 04: National Annenberg Election Survey.* 21 Sept. 2004. Web. http://www.annenbergpublicpolicycenter.org/downloads/political_communication/naes/2004_03_late-night-knowledge-2_9-21_pr.pdf

23. Kull, Steven, et al. "Misperceptions, the Media and the Iraq War." *The PIPA/ Knowledge Networks Poll.* 2 Oct. 2003. Web. http://www.pipa.org/OnlineReports/Iraq/IraqMedia_Oct03/IraqMedia_Oct03_rpt.pdf

24. "Public Knowledge of Current Affairs Little Changed by News and Information Revolutions." *Pew Research Center for the People & the Press.* 15 Apr. 2007. Web. http://www.people-press.org/2007/04/15/public-knowledge-of-current-affairs-little-changed-by-news-and-information-revolutions/

25. "Ron Paul's Colbert Bump." *Colbert Nation.* 21 June 2007. Web. http://www.colbertnation.com/the-colbert-report-videos/88989/june-21–2007/ron-paul-s-colbert-bump

26. Collett-White, Mike. "'Capitalism Is Evil,' says New Michael Moore Film." *Reuters.* 6 Sept. 2009. Web. http://www.reuters.com/article/2009/09/06/us-venice-capitalism-idUSTRE5850F320090906

27. "2010 Redistricting Yields New Breed of Recalcitrant Republicans." *MSNBC.* 30 Sept. 2013. Web. http://www.msnbc.com/rachel-maddow-show/2010-redistricting-yields-new-breed

28. Ibid.

2 Comedy U: Lessons Learned Where You Least Expect It

1. Kull, Steven, et al. "Misperceptions, the Media and the Iraq War." Program on International Policy Attitudes/Knowledge Networks. 2 Oct. 2003. Web. http://www.pipa.org/OnlineReports/Iraq/IraqMedia_Oct03/IraqMedia_Oct03_rpt.pdf

2. Rabin, Nathan. "Stephen Colbert." *A.V. Club.* 25 Jan. 2006. Web. http://www.avclub.com/article/stephen-colbert-13970

3. Lewis, Charles, and Mark Reading-Smith. "False Pretenses." *The Center for Public Integrity.* 23 Jan. 2008. Web. http://www.publicintegrity.org/2008/01/23/5641/false-pretenses

4. Giroux, Henry A. "Chartering Disaster: Why Duncan's Corporate-Based Schools can't Deliver an Education that Matters." *Truthout.* 21 June 2010. Web. http://www.truth-out.org/archive/item/90213:chartering-disaster-why-duncans-corporatebased-schools-cant-deliver-an-education-that-matters

5. The following summary of statistics on these cuts comes from the Consortium of Social Science Associations Washington Update: "Education Department Eliminates and Reduces Many Programs as a Result of FY 2011 Appropriations." *COSSA: Washington Update.* 16 May 2011. Web. http://archive.constantcontact.com/fs021/1102766514430/archive/1105558801940.html#LETTER.BLOCK11

6. Ibid.

7. Giroux, Henry A., and Kenneth Saltman. "Obama's Betrayal of Public Education? Arne Duncan and the Corporate Model of Schooling." *Truthout.* 17 Dec. 2008. Web. http://www.truth-out.org/archive/item/81572:obamas-betrayal-of-public-education-arne-duncan-and-the-corporate-model-of-schooling

8. Hayes, Dianne. "When Academic Freedom and Corporate-sponsored Professorships Collide." *Diverse Issues in Higher Education.* 10 Nov. 2006. Web. http://diverseeducation.com/article/6638/

9. Chea, Terence. "UC Berkeley's BP Deal Tainted by Oil Spill: $500 Million Research Agreement at Stake." *HuffPost College.* 31 July 2010. Web. http://www.huffingtonpost.com/2010/07/31/uc-berkeleys-bp-deal-tain_n_666355.html

10. Ibid.

11. "Monitoring Middle East Studies on Campus." *Campus Watch.* Web. http://www.campus-watch.org/about.php

12. "Tim Russert." *NBC News.* 13 June 2008. Web. http://www.nbcnews.com/id/4459759/ and "Red States and Blue States." *Wikipedia.* Web. http://en.wikipedia.org/wiki/Red_states_and_blue_states

13. "Obama Praises Islam as 'Great Religion.'" *Fox News Politics.* 1 Sept. 2009. Web. http://www.foxnews.com/politics/2009/09/01/obama-praises-islam-great-religion/

14. Boston, Rob. "5 Sneaky Ways Fundamentalists are Trying to Slip Christian Creationism into America's Public Schools." *AlterNet*. 3 July 2013. Web. http://www.alternet.org/belief/public-schools?page=0%2C0

15. "Creation and Evolution in Public Education." *Wikipedia*. Web. http://en.wikipedia.org/wiki/Creation_and_evolution_in_public_education#United_States

16. "About SAF." *Students for Academic Freedom*. 22 May 2006. Web. http://www.studentsforacademicfreedom.org/about/

17. "9/11 First Responders React to the Senate Filibuster." *The Daily Show*. 17 Dec. 2010. Web. http://www.thedailyshow.com/watch/thu-december-16--2010/9--11-first-responders-react-to-the-senate-filibuster

18. Carter, Bill, and Brian Stelter. "In 'Daily Show' Role on 9/11 Bill, Echoes of Murrow." *The New York Times*. 26 Dec. 2010. Web. http://www.nytimes.com/2010/12/27/business/media/27stewart.html?pagewanted=all&_r=0

19. http://www.nationaljournal.com/magazine/these-10-districts-are-most-likely-to-fire-their-congressmen-20131024

20. Pratt, Eric. "*Fahrenheit 9/11* in the Classroom?" *Gun Owners of America*. 2 Sept. 2004. Web. https://gunowners.org/op0443htm.htm

21. Ibid.

22. "View the *Fahrenheit 9/11* Teacher's Guide." *Fahrenheit 9/11*. Web. http://www.fahrenheit911.com/library/book/index.php

23. "Frequently Asked Questions." *The Yes Men*. Web. http://theyesmen.org/faq

24. Ibid.

25. "About." *Pat Paulsen for President*. Web. http://www.paulsen.com/pat/about/

26. "Indecision 2008: Don't F%#k This Up America—Presidential Bid." *Colbert Nation*. 16 Oct. 2007. Web. http://www.colbertnation.com/the-colbert-report-videos/118597/october-16-2007/indecision-2008--don-t-f--k-this-up-america---presidential-bid

27. "'Meet the Press' Transcript for Oct. 21, 2007." *Meet the Press*. 21 Oct. 2007. Web. http://www.nbcnews.com/id/21407008/ns/meet_the_press/t/meet-press-transcript-oct/#.UszvVGRDsvo

28. Montopoli, Brian. "Stephen Colbert Isn't Really Running for President." *CBSNews*. 13 Jan. 2012. Web. http://www.cbsnews.com/news/stephen-colbert-isnt-really-running-for-president/

29. "Colbert Super PAC—Not Coordinating with Stephen Colbert." *The Daily Show*. 17 Jan. 2012. Web. http://www.thedailyshow.com/watch/tue-january-17-2012/colbert-super-pac---not-coordinating-with-stephen-colbert

30. Vogel, Kenneth P. "Colbert Files Papers to Run for President." *Politico*. 1 Nov. 2007. Web. http://www.politico.com/news/stories/1107/6672.html

31. Liptak, Adam. "Justices, 5–4, Reject Corporate Spending Limit." *The New York Times*. 21 Jan. 2010. Web. http://www.nytimes.com/2010/01/22/us/politics/22scotus.html?pagewanted=all

32. "Obama Criticizes Campaign Finance Ruling." *Political Ticker*. 21 Jan. 2010. Web. http://politicalticker.blogs.cnn.com/2010/01/21/obama-criticizes-campaign-finance-ruling/

33. "Super PACs." *OpenSecrets.org.* Web. http://www.opensecrets.org/pacs/super-pacs.php?cycle=2012

34. http://www.washingtonpost.com/blogs/the-fix/wp/2013/05/13/what-is-a-501c4-anyway/

35. Weigel, David. "Colbert Pays Tribute to the Tim Pawlenty Web Ad." *Slate.* 23 Mar. 2011. Web. http://www.slate.com/blogs/weigel/2011/03/23/colbert_pays_tribute_to_the_tim_pawlenty_web_ad.html

36. Winkler, Jeff. "Colbert's Super PAC Launches First TV Ad Supporting 'Rick Parry.'" *The Daily Caller.* 10 Aug. 2011. Web. http://dailycaller.com/2011/08/10/colberts-super-pac-launches-first-tv-ad-supporting-rick-parry/

37. Ibid.

38. Ibid.

39. "Super PAC Ad—Episode 4: A New Hope." *Colbert Nation.* 11 Aug. 2011. Web. http://www.colbertnation.com/the-colbert-report-videos/394434/august-11--2011/super-pac-ad---rick-perry

40. "Colbert Super PAC Ad—Attack in B Minor for Strings." *Colbert Nation.* 15 Jan. 2012. Web. http://www.colbertnation.com/the-colbert-report-videos/405930/january-15--2012/colbert-super-pac-ad---attack-in-b-minor-for-strings

41. Ibid.

42. "Colbert: 'Re-Becoming' The Nation we Always were." *North County Public Radio.* 4 Oct. 2012. Web. http://www.northcountrypublicradio.org/news/npr/162304439/colbert-re-becoming-the-nation-we-always-were

43. Vogel, Kenneth P. "Stephen Colbert at the FEC? Really." *Politico.* 13 May 2011. Web. http://www.politico.com/news/stories/0511/54946.html

44. Shear, Michael D. "Colbert Gets Permission to Form Super PAC." *The Caucus: The Politics and Government Blog of* The Times. 30 June 2011. Web. http://thecaucus.blogs.nytimes.com/2011/06/30/colbert-gets-permission-to-form-super-pac/?_r=0

45. http://www.atlawblog.com/2013/05/comedian-stephen-colbert-takes-on-irs-scandal-with-d-c-lawyers-help/

46. "Colbert Super PAC—Trevor Potter & Stephen's Shell Corporation." *Colbert Nation.* 29 Sept. 2011. Web. http://www.colbertnation.com/the-colbert-report-videos/398531/september-29-2011/colbert-super-pac---trevor-potter---stephen-s-shell-corporation

47. Rufca, Sarah. "Perry Comedy Team." *Culture Map Austin.* 19 Aug. 2011. Web. http://austin.culturemap.com/news/city-life/atx-08-19-11-revenge-for-parry-ads-rick-perry-poaches-stephen-colberts-pac-man/

48. Schouten, Fredreka, and Maureen Groppe. "Crop of College Super PACs Answers Call of Stephen Colbert." *USA Today.* 7 May 2012. Web. http://usatoday30.usatoday.com/news/politics/story/2012-05-04/super-PAC-spinoff-stephen-colbert/54746928/1

49. *Stephen Colbert Super PAC.* Web. http://www.colbertsuperpac.com/archive/033012.html

50. "The Name of Mitt Romney's Super PAC Makes No Sense." *BuzzFeed.* 18 April 2012. Web. http://www.buzzfeed.com/buzzfeedpolitics/the-name-of-mitt-romneys-super-pac-makes-no-s

51. Schouten and Groppe, "Crop." http://usatoday30.usatoday.com/news/politics/story/2012-05-04/super-PAC-spinoff-stephen-colbert/54746928/1

52. Bingham, Amy. "Stephen Colbert's Super PAC Hauls in More than $1 Million." *The Note.* 31 Jan. 2012. Web. http://abcnews.go.com/blogs/politics/2012/01/stephen-colberts-super-pac-hauls-in-more-than-1-million/

53. Vogel, "Stephen Colbert." http://www.politico.com/news/stories/0511/54946.html#ixzz2q2b0YBf8

54. Schouten and Groppe, "Crop." http://usatoday30.usatoday.com/news/politics/story/2012-05-04/super-PAC-spinoff-stephen-colbert/54746928/1

55. "Colbert Super PAC Raises $1 million; Non-satirical PACs to Follow." *NBC Politics.* 31 Jan. 2012. Web. http://nbcpolitics.nbcnews.com/_news/2012/01/31/10278617-colbert-super-pac-raises-1-million-non-satirical-pacs-to-follow

56. Levinthal, Dave. "Stephen Colbert's Super PAC Spawns Mini PACs." *Politico.* 4 May 2012. Web. http://www.politico.com/news/stories/0512/75942.html

57. Leven, Rachel. "Super-PACs: So Easy, a College Student can Do it." *The Hill.* 28 Mar. 2012. Web. http://thehill.com/business-a-lobbying/218773-super-pacs-so-easy-a-college-student-can-do-it

58. Kingkade, Tyler. "Stephen Colbert's Super PAC Inspires College Students to Create Campus Chapters." *HuffPost College.* 9 May 2012. Web. http://www.huffingtonpost.com/2012/05/09/college-student-stephen-colbert-super-pac_n_1498494.html

59. Levinthal, "Stephen Colbert's Super PAC." http://www.politico.com/news/stories/0512/75942_Page2.html

60. Kurp, Josh. "Stephen Colbert has Inspired Bored College Students to Begin Ironic Super PACs." *Warming Glow.* 21 May 2012. Web. http://www.uproxx.com/tv/2012/05/stephen-colbert-has-inspired-bored-college-students-to-begin-ironic-super-pacs/

61. Schouten and Groppe, "Crop." http://usatoday30.usatoday.com/news/politics/story/2012-05-04/super-PAC-spinoff-stephen-colbert/54746928/1

62. Riley, Charles. "Colbert Spawns Army of Crazy Super PACs." *CNN Money.* 21 May 2012. Web. http://money.cnn.com/2012/05/21/news/economy/colbert-super-pac/

63. Ibid.

64. Levinthal, "Stephen Colbert's Super PAC." http://www.politico.com/news/stories/0512/75942_Page2.html#ixzz2q1aXkuDK

65. Maisel, Remy. Twitter post. 4 May 2012. Web. https://twitter.com/remeanie/statuses/198507237981954048

66. Rettoun, Hannah. "Colbert Super PAC Super Fun Pack Treasure Hunt Solved!" *Charged.fm.* 3 July 2012. Web. http://www.charged.fm/blog/post/2382/colbert-super-pac-super-fun-pack-treasure-hunt-solved

67. Levinthal, Dave. "Colbert Donates Super PAC Funds to Charity." *Politico.* 14 Dec. 2012. Web. http://www.politico.com/blogs/media/2012/12/colbert-donates-super-pac-funds-to-charity-151964.html

3   Some of the News That's Fit to Print: Satire and the Changing News Cycle

1. Williams, Scott. "Murdoch Names Ailes to Launch 24-hour TV News Channel." *AP News Archive.* 30 Jan. 1996. Web. http://www.apnewsarchive.com/1996/ Murdoch-Names-Ailes-to-Launch-24-Hour-TV-News-Channel/id-08ff251 f11de3a8ccc5ee108c77e7281

2. Sherman, Gabriel. "The Elephant in the Green Room." *New York Magazine.* 22 May 2011. Web. http://nymag.com/news/media/roger-ailes-fox-news-2011-5/

3. Corn, David. "Did Chris Wallace Really Say Fox News Isn't Fair and Balanced?" *Mother Jones.* 20 June 2011. Web. http://www.motherjones.com/mojo/2011/06/ chris-wallace-jon-stewart-fox

4. Decker, Henry. "5 Examples of Fox News' 'Fair and Balanced' Obama Coverage." *The National Memo.* 29 Jan. 2013. Web. http://www.nationalmemo. com/5-examples-of-fox-news-fair-and-balanced-obama-coverage/

5. Decker, Henry. "Sean Hannity Breaks The Bank for Insane Anti-Obama Painting." *The National Memo.* 3 April 2012. Web. http://www.nationalmemo. com/sean-hannity-breaks-the-bank-for-insane-anti-obama-painting/

6. Easley, Jason. "Fair and Balanced Fraud Exposed: 94% of Fox News Viewers Are Republicans." *PoliticusUSA.* 8 July 2013. Web. http://www.politicususa. com/2013/07/08/fair-balanced-fraud-exposed-94-fox-news-viewers-republi-cans.html

7. "Context of '1995: Fox News Registers 'Fair and Balanced' Slogan, Authors Claim Disproportionately Presents Conservative Viewpoints.'" *History Commons.* Web. http://www.historycommons.org/context.jsp?item=a0708 foxfairbalanced

8. Auletta, Ken. "Vox Fox: How Roger Ailes and Fox News Are Changing Cable News." *Ken Auletta.* 26 May 2003. Web. http://www.kenauletta.com/voxfox. html

9. "Fox News Channel—Fair & Balanced." *The Daily Show.* 20 June 2011. Web. http://www.thedailyshow.com/watch/mon-june-20--2011/fox-news-channel---fair---balanced

10. Dudak, Gary. "11 Direct Effects 9/11 Had on the Sports and Entertainment Industries." *Mandatory.* 11 Sept. 2012. Web. http://www.mandatory.com/ 2012/09/11/11-direct-effects-9–11-had-on-the-sports-and-entertainment-indus/2

11. "'SNL' Skewers 'Fox and Friends' With Bin Laden Anniversary." *HuffPost Comedy.* Web. 6 May 2012. http://www.huffingtonpost.com/2012/05/06/ snl-skewers-fox-and-friends-fox-news-bin-laden_n_1488102.html

12. "Bill Maher on FOX News: 'Facts Never Get in the Way of their Talking Points.'" *Piers Morgan Live.* 29 Oct. 2013. Web. http://piersmorgan.blogs.cnn. com/2013/10/29/bill-maher-of-fox-news-facts-never-get-in-the-way-of-their-talking-points/

13. "Fox Falls for Fake Story about Obama Personally Funding Muslim Museum during Shutdown." *Media Matters for America.* 5 Oct. 2013. Web. http://mediamatters.org/print/blog/2013/10/05/fox-falls-for-fake-story-about-obama-personally/196304

14. Edwards, David. "Fox Nation Readers Confuse Onion Article with Real News." *The Raw Story.* 26 Nov. 2010. Web. http://www.rawstory.com/rs/2010/11/26/fox-nation-readers-confuse-onion-article-real-news/

15. Ibid.

16. "Stephen Colbert." *Wikiquote.* Web. http://en.wikiquote.org/wiki/Stephen_Colbert

17. Fickling, David. "Geneva Conventions Vague, says Bush." *The Guardian.* 15 Sept. 2006. Web. http://www.theguardian.com/world/2006/sep/15/usa.davidfickling1

18. Daley, David. "Paul Auster: "I Think of the Right-wing Republicans as Jihadists." *Salon.* 19 Aug. 2012. Web. http://www.salon.com/2012/08/19/paul_auster_i_think_of_the_right_wing_republicans_as_jihadists/

19. Brayton, Ed. "Dan Savage Reads Sarah Palin's Book." *Freethought Blogs.* 22 Dec. 2013. Web. http://freethoughtblogs.com/dispatches/2013/12/22/dan-savage-reads-sarah-palins-book/

20. Farsetta, Diane, and Daniel Price. "Fake TV News: Widespread and Undisclosed." *PR Watch.* 6 Apr. 2006. Web. http://www.prwatch.org/fakenews/execsummary

21. "The Democratic Party: A Very Lucky Crew." *The O'Reilly Factor.* 14 Feb. 2013. Web. http://www.foxnews.com/on-air/oreilly/2013/02/15/bill-oreilly-democratic-party-very-lucky-crew

22. "Concentration of Media Ownership." *Wikipedia.* Web. http://en.wikipedia.org/wiki/Concentration_of_media_ownership

23. "Public Knowledge of Current Affairs Little Changed by News and Information Revolutions." *Pew Research Center for the People & the Press.* 15 Apr. 2007. Web. http://www.people-press.org/2007/04/15/public-knowledge-of-current-affairs-little-changed-by-news-and-information-revolutions/

24. "TV Nation." *Wikipedia.* Web. http://en.wikipedia.org/wiki/TV_Nation

25. Miller, Geoffrey. "Rev. of *The Best of the Awful Truth*, dir. Michael Moore." *DVD Verdict.* 8 Sept. 2006. Web. http://www.dvdverdict.com/reviews/bestawfultruth.php

26. "*The Awful Truth* (TV Series)." *Wikipedia.* Web. http://en.wikipedia.org/wiki/The_Awful_Truth_%28TV_series%29

27. "Better Know a District—Georgia's 8th—Lynn Westmoreland." *Colbert Nation.* 14 June 2006. Web. http://www.colbertnation.com/the-colbert-report-videos/70730/june-14-2006/better-know-a-district---georgia-s-8th---lynn-westmoreland

28. Mitchell, Amy, et al. "The Role of News on Facebook: Common yet Incidental." *Pew Research Journalism Project.* 24 Oct. 2013. Web. http://www.journalism.org/2013/10/24/the-role-of-news-on-facebook/

29. Mitchell, Amy. "The State of the News Media 2013: An Annual Report on American Journalism." *The Pew Research Center's Project for Excellence in Journalism.* Web. http://stateofthemedia.org/
30. Ibid.
31. http://www.timepolls.com/hppolls/archive/poll_results_417.html
32. Moran, Douglas. "Why We Trust Jon Stewart." *Random Blather.* 10 Aug. 2009. Web. http://open.salon.com/blog/douglas_moran/2009/08/10/why_we_trust_jon_stewart
33. Chris Raphael, "Politically Incorrect: A Eulogy." *The Big Story.* June 3, 2002. Web. http://thebigstory.org/ov/ov-politicallyincorrect.html
34. Hamm, Theodore. "Reading The Onion Seriously." *In These Times.* 26 June 2008. Web. http://www.inthesetimes.com/article/3778/
35. Narr, Bill Moyers. "Buying the War." *Bill Moyers Journal.* 25 April 2007. Web. Transcript. http://www.pbs.org/moyers/journal/btw/transcript1.html
36. "Freedoms Curtailed in Defense of Liberty." *The Onion.* 10 Oct. 2001. Web. http://www.theonion.com/articles/freedoms-curtailed-in-defense-of-liberty,213/
37. Ibid.
38. "About." *Americans for Fairness in Awarding Journalism Prizes.* Web. http://afajp.tumblr.com/about
39. "*Farenheit 9/11.*" *Wikipedia.* Web. http://en.wikipedia.org/wiki/Fahrenheit_9/11
40. Ibid.
41. Ibid.
42. "The New York Times Special Edition." *Steve Lambert.* 1 Nov. 2008. Web. http://visitsteve.com/made/the-ny-times-special-edition/
43. "The Yes Men." *Wikipedia.* Web. http://en.wikipedia.org/wiki/The_Yes_Men
44. "The New York Times Special Edition." *Steve Lambert.* Web. http://visitsteve.com/made/the-ny-times-special-edition/
45. "New York Times Special Edition." *The Yes Men.* Web. http://theyesmen.org/hijinks/newyorktimes
46. "CNBC Financial Advice." *The Daily Show.* 4 Mar. 2009. Web. http://www.thedailyshow.com/watch/wed-march-4-2009/cnbc-financial-advice
47. Lieberman, David. "Jim Cramer Takes his Lumps on 'The Daily Show.'" *USA Today.* 13 Mar. 2009. Web. http://usatoday30.usatoday.com/money/media/2009-03-12-jim-cramer-appears-on-jon-stewart-show-daily-show_N.htm
48. "Exclusive—Jim Cramer Extended Interview Pt. 1." *The Daily Show.* 13 Mar. 2009. Web. http://thedailyshow.cc.com/videos/fttmoj/exclusive---jim-cramer-extended-interview-pt--1
49. "Newsmakers: Jon Stewart v. Jim Cramer." *Newsweek.* 13 Mar. 2009. Web. http://www.newsweek.com/newsmakers-jon-stewart-vs-jim-cramer-76533
50. Fallows, James. "It's True: Jon Stewart has become Edward R. Murrow." *The Atlantic.* 13 Mar. 2009. Web. http://www.theatlantic.com/technology/archive/2009/03/it-apos-s-true-jon-stewart-has-become-edward-r-murrow-updated/9731/

51. "Obama Spokesman 'Enjoyed' Lashing of CNBC Host." *USA Today*. 13 Mar. 2009. Web. http://usatoday30.usatoday.com/life/television/news/2009-03-13-obama-cramer-stewart_N.htm

52. "Jon Stewart's 2009 Criticism of CNBC." *Wikipedia*. Web. http://en.wikipedia.org/wiki/Jon_Stewart%27s_2009_criticism_of_CNBC#cite_note-34

53. "Dan Quayle Quotes." *Brainy Quote*. Web. http://www.brainyquote.com/quotes/authors/d/dan_quayle.html

54. "Vice Presidential Candidacy of Sarah Palin." *Wikipedia*. Web. http://en.wikipedia.org/wiki/Vice_presidential_candidacy_of_Sarah_Palin#cite_ref-game_10-0

55. "Sarah Palin Interviews with Katie Couric." *Wikipedia*. Web. http://en.wikipedia.org/wiki/Sarah_Palin_interviews_with_Katie_Couric

56. "*Saturday Night Live* Parodies of Sarah Palin." *Wikipedia*. Web. http://en.wikipedia.org/wiki/Saturday_Night_Live_parodies_of_Sarah_Palin

57. "Sarah Palin Interviews with Katie Couric." http://en.wikipedia.org/wiki/Sarah_Palin_interviews_with_Katie_Couric

58. Ibid.

59. "Fox News Confuses Tina Fey for Sarah Palin." *YouTube*. Web. http://www.youtube.com/watch?v=Rg_ghEixfSg#t=10

4 The Dynamic Duo: Jon Stewart and Stephen Colbert Redefine Political Satire

1. "Stephen's Emmy Awards." *Colbert Nation*. 24 Sept. 2013. Web. http://thecolbertreport.cc.com/videos/ecu59e/stephen-s-emmy-awards

2. "The Daily Show with Jon Stewart: Indecision 2004." *Peabody Awards*. Web. http://peabodyawards.com/past-winners/award/?pbaward=1387&pb_search=1&pb_title=&pb_year=1&pb_porg=&pb_query=2004

3. "The Colbert Report (Comedy Central)." *Peabody Awards*. Web. http://peabodyawards.com/past-winners/award/?pbaward=1481&pb_search=1&pb_title=1&pb_year=&pb_porg=&pb_query=colbert

4. "History: Timeline of the George Foster Peabody Awards." *Peabody Awards*. Web. http://peabodyawards.com/about-the-peabody/history/

5. MacGregor, Jeff. "Past Jonathan Swift to Linda Tripp (Yeah. Whatever.)." *The New York Times*. 23 Aug. 1998. Web. http://www.nytimes.com/1998/08/23/arts/television-past-jonathan-swift-to-linda-tripp-yeah-whatever.html?pagewanted=all

6. P., Ken. "An Interview with Stephen Colbert." *IGN*. 11 Aug. 2003. Web. http://www.ign.com/articles/2003/08/11/an-interview-with-stephen-colbert?page=6

7. Ibid.

8. "Carell—Colbert—10 F#@king Years—Even Stevphen." *The Daily Show*. 19 Sept. 2006. Web. http://www.thedailyshow.com/watch/tue-september-19-2006/10-f—king-years—even-stevphen.

9. "Comic Release/'Daily Show' Host Jon Stewart Is TV's King of Irony." *SF Gate.* 23 Apr. 2002. Web. http://www.sfgate.com/entertainment/article/Comic-release-Daily-Show-host-Jon-Stewart-is-2847806.php#page-2

10. Sternbergh, Adam. "Stephen Colbert Has America by the Ballots." *New York Magazine.* 8 Oct. 2006. Web. http://nymag.com/news/politics/22322/

11. Levin, Gary. "First 'Stewart,' now 'Colbert.'" *USA Today.* 13 Oct. 2005. Web. http://www.usatoday.com/life/television/news/2005–10–13-colbert_x.htm

12. Ibid.

13. Ibid.

14. *"The Colbert Report." Wikipedia.* Web. http://en.wikipedia.org/wiki/The_Colbert_Report

15. Ibid.

16. "Infotainment." *Wikipedia.* Web. http://en.wikipedia.org/wiki/Infotainment

17. Solomon, Deborah. "Questions for Stephen Colbert: Funny about the News." *The New York Times Magazine.* 25 Sept. 2005. Web. http://www.nytimes.com/2005/09/25/magazine/25questions.html

18. "The Colbert Report—Introduction." *The Colbert Report.* 17 Oct. 2005. Web. http://www.colbertnation.com/the-colbert-report-videos/180900/october-17–2005/intro—10–17–05

19. Gross, Terry. "A Fake Newsman's Fake Newsman: Stephen Colbert." *Fresh Air from WHYY.* 24 Jan. 2005. Web. http://www.npr.org/templates/story/story.php?storyId=4464017

20. Lederman, Diane. "Ted Koppel: Stephen Colbert, Jon Stewart 'Doing a Better Job than the Real Journalists.'" *Mass Live.* 4 May 2012. Web. http://www.masslive.com/news/index.ssf/2012/05/ted_koppel_to_speak_at_umass_g_1.html

21. Bergman, Cory. "DNC: A Serious Interview with Jon Stewart (with Ted Koppel)." *Free Republic.* 29 Jul. 2004. Web. http://www.freerepublic.com/focus/f-news/1181311/posts

22. "Jon Stewart Crushes Bill O'Reilly in Debate." *YouTube.* 9 Oct. 2012. Web. http://www.youtube.com/watch?v=CK03KI6WMz4

23. "David Folkenflik." *Colbert Nation.* 4 Nov. 2013. Web. http://www.colbertnation.com/the-colbert-report-videos/430203/november-04-–2013/david-folkenflik

24. "Daily/Colbert—Just a Quickie." *The Daily Show.* 17 Sept. 2008. Web. http://www.thedailyshow.com/watch/wed-september-17-–2008/daily-colbert—just-a-quickie

25. "US Comics Unveil Dueling DC Political Rallies." *AFP.* 17 Sept. 2010. http://www.google.com/hostednews/afp/article/ALeqM5gkOsOs61eFqq5znyHyVThYNAGTDw

26. "Rally to Restore Sanity and/or Fear." *Wikipedia.* Web. http://en.wikipedia.org/wiki/Rally_to_Restore_Sanity_and/or_Fear#cite_note-AFP-4

27. Halloran, Liz. "Glenn Beck Comes To D.C., Controversy Follows." *NPR.* 27 Aug. 2010. Web. http://www.npr.org/templates/story/story.php?storyId=129449408

28. Avlon, John. "I Have a Nightmare." *The Daily Beast.* 15 May 2010. Web. http://www.thedailybeast.com/articles/2010/08/27/glenn-beck-sarah-palin-rally-a-martin-luther-king-nightmare.html
29. Ibid.
30. Ibid.
31. *Rally to Restore Sanity.* Web. http://www.rallytorestoresanity.com/
32. *March to Keep Fear Alive.* Web. http://www.keepfearalive.com/
33. Corvette, Jenny. "Glenn Beck's Top Ten Dumbest Quotes." *Yahoo! Voices.* 11 Dec. 2009. Web. http://voices.yahoo.com/glenn-becks-top-ten-dumbest-quotes-5055452.html?cat=9
34. Hawkins, John. "Let Sarah Speak: The 20 Best Quotes from Sarah Palin." *Townhall.* 21 Aug. 2012. Web. http://townhall.com/columnists/johnhawkins/2012/08/21/let_sarah_speak_the_20_best_quotes_from_sarah_palin/page/full
35. Kurtzman, Daniel. "Ann Coulter Quotes." *About.com.* Web. http://politicalhumor.about.com/od/funnyquotes/a/anncoulter.htm
36. Clifton, Allen. "Satire Has Become Reality: Rush Limbaugh Attacks Pope Francis for Acting Like a Christian." *Forward Progressives.* 30 Nov. 2013. Web. http://www.forwardprogressives.com/satire-has-become-reality-rush-limbaugh-attacks-pope-francis-for-acting-like-a-christian/
37. "Rally to Restore Sanity and/or Fear." *Wikipedia.* Web. http://en.wikipedia.org/wiki/Rally_to_Restore_Sanity_and/or_Fear#cite_note-26
38. "Obama Plugs Jon Stewart Rally." *NBC News.* 29 Sept. 2010. Web. http://firstread.nbcnews.com/_news/2010/09/29/5203437-obama-plugs-jon-stewart-rally
39. Firecloud, Johnny. "Metal Meets Folk Meets Soul at the Rally to Restore Sanity." *Crave Online.* 31 Oct. 2010. Web. http://www.craveonline.com/music/articles/132858-metal-meets-folk-meets-soul-at-the-rally-to-restore-sanity
40. Ibid.
41. Ibid.
42. Strauss, Neil. "Stephen Colbert on Deconstructing the News, Religion and the Colbert Nation: More from Neil Strauss' Conversation with TV's Most Dangerous Man." *Rolling Stone.* 2 Sept. 2009. Web. http://www.rollingstone.com/culture/news/stephen-colbert-on-deconstructing-the-news-religion-and-the-colbert-nation-20090902
43. Rose, Charlie. "A Conversation with Comedian Stephen Colbert." *Charlie Rose.* Web. http://www.charlierose.com/view/interview/93
44. Sternbergh, Adam. "Stephen Colbert Has America by the Ballots." *New York Magazine.* 8 Oct. 2006. Web. http://nymag.com/news/politics/22322/
45. Ibid.
46. "Tip/Wag—Joe Reed & Levi's Ex-Girlfriend Jeans." *Colbert Nation.* 28 Feb. 2011. Web. http://www.colbertnation.com/the-colbert-report-videos/375740/february-28–2011/tip-wag—-joe-reed—-levi-s-ex-girlfriend-jeans
47. "A Few Very Specific Men." *The Daily Show.* 15 Aug. 2012. Web. http://www.thedailyshow.com/watch/wed-august-15-–2012/a-few-very-specific-men
48. "The Parent Company Trap." *The Daily Show.* 23 Aug. 2010. Web. http://www.thedailyshow.com/watch/mon-august-23–2010/the-parent-company-trap

49. "Nancy Pelosi." *The Daily Show.* 9 Nov. 2011. Web. http://thedailyshow.cc.com/videos/8h7ys1/nancy-pelosi

50. "The Daily Show with Jon Stewart: Indecision 2004." *Peabody Awards.*

51. "Harvey Mansfield." *Colbert Nation.* 5 Apr. 2006. Web. http://www.colbertnation.com/the-colbert-report-videos/61315/april-05–2006/harvey-mansfield

52. P., Ken. "An Interview with Stephen Colbert." http://www.ign.com/articles/2003/08/11/an-interview-with-stephen-colbert?page=4

53. Ibid.

54. Gross, Terry. "Bluster and Satire: Stephen Colbert's 'Report.'" *Fresh Air from WHYY.* 7 Dec. 2005. http://www.npr.org/templates/story/story.php?storyId=5040948&ps=rs

5   When I Mock You, I Make You Better: How Satire Works

1. Suskind, Ron. "Faith, Certainty and the Presidency of George W. Bush." *The New York Times.* 17 Oct. 2004. Web. http://www.nytimes.com/2004/10/17/magazine/17BUSH.html

2. "Stephen Colbert at the White House Correspondents Dinner." *YouTube.* 14 Nov. 2011. Web. http://www.youtube.com/watch?feature=player_embedded&v=CWqzLgDc030

3. "Transcript: Bill Moyers Interviews Jon Stewart." *NOW.* 11 July 2003. Web. http://www.pbs.org/now/transcript/transcript_stewart.html

4. "*Saturday Night Live* (season 27)." *Wikipedia.* Web. http://en.wikipedia.org/wiki/Saturday_Night_Live_%28season_27%29

5. Williams, Zoe. "The Final Irony." *The Guardian.* 27 June 2003. Web. http://www.theguardian.com/theguardian/2003/jun/28/weekend7.weekend2

6. Nunberg, Geoffrey. "Since Sept. 11, We're Watching Our Words." *Los Angeles Times.* 4 Nov. 2001. Web. http://articles.latimes.com/2001/nov/04/opinion/op-65510

7. Ibid.

8. Ibid.

9. Ibid.

10. Williams, Zoe. "The Final Irony." *The Guardian.* 27 June 2003. Web.

11. "U.S. Vows to Defeat Whoever it Is we're at War with." *The Onion.* 26 Sept. 2001. Web. http://www.theonion.com/articles/us-vows-to-defeat-whoever-it-is-were-at-war-with

12. "Mika Brzezinski Experiences Palin Fatigue." *Colbert Nation.* 18 Jan. 2011. Web. http://www.colbertnation.com/the-colbert-report-videos/371413/january-18--2011/mika-brzezinski-experiences-palin-fatigue

13. "Mika Brzezinski Experiences Palin Fatigue." *Colbert Nation.* ibid.

14. Almond, Steve. "The Joke's On You." *The Baffler.* 20 Aug. 2012. Web. http://www.thebaffler.com/salvos/the-jokes-on-you

15. "The Parent Company Trap." *The Daily Show.* 23 Aug. 2010. Web. http://www.thedailyshow.com/watch/mon-august-23--2010/the-parent-company-trap

16. Ibid.
17. Almond, Steve. "The Joke's On You." *The Baffler* 20. 2012. Web. http://www.thebaffler.com/past/the_jokes_on_you
18. "The Yes Men Fix the US Chamber of Commerce." *YouTube.* 19 Oct. 2009. Web. http://www.youtube.com/watch?v=D67LYEacBoE
19. Rushdie, Salman. "Ugly Phrase Conceals an Uglier Truth." *The Sydney Morning Herald.* 10 Jan. 2006. Web. http://www.smh.com.au/news/opinion/ugly-phrase-conceals-an-uglier-truth/2006/01/09/1136771496819.html?page=fullpage#contentSwap2
20. Ibid.
21. Sternbergh, Adam. "Stephen Colbert Has America by the Ballots." *New York Magazine.* 22 Mar. 2014. Web. http://nymag.com/news/politics/22322/
22. Ibid.
23. "Intro—4/3/08." *Colbert Nation.* 3 Apr. 2008. Web. http://www.colbertnation.com/the-colbert-report-videos/164890/april-03-2008/intro---4-3-08
24. "Intro—11/14/12." *Colbert Nation.* 14 Nov. 2012. Web. http://www.colbertnation.com/the-colbert-report-videos/421263/november-14-2012/intro---11-14-12
25. Gross, Terry. "Bluster and Satire: Stephen Colbert's 'Report.'" *Fresh Air from WHYY.* 7 Dec. 2005. Web. http://www.npr.org/templates/story/story.php?storyId=5040948
26. Ibid.
27. Brady, Christian. "Satire, What Is it Good for?" *Blogging the Academy.* 14 Oct. 2013. Web. http://sites.psu.edu/bradypla/tag/satire/
28. Ibid.
29. Jenkins, Henry. "Manufacturing Dissent: An Interview with Stephen Duncombe (Part Two)." *Confessions of an Aca-Fan: The Official Weblog of Henry Jenkins.* 24 July 2007. Web. http://henryjenkins.org/2007/07/manufacturing_dissent_an_inter_1.html#sthash.PwHWw0ur.dpuf
30. Ibid.
31. Albertson, Eric. "Smarm, Snark, and Digital Discourse." *The Brooklyn Quarterly.* Web. http://brooklynquarterly.org/smarm-and-stature/
32. Ibid.
33. Ibid.
34. Scocca, Tom. "On Smarm." *Gawker.* 5 Dec. 2013. Web. http://gawker.com/on-smarm-1476594977
35. Ibid.
36. Gladwell, Malcolm. "Being Nice Isn't Really so Awful." *The New Yorker.* 11 Dec. 2013. Web. http://www.newyorker.com/online/blogs/books/2013/12/dave-eggers-tom-scocca-and-being-nice.html
37. Edwards, David. "Stephen Colbert: 'Sarah Palin Is a F**cking Retard!'" *AlterNet.* 9 Feb. 2010. Web. http://www.alternet.org/story/145627/stephen_colbert%3A_%27sarah_palin_is_a_f**cking_retard%27
38. "Colbert: Sarah Palin Is a F--king Retard." *Crooks and Liars.* 9 Feb. 2010. Web. http://crooksandliars.com/scarce/colbert-sarah-palin-f-king-retard
39. Ibid.

40. "Sarah Palin Uses a Hand-O-Prompter." *Colbert Nation.* 8 Feb. 2010. Web. http://www.colbertnation.com/the-colbert-report-videos/264042/february-08--2010/sarah-palin-uses-a-hand-o-prompter

41. Ibid.

42. Kavanah, Jim. "Cain: 'America's too Uptight!'" *CNN.* 14 Sept. 2011. Web. http://www.cnn.com/2011/POLITICS/09/12/debate.cain.humor/index.html

43. Saulny, Susan, and Sarah Wheaton. "Cain Says His Deadly Fence Plan Was 'a Joke.'" *The New York Times.* 16 Oct. 2011. Web. http://thecaucus.blogs.nytimes.com/2011/10/16/cain-says-his-deadly-fence-plan-was-a-joke/

44. Balz, Dan. "From doubts to confidence to defeat." *The Washington Post.* 27 Jul. 2013. Web. http://www.washingtonpost.com/sf/feature/wp/2013/07/27/from-doubts-to-confidence-to-defeat/

45. "Today's Journalists Less Prominent." *Pew Research Center for the People & the Press.* 8 Mar. 2007. Web. http://www.people-press.org/2007/03/08/todays-journalists-less-prominent/

46. *Mitt.* Dir. Greg Whiteley. Netflix, 2014. Web. http://movies.netflix.com/Movie/Mitt/70296733; "Shorts/Mitt Romney Style (Gangnam Style Parody)." *CollegeHumor.* 2 Oct. 2012. Web. http://www.collegehumor.com/video/6830834/mitt-romney-style-gangnam-style-parody

6   Mesmerized Millennials and BYTE-ing Satire: Or How Today's Young Generation Thinks

1. "'Stoned Slackers' Watch Jon Stewart." *Today.* 28 Sept. 2004. Web. http://www.today.com/id/6117542#.UtlYdvYo7Jw

2. Carr, Nicholas. "Is Google Making Us Stupid?" *The Atlantic.* 1 July 2008. Web. http://www.theatlantic.com/magazine/archive/2008/07/is-google-making-us-stupid/6868/

3. Ibid.

4. "Colbert—Bloggers." *The Daily Show.* 16 Feb. 2005. Web. http://www.thedaily-show.com/watch/wed-february-16–2005/bloggers

5. "Beau Willimon." *Colbert Nation.* 5 Mar. 2014. Web. http://thecolbertreport.cc.com/full-episodes/gj1fhn/march-5--2014---beau-willimon

6. Lowrey, Annie. "Do Millennials Stand a Chance in the Real World." *The New York Times.* 26 Mar. 2013. Web. http://www.nytimes.com/2013/03/31/magazine/do-millennials-stand-a-chance-in-the-real-world.html?pagewanted=all&_r=0

7. "Why Generation Y Yuppies Are Unhappy." *HuffPost College.* 15 Sept. 2013. Web. http://www.huffingtonpost.com/wait-but-why/generation-y-unhappy_b_3930620.html

8. "20 Job Rules for Millennials." *Forbes.* Web. http://www.forbes.com/pictures/eeel45ggdk/1-keep-working-at-something/

9. Harvey, Paul. "As College Graduates Hit the Workforce, So Do More Entitlement-Minded Workers." *University of New Hampshire Media Relations.* 17 May 2010. Web. http://www.unh.edu/news/cj_nr/2010/may/lw17gen-y.cfm

10. "Glenn Beck on this Generation of Kids—The Me Generation." *YouTube*. 27 Oct. 2009. Web. https://www.youtube.com/watch?v=XQYC1sY3jp4

11. Crockett, Emily. "Why Millennials Aren't Lazy, Entitled Narcissists." *Generation Progress*. 14 May 2013. Web. http://genprogress.org/voices/2013/05/14/18884/why-millennials-arent-lazy-entitled-narcissists/

12. Stewart, Brian, and Abraham White. "It's Clear: Young Voters Turned Out in Record Numbers." *Generation Progress*. 7 Nov. 2012. Web. http://genprogress.org/voices/2012/11/07/18183/its-clear-young-people-turned-out-to-vote-in-record-numbers/

13. "Millennials Lead the Nation in Service to Our Country." *NDN*. 19 Aug. 2009. Web. http://ndn.org/blog/2009/08/millennials-lead-nation-service-our-country

14. Klein, Ezra. "Joel Stein is Wrong about Millennials, in One Chart." *The Washington Post*. 9 May 2013. Web. http://www.washingtonpost.com/blogs/wonkblog/wp/2013/05/09/joel-stein-is-wrong-about-millennials-in-one-chart/

15. Reeve, Elspeth. "Every Every Every Generation Has Been the Me Me Me Generation." *The Wire*. 9 May 2013. Web. http://www.thewire.com/national/2013/05/me-generation-time/65054/

16. Lowrey, Annie. "Do Millennials Stand a Chance?"

17. Goodman, William. "Millennials 'Apologize' for Being So Terrible." *HuffPost College*. 19 Sept. 2013. Web. http://www.huffingtonpost.com/2013/09/19/millennials-apologize-parody_n_3950696.html

18. Ibid.

19. "Scene from a Satirical Papyrus." *The British Museum*. Web. http://www.britishmuseum.org/explore/highlights/highlight_objects/aes/s/scene_from_a_satirical_papyrus.aspx

20. "The Flip Side: Video Shows what Happens when Men and Women Switch Roles." *The Huffington Post*. 3 Dec. 2012. Web. http://www.huffingtonpost.com/2012/11/30/flip-side-video_n_2220370.html

21. "The Me Generation Meets Generation Me." 20 June 2013. Web. http://www.nielsen.com/us/en/newswire/2013/the-me-generation-meets-generation-me.html

22. Navasky, Victor. "15 Historic Cartoons that Changed the World." *BuzzFeed*. 2 May 2013. Web. http://www.buzzfeed.com/victornavasky/15-historic-cartoons-that-changed-the-world

23. *Punch*. Web. punch.co.uk

24. Lorusso, Lorenzo. "Neuroscience by Caricature in Europe Throughout the Ages." Web. http://neuro-caricatures.eu/caricatural-journals

25. *Punch*. http://punch.co.uk/

26. Stannard, Ed. "New Haven Creator of 'Being Liberal' Facebook Page Comes Out from Behind Screen." *New Haven Register*.18 Feb. 2013. Web. http://www.nhregister.com/general-news/20130218/new-haven-creator-of-being-liberal-facebook-page-comes-out-from-behind-screen

27. *Being Liberal*. Web. http://beingliberal.tumblr.com/

28. Rusli, Evelyn M. "Facebook Buys Instagram for $1 Billion." *The New York Times.* 9 Apr. 2012. Web. http://dealbook.nytimes.com/2012/04/09/facebook-buys-instagram-for-1-billion/?_php=true&_type=blogs&_r=0

29. Nunberg, Geoff. "Narcissistic or Not, 'Selfie' Is Nunberg's Word of the Year." *NPR.* 19 Dec. 2013. Web. http://www.npr.org/2013/12/19/255294091/narcissistic-or-not-selfie-is-nunbergs-word-of-the-year

30. Rutledge, Pamela. "Positively Media." *Psychology Today.* 18 Apr. 2013. Web. http://www.psychologytoday.com/blog/positively-media/201304/selfies-narcissism-or-self-exploration

31. Dominguez, Trace. Twitter post. 30 Sept. 2013. Web. https://twitter.com/trace501/statuses/384802367066996736

32. "Colbert Praises Chuck Grassley's Mystifying Twitter Feed." *HuffPost Comedy.* 11 Apr. 2012. Web. http://www.huffingtonpost.com/2012/04/11/colbert-praises-chuck-grassleys-twitter_n_1417873.html

33. "I Got the Tweets like Grassley." *Colbert Nation.* 10 Apr. 2012. Web. http://thecolbertreport.cc.com/videos/qu7492/i-got-the-tweets-like-grassley

34. Ungerleider, Neal. "Using Vine to Cover Breaking News." *Fast Company.* 7 Feb. 2013. Web. http://www.fastcompany.com/3005630/fast-feed/using-vine-cover-breaking-news

35. https://vine.co/v/hHDYAmtPBYV

36. http://www.huffingtonpost.com/2008/06/09/fox-anchor-calls-obama-fi_n_106027.html

37. Seltzer, Cassandra. Tumblr. Web. http://benjaminskanklin.tumblr.com/post/74013848508/hey-girl-let-me-give-you-the-ol-runners-up-try

38. Stern, Marlow. "Romney's 'Binders Full of Women' Comment Sets Internet Ablaze." *The Daily Beast.* 17 Oct. 2012. Web. http://www.thedaily-beast.com/articles/2012/10/17/mitt-romney-s-binders-full-of-women-com-ment-sets-internet-ablaze.html

39. "IAmA." *Reddit.* Web. http://www.reddit.com/r/IAmA

40. "I am Barack Obama, President of the United States—AMA." *Reddit.* Web. http://www.reddit.com/r/IAmA/comments/z1c9z/i_am_barack_obama_president_of_the_united_states/

41. Kolawole, Emi. "President Obama's Reddit AMA: Top Five Most Awesome Questions." *The Washington Post.* 29 Aug. 2012. Web. http://www.washington-post.com/blogs/innovations/post/president-obamas-reddit-ama-top-five-most-awesome-questions/2012/08/29/d3f2c1aa-f21a-11e1-adc6-87dfa8eff430_blog.html

42. "Shorts/Mitt Romney Style." *CollegeHumor.* 2 Oct. 2012. Web. http://www.collegehumor.com/video/6830834/mitt-romney-style-gangnam-style-parody

43. Chen, Adrian. "11-Year-Old Viral Video Star Placed under Police Protection after Death Threats." *Gawker.* 18 Jul. 2010. Web. http://gawker.com/5590166/11-year-old-viral-video-star-placed-under-police-protection-after-death-threats

44. Carr, David. "Two Guys Made a Website, and This Is What They Got." *The New York Times*. 9 Jul 2012. Web. http://mediadecoder.blogs.nytimes.com/2012/07/09/two-guys-made-a-web-site-and-this-is-what-they-got/?_php=true&_type=blogs&_r=0

45. "Upworthy is . . ." *UpWorthy*. Web. http://www.upworthy.com/about

46. Pfeiffer, Sacha. "In Colbert 101, Students Study Comic's Inner Socrates." *90.9 WBUR*. 6 May 2011. Web. http://www.wbur.org/2011/05/06/bu-colbert-class

47. O'Hara, Jessica. Email message to author. 30 January 2014.

48. "Likes don't Save Lives UNICEF Sweden the Restaurant." *YouTube*. 4 Mar. 2014. Web. https://www.youtube.com/watch?v=Mkglaq4_5Sk

49. Livingston, Geoff. "HOW TO: Turn Slacktivists into Activists with Social Media." *Mashable*. 13 May 2010. Web. http://mashable.com/2010/05/13/slacktivists-activists-social-media/

50. Ibid. "HOW TO: Turn Slacktivists into Activists with Social Media." *Mashable*. 13 May 2010. Web. http://mashable.com/2010/05/13/slacktivists-activists-social-media/

51. Ibid.

52. Ibid.

7 Savin' Franklin: Satire Defends Our National Values

1. "Super Bowl Advertising." *Wikipedia*. Web. http://en.wikipedia.org/wiki/Super_Bowl_advertising

2. Smerconish, Michael. "The Pulse: After the Song, Grating Notes." *Philly.com*. 8 Feb. 2014. Web. http://www.philly.com/philly/columnists/michael_smerconish/20140209_The_Pulse__After_the_song__grating_notes.html

3. Ibid.

4. Poniewozik, James. "Coca-Cola's 'It's Beautiful' Super Bowl Ad Brings Out Some Ugly Americans." *TIME*. 2 Feb. 2014. Web. http://entertainment.time.com/2014/02/02/coca-colas-its-beautiful-super-bowl-ad-brings-out-some-ugly-americans/

5. Isquith, Elias. "Glenn Beck Calls Coca-Cola's Multilingual Super Bowl Commercial an 'In Your Face' Attempt to 'Divide People.'" *Salon*. 3 Feb. 2014. Web. http://www.salon.com/2014/02/03/glenn_beck_calls_coca_colas_multilingual_super_bowl_commercial_an_in_your_face_attempt_to_divide_people/

6. Leahy, Michael Patrick. "Why Coca-Cola's Multicultural 'America the Beautiful' Ad was Offensive." *Breitbart*. 2 Feb. 2014. Web. http://www.breitbart.com/Big-Government/2014/02/02/Why-Coca-Cola-America-The-Beautiful-Ad-Was-Offensive?utm_source=twitterfeed&utm_medium=twitter

7. Garcia, Arturo. "WATCH: Jon Stewart's Funny, Poignant Rebuke to Racists Upset by Coke's Super Bowl Ad." *The Raw Story*. 7 Feb. 2014. Web. http://www.rawstory.com/rs/2014/02/07/watch-jon-stewarts-funny-poignant-rebuke-to-racists-upset-by-cokes-super-bowl-ad/

8. Tesfaye, Sophia. "'Road to Perdition': Right-Wing Media React to Multicultural Coca-Cola Super Bowl Ad." *Media Matters.* 3 Feb. 2014. Web. http://media-matters.org/research/2014/02/03/road-to-perdition-right-wing-media-react-to-mul/197898

9. "Hop on Pop." *The Daily Show.* 6 Feb. 2014. Web. http://www.thedaily-show.com/watch/thu-february-6--2014/hop-on-pop

10. Ibid.

11. "Coca-Cola's Diverse 'America the Beautiful' Ad." *Colbert Nation.* 3 Feb. 2014. Web. http://www.colbertnation.com/the-colbert-report-videos/432753/february-03-2014/coca-cola-s-diverse—america-the-beautiful—ad

12. Ibid.

13. "Anti-intellectualism." *Wikipedia.* Web. http://en.wikipedia.org/wiki/Anti-intellectualism

14. Wikipedia cites: Hofstadter, Richard. *Anti-intellectualism in American Life.* 1962. New York: Vintage, 1996. Print. "Anti-intellectualism." *Wikipedia.* Web. http://en.wikipedia.org/wiki/Anti-intellectualism

15. Wikipedia cites: Sowell, Thomas. *The Quest for Cosmic Justice.* New York: Simon & Schuster, 2001. "Anti-intellectualism." *Wikipedia.* Web. http://en.wikipedia.org/wiki/Anti-intellectualism

16. Wikipedia cites: Hofstadter, Richard. *Anti-intellectualism in American Life.* 1962. New York: Vintage, 1996. Print. "Anti-intellectualism." *Wikipedia.* Web. http://en.wikipedia.org/wiki/Anti-intellectualism

17. Peterson cites: Freud, Sigmund. *Jokes and their Relation to the Unconscious.* Trans. James Strachey New York: Norton, 1963.

18. Goodwin, Doris Kearns. *Team of Rivals*: The Political Genius of Abraham Lincoln. New York: Simon & Schuster, 2006. Cited in Wickman, Forrest. "How Accurate Is *Lincoln?" Slate.* 9 Nov. 2012. Web. http://www.slate.com/blogs/browbeat/2012/11/09/lincoln_historical_accuracy_sorting_fact_from_fiction_in_the_steven_spielberg.html

19. Peterson cites: Madison, James. "Federalist Fifty-one." *The Federalist Papers.* Ed. Clinton Rossiter. New York: Signet, 1961.

20. Strle, Zako. "New Bush Memoir Hails Choking on Pretzel as Top Decision Point." *The Spoof!* 26 Nov. 2010. Web. http://www.thespoof.com/news/us/87200/new-bush-memoir-hails-choking-on-pretzel-as-top-decision-point

21. Quoted in Trachtenberg, Jeffrey A. "Mark Twain's New Book." *WSJ.* 18 Apr. 2009. Web. http://online.wsj.com/article/SB124000246279630121.html

22. "The Wørd: Swift Payment." *Colbert Nation.* 13 Dec. 2010. Web. http://thecol-bertreport.cc.com/videos/c1yv8b/the-word--swift-payment

23. "Better Know a Founder." *Colbert Nation.* 1 Mar. 2006. Web. http://www.colbertnation.com/the-colbert-report-videos/59707/march-01-2006/better-know-a-founder---benjamin-franklin

24. Bliss, Don. "Stephen Colbert Hill Visit: A Twist on Twain." *The Washington Post.* 28 Sept. 2010. Web. http://www.washingtonpost.com/wp-dyn/content/article/2010/09/27/AR2010092706125.html

25. "The Wørd: Swift Payment." *Colbert Nation.* 13 Dec. 2010. Web. http://thecol-bertreport.cc.com/videos/c1yv8b/the-word---swift-payment

26. Stratton, Allegra. "2007 Is America's Deadliest Year in Iraq." *The Guardian*. 31 Dec. 2007. Web. http://www.theguardian.com/world/2007/dec/31/usa.iraq

27. Sarat quotes: Gates Jr., Henry Louis. "Patriotism." *Nation*. July 15/22, 1991, 91.

28. Michaels quoted in: Pennington, Gail. "People in the News." *St. Louis Post-Dispatch*. 29 Sept. 2001. Quoted in Peterson 197.

29. Saletan, William. "Imperial President." *Slate*. 2 Sept. 2004. Web. http://www.slate.com/articles/news_and_politics/ballot_box/2004/09/imperial_president.1.html

30. Krugman, Paul. "The Last Refuge." *The New York Times*. 8 Apr. 2003. Web. http://www.nytimes.com/2003/04/08/opinion/the-last-refuge.html

31. "September 11, 2001." *The Daily Show*. 21 Sept. 2001. Web. http://thedaily-show.cc.com/videos/1q93jy/september-11--2001

32. Lewis cites: Kushner, Malcolm. "Unleash USA's Secret Weapon: Humor." *USA Today*. 4 Oct. 2001. Web. http://usatoday30.usatoday.com/news/comment/2001-10-05-opline.htm

33. Peterson cites: Reeves, Richard. "Patriotism Calls Out the Censor." *The New York Times*. 1 Oct. 2001. Web. http://www.nytimes.com/2001/10/01/opinion/patriotism-calls-out-the-censor.html

34. "Mess O'Potamia—He Said, Sheehan Said." *The Daily Show*. 25 Aug. 2005. Web. http://www.thedailyshow.com/watch/thu-august-25--2005/mess-o-potamia---he-said--sheehan-said

35. Sprung, Shlomo. "25 More Signs that America Is not the Greatest Country on Earth." *Business Insider*. 25 Jun. 2012. Web. http://www.businessinsider.com/here-are-25-more-signs-that-america-is-not-1-2012-6

36. "Bill O'Reilly." *The Colbert Report*. 18 Jan. 2007. Web. http://thecolbertreport.cc.com/videos/9seimt/bill-o-reilly

37. "On Topic—In the News—The Real America." *The Daily Show*. 17 May 2010. Web. http://www.thedailyshow.com/watch/mon-may-17-2010/on-topic--in-the-news---the-real-america

38. "Quiz: Are you a Real American?" *The Daily Show*. 20 Oct. 2008. Web. http://www.thedailyshow.com/watch/mon-october-20--2008/quiz--are-you-a-real-american

8 Laughing So Hard I Could Cry: Analyzing the Satire Scare

1. Shackle, Samira. "The NS Interview—PJ O'Rourke." *New Statesman*. 9 Jan. 2012. Web. http://www.newstatesman.com/north-america/2012/01/barack-obama-interview-tea

2. Zwicky, Arnold. "The Dangers of Satire." *Language Log*. 30 Jul. 2008. Web. http://languagelog.ldc.upenn.edu/nll/?p=369

3. "America Is a Joke." *New York Magazine*. Web. http://nymag.com/arts/tv/profiles/68086/index1.html

4. Ibid. http://nymag.com/arts/tv/profiles/68086/index1.html

5. Kakutani, Michiko. "Is Jon Stewart the Most Trusted Man in America?" *The New York Times*. 15 Aug. 2008. Web. http://www.nytimes.com/2008/08/17/arts/television/17kaku.html?pagewanted=all

6. "CNN Newsroom: CNN: Is Jon Stewart a Journalist or Comedian?" *YouTube.* 28 Dec. 2010. Web. https://www.youtube.com/watch?v=U1p3RWpZP3c

7. Carter, Bill, and Brian Stelter. "In 'Daily Show' Role on 9/11 Bill, Echoes of Murrow." *The New York Times.* 26 Dec. 2010. Web. http://www.nytimes.com/2010/12/27/business/media/27stewart.html?pagewanted=all

8. Lederman, Diane. Ted Koppel: Stephen Colbert, Jon Stewart 'Doing a Better Job than the Real Journalists.'" *Mass Live.* 4 May 2012. Web. http://www.masslive.com/news/index.ssf/2012/05/ted_koppel_to_speak_at_umass_g_1.html

9. *Poynter.* 15 Oct. 2011. Web. http://www.poynter.org/latest-news/mediawire/191625/stephen-colbert-i-care-about-the-news/

10. Young, Dannagal Goldthwaite. "Daily Show Viewers Knowledgeable about Presidential Campaign, National Annenberg Election Survey Shows." *NAES 04: National Annenberg Election Survey.* 21 Sept. 2004. Web. http://www.annenbergpublicpolicycenter.org/downloads/political_communication/naes/2004_03_late-night-knowledge-2_9-21_pr.pdf

11. Ibid.

12. Linkins, Jason, and Elyse Siegel. "CNN Is Terrible. Here's Why." *The Huffington Post.* 4 May 2012. Web. http://www.huffingtonpost.com/2012/05/04/cnn-is-terrible-heres-why_n_1478927.html

13. "Rally to Restore Sanity Announcement." *The Daily Show.* 16 Sept. 2010. Web. http://thedailyshow.cc.com/video-playlists/pj77i8/daily-show-15117

14. Stewart, Brian, and Abraham White. "It's Clear: Young Voters Turned Out in Record Numbers." *Generation Progress.* 7 Nov. 2012. Web. http://genprogress.org/voices/2012/11/07/18183/its-clear-young-people-turned-out-to-vote-in-record-numbers/

15. Winograd, Morley, and Michael D. Hais. "Millennials Lead the Nation in Service to our Country." *NDN.* 19 Aug. 2009. Web. http://ndn.org/blog/2009/08/millennials-lead-nation-service-our-country

16. "SURVEY: Daily Show/Colbert Viewers Most Knowledgeable, Fox News Viewers Rank Lowest." *Think Progress.* 16 Apr. 2007. Web. http://thinkprogress.org/default/2007/04/16/11946/daily-show-fox-knowledge/#

17. Beaujon, Andrew. "Survey: NPR's Listeners Best-informed, Fox Viewers Worst-informed." *Poynter.* 23 May 2012. Web. http://www.poynter.org/latest-news/mediawire/174826/survey-nprs-listeners-best-informed-fox-news-viewers-worst-informed/

9   I'm Not Laughing at You, I'm Laughing With You: How to Stop Worrying and Love the Laughter

1. "Boston Tea Party." *Wikipedia.* Web. http://en.wikipedia.org/wiki/Boston_Tea_Party

2. Ruhl, Lisa. "VIDEO: Paul Ryan Says Democrats Offering 'a Full Stomach and an Empty Soul.'" *Washington Examiner.* 6 Mar. 2014. Web. http://washingtonexaminer.com/video-paul-ryan-says-democrats-offering-full-stomachs-and-empty-soul/article/2545192

3. Ibid.

4. Ibid.

5. Ibid.

6. "The Amazing Base—Power of Love." *The Daily Show*. 10 Mar. 2014. Web. http://www.thedailyshow.com/watch/mon-march-10-2014/the-amazing-base---power-of-love

7. Ibid.

8. "Transcript: Bill Moyers Interviews Jon Stewart." *NOW*. 11 Jul. 2003. Web. http://www.pbs.org/now/transcript/transcript_stewart.html

9. "'Stoned Slackers' Watch Jon Stewart?" *Today*. 28 Sept. 2004. Web. http://www.today.com/id/6117542/ns/today-today_entertainment/t/stoned-slackers-watch-jon-stewart/#.UyYaSl5simk

10. "Jon Kyle Tweets not Intended to Be Factual Statements." *Colbert Nation*. 12 Apr. 2011. Web. http://www.colbertnation.com/the-colbert-report-videos/381484/april-12-2011/jon-kyl-tweets-not-intended-to-be-factual-statements

11. Dugan, Lauren. "Colbert Tweets: 'Jon Kyl's Knees Bend Both Ways. He's Part Racehorse #NotIntendedToBeAFactualStatement." *All Twitter*. 14 Apr. 2011. Web. http://www.mediabistro.com/alltwitter/colbert-tweets-jon-kyls-knees-bend-both-ways-hes-part-racehorse-notintendedtobeafactualstatement_b7135

12. Bichlbaum, Andy. "Wall Street Bull Survives Attack by Matador; Clowns Arrested." *Yes Lab*. 9 Nov. 2011. Web. http://yeslab.org/bull

13. Ibid.

14. Ibid.

15. Gillmore, Frederick. "Occupy Wall Street Has Been Effective." *The Wall Street Journal*. 7 Feb. 2012. Web. http://online.wsj.com/news/articles/SB10001424052970203711104577199763603095798

16. "We Need Homes, Not Jails." *Occupy Wall Street*. 28 Feb. 2014. Web. http://occupywallst.org/article/we-need-homes-not-jails/

17. Derickson. "Millennials & Social Activism." *e-Strategy Trends*.16 Aug. 2012. Web. http://trends.e-strategyblog.com/2012/08/16/millennials-social-activism-infographic/2891

18. Occupy Wall Street. Twitter post. 28 Feb. 2014. Web. https://twitter.com/OccupyWallSt/status/439395166399787008. See OccupyWallSt.org

19. Colbert, Stephen. "Stephen Colbert's Address to the Graduates." *AlterNet*. 5 Jun. 2006. Web. http://www.alternet.org/story/37144/stephen_colbert%27s_address_to_the_graduates

20. Giroux, Henry A. "Henry A. Giroux: The Occupy Movement and the Politics of Educated Hope." *Truthout*. Web.http://truth-out.org/news/item/9237-the-occupy-movement-and-the-politics-of-educated-hope

21. "Story." *The Yes Men Fix the World*. Web. http://theyesmenfixtheworld.com/story.htm

Works Cited

Achter, Paul. "Comedy in Unfunny Times: News Parody and Carnival After 9/11." *Critical Studies in Media Communication* 25.3 (2008): 274–303. *Taylor & Francis Online*. Web.

Baek, Young Min, and Magdalena E.Wojcieszak. "Don't Expect Too Much! Learning from Late-Night Comedy and Knowledge Item Difficulty." *Communication Research* 36.6 (2009): 783–809. *SAGE*. Web.

Baumgartner, Jody C., and Jonathan S. Morris. "One 'Nation,' Under Stephen? The Effects of *The Colbert Report* on American Youth." *Journal of Broadcasting & Electronic Media* 52.4 (2008): 622–43. *Taylor & Francis Online*. Web.

———. "Stoned Slackers or Super Citizens? *The Daily Show* Viewing and Political Engagement of Young Adults." *The Stewart/Colbert Effect: Essays on the Real Impact of Fake News*. Ed. Amarnath Amarasingam. Jefferson: McFarland, 2011. 63–78. Print.

———. "The Daily Show Effect: Candidate Evaluations, Efficacy, and American Youth." *American Politics Research,* 34, (2006): 341–366.

Baym, Geoffrey. "The Daily Show: Discursive Integration and the Reinvention of Political Journalism." *Political Communication* 22.3 (2005): 259–76. Print.

———. *From Cronkite to Colbert: The Evolution of Broadcast News*. Boulder: Paradigm, 2009. Print.

———. "Representation and the Politics of Play: Stephen Colbert's Better Know a District." *Political Communication* 24.4 (2007): 359–76. *Taylor & Francis Online*. Web.

———. "Stephen Colbert's Parody of the Postmodern." *Satire TV: Politics and Comedy in the Post-Network Era*. Eds. Jonathan Alan Gray, Jeffrey P. Jones, and Ethan Thompson. New York: NYU Press, 2009. 124–46. Print.

Becker, Amy B., Michael A. Xenos, and Don J. Waisanen. "Sizing Up *The Daily Show* Perceptions of Political Comedy Programming." *The Atlantic Journal of Communication* 18.3 (2010): 144–57. *Taylor & Francis Online*. Web.

Bennett, Lance W., and William Serrin. "The Watchdog Role." *The Press*. Eds. Geneva Overholser, and Kathleen Hall Jamieson. Oxford: Oxford UP, 2005. 169–88. Print.

Berlant, Lauren. "The Epistemologies of State Emotions." *Dissent in Dangerous Times*. Ed. Austin Sarat. Ann Arbor: University of Michigan Press, 2005. 46–80. Print.

Boler, Megan. (Ed. and "Introduction"). *Digital Media and Democracy: Tactics in Hard Times*. Cambridge: MIT, 2008. Print.

Boler, Megan, and Stephen Turpin. "*The Daily Show* and *Crossfire*: Satire and Sincerity as Truth to Power." *Digital Media and Democracy: Tactics in Hard Times*. Ed. Megan Boler. Cambridge: MIT, 2008. 383–404. Print.

Brock, David, and Ari Rabin-Havt. *The Fox Effect: How Roger Ailes Turned a Network into a Propaganda Machine*. New York: Random House, 2012. Print.

Brown, Wendy. "Political Idealization & Its Discontents." *Dissent in Dangerous Times*. Ed. Austin Sarat. Ann Arbor: University of Michigan Press, 2005. 23–45. Print.

Cao, Xiaoxia. "Hearing It from Jon Stewart: The Impact of *The Daily Show* on Public Attentiveness to Politics." *International Journal of Public Opinion Research* 22.1 (2010): 26–46. *Oxford Journals*. Web.

Cao, Xiaoxia, and Paul R. Brewer. "Political Comedy Shows and Public Participation in Politics." *International Journal of Public Opinion Research* 20.1 (2008): 90–9. *Oxford Journals*. Web.

Colebrook, Claire. *Irony*. New York: Routledge, 2004. Print.

Compton, Josh. "Introduction: Surveying Scholarship on *The Daily Show* and *The Colbert Report*." *The Stewart/Colbert Effect: Essays on the Real Impact of Fake News*. Ed. Amarnath Amarasingam. Jefferson: McFarland, 2011. 9–24. Print.

Dahlgren, Robert L. "Fahrenheit 9/11 in the Classroom." *Teacher Education Quarterly* 36.1 (2009): 25–43. Institute of Education Sciences. Web.

Dalton, Russell. *The Good Citizen: How a Younger Generation Is Reshaping American Politics*. Washington, DC: CQ Press, 2009. Print.

Day, Amber. *Satire and Dissent: Interventions in Contemporary Political Debate*. Bloomington: Indiana UP, 2011. Print.

Debrix, François. *Tabloid Terror: War, Culture, and Geopolitics*. New York: Routledge, 2008. Print.

Demers, David. *Dictionary of Mass Communication & Media Research: A Guide for Students, Scholars and Professionals*. Spokane: Marquette, 2005. Print.

Denby, David. *Snark*. New York: Simon & Schuster, 2009. Print.

Di Leo, Jeffrey R., Henry A. Giroux, Sophia A. McClennen and Kenneth J. Saltman. *Neoliberalism, Education, Terrorism: Contemporary Dialogues*. Boulder: Paradigm, 2013. Print.

Duncombe, Stephen. *Dream: Re-Imagining Progressive Politics in an Age of Fantasy*. New York: New Press, 2007. Print.

Feldman, Lauren, Anthony Leiserowitz, and Edward Maibach. "The Science of Satire: *The Daily Show* and *The Colbert Report* as Sources of Public Attention to Science and the Environment." *The Stewart/Colbert Effect: Essays on the Real Impact of Fake News*. Ed. Amarnath Amarasingam. Jefferson: McFarland, 2011. 25–46. Print.

Fowler, James H. "The Colbert Bump in Campaign Donations: More Truthful than Truthy." *PS: Political Science & Politics*. 41.3 (2008): 533–9. *APSA*. Web.

Giroux, Henry A. *The Abandoned Generation: Democracy Beyond the Culture of Fear*. New York: Palgrave Macmillan, 2003. Print.

———. *Hearts of Darkness: Torturing Children in the War on Terror*. Boulder: Paradigm, 2010. Print.

————. *Public Spaces/Private Lives: Beyond the Culture of Cynicism.* New York: Rowman and Littlefield, 2001. Print.

————. *The Terror of Neoliberalism: The New Authoritarianism and the Eclipse of Democracy.* Boulder: Paradigm, 2002. Print.

————. *Youth in a Suspect Society: Democracy or Disposability?* New York: Palgrave Macmillan, 2009. Print.

Giroux, Henry A., and Susan Searls Giroux. *Take Back Higher Education.* New York: Palgrave Macmillan, 2004. Print.

Goodman, Amy, and David Goodman. *Static: Government Liars, Media Cheerleaders, and the People Who Fight Back.* New York: Hyperion, 2006. Print.

Gournelos, Ted, and Viveca Greene. *A Decade of Dark Humor: How Comedy, Irony, and Satire Shaped Post-9/11 America.* Jackson: UP of Mississippi, 2011. Print.

Granger, Bruce Ingham. *Political Satire in the American Revolution, 1763–1783.* Ithaca: Cornell UP, 1960. Print.

Gray, Jonathan, Jeffrey P. Jones, and Ethan Thompson. *Satire TV: Politics and Comedy in the Post Network Era.* New York: NYU Press, 2009. Print.

Greene, Viveca. "Critique, Counternarratives, and Ironic Intervention in *South Park* and Stephen Colbert." *A Decade of Dark Humor: How Comedy, Irony, and Satire Shaped Post-9/11 America.* Eds. Ted Gournelos and Viveca Greene. Jackson: UP of Mississippi, 2011. 119–36. Print.

Gurney, David. "Everything Changes Forever (Temporarily): Late-Night Television Comedy 9/11." *A Decade of Dark Humor: How Comedy, Irony, and Satire Shaped Post-9/11 America.* Eds. Ted Gournelos and Viveca Greene. Jackson: UP of Mississippi, 2011. 3–19. Print.

Gusterson, Hugh. 2005. "The Weakest Link? Academic Dissent in the 'War on Terrorism.'" *Dissent in Dangerous Times.* Ed. Austin Sarat. Ann Arbor: University of Michigan Press, 2005. 81–110. Print.

Habermas, Jürgen. *The Structural Transformation of the Public Sphere: An Inquiry into a Category of Bourgeois Society.* Trans. Thomas Burger. Cambridge: MIT Press, 1991. Print.

Hall, Sean. *This Means This, This Means That: A User's Guide to Semiotics.* London: Laurence King, 2007.

Hariman, Robert. "Political Parody and Public Culture." *Quarterly Journal of Speech* 94.3 (2008): 247–72. *Taylor & Francis Online.* Web.

Hart, Roderick P., and E. Johanna Hartelius. "The Political Sins of Jon Stewart." *Critical Studies in Media Communication* 24.3 (2007): 263–72. *Taylor & Francis Online.* Web.

Haugerud, Angelique. *No Billionaire Left Behind: Satirical Activism in America.* Stanford: Stanford UP, 2013. Print.

Hauser, Gerard A. "Civil Society and the Principle of the Public Sphere." *Philosophy and Rhetoric* 31.1 (1998): 19–40. *JSTOR.* Web.

Hoffman, Lindsay H., and Dannagal G. Young. "Satire, Punch Lines, and the Nightly News: Untangling Media Effects on Political Participation." *Communication Research Reports* 28.2 (2011): 159–68. *Taylor & Francis Online.* Web.

Hoffman, Lindsay H., and Tiffany L. Thomson. "The Effect of Television Viewing on Adolescents' Civic Participation: Political Efficacy as a Mediating

Mechanism." *Journal of Broadcasting & Electronic Media* 53.1 (2009): 3–21. *Taylor & Francis Online*. Web.

Holloway, David. "Republican Decline and Culture Wars in 9/11 Humor." *A Decade of Dark Humor: How Comedy, Irony, and Satire Shaped Post-9/11 America*. Eds. Ted Gournelos and Viveca Greene. Jackson: UP of Mississippi, 2011. 99–118. Print.

Jenkins, Henry. *Convergence Culture: Where Old and New Media Collide*. New York: New York UP, 2006. Print.

→Jones, Jeffrey P. *Entertaining Politics: Satiric Television and Political Engagement*. 2nd ed. Lanham: Rowman and Littlefield, 2010. Print.

———. "With All Due Respect: Satirizing Presidents from *Saturday Night Live* to Lil' Bush." *Satire TV: Politics and Comedy in the Post-Network Era*. Eds. Jonathan Gray, Jeffrey P. Jones, and Ethan Thompson. New York: NYU Press, 2009. 37–63. Print.

Kapitulik, Brian P., Hilton Kelly, and Dan Clawson. "Critical Experiential Pedagogy: Sociology and the Crisis in Higher Education." *The American Sociologist* 38.2 (2007): 135–58. *Springer Link*. Web.

Kellner, Douglas. *Media Culture: Cultural Studies, Identity and Politics between the Modern and the Postmodern*. New York: Routledge, 2003. Print.

Kim, Young Mie, and John Vishak. "Just Laugh! You Don't Need to Remember: The Effects of the Entertainment Media on Political Information Acquisition and Processing in Political Judgment." *Journal of Communication* 58 (2008): 338–60. *Boise State University*. Web.

Kuhrik, Marilee, Nancy Kuhrik, and Paula A. Berry. "Facilitating Learning with Humor." *Journal of Nursing Education* 36 (1997): 332–4. *EBSCOhost*. Web.

LaMarre, Heather L., Kristen D. Landreville, and Michael A. Beam. "The Irony of Satire: Political Ideology and the Motivation to See What You Want to See in *The Colbert Report*." *The International Journal of Press/Politics* 14.2 (2009): 212–31. Print.

Lewis, Paul. *Cracking Up: American Humor in a Time of Conflict*. Chicago: University of Chicago Press, 2006. Print.

MacMullan, Terrance. "Jon Stewart and the New Public Intellectual." *The Daily Show and Philosophy: Moments of Zen in the Art of Fake News*. Ed. Jason Holt. Malden: Blackwell, 2007. 57–68. Print.

Martin, Jerry L., and Anne D. Neal. "Defending Civilization: How Our Universities Are Failing America and What Can Be Done about it." *The American Council of Trustees and Alumni*. February 2002. Web.

McBeth, Mark K., and Randy S. Clemons. "Is Fake News the Real News?" *The Stewart/Colbert Effect: Essays on the Real Impact of Fake News*. Ed. Amarnath Amarasingam. Jefferson: McFarland, 2011. 63–78. Print.

McClennen, Sophia A. *Colbert's America: Satire and Democracy*. New York: Palgrave Macmillan, 2012. Print.

Mercer, Rick. *Rick Mercer Report: The Paperback Book*. Toronto: Anchor, 2007. Print.

Michels, Steven, and Michael Ventimiglia. "Can *The Daily Show* Save Democracy? Jon Stewart as the Gadfly of Gotham." *The Daily Show and Philosophy: Moments of Zen in the Art of Fake News.* Ed. Jason Holt. Malden: Blackwell, 2007. 81–92. Print.

Morreale, Joanne. "Jon Stewart and *The Daily Show*: I Thought You Were Going to Be Funny!" *Satire TV: Politics and Comedy in the Post-Network Era.* Eds. Jonathan Gray, Jeffrey P. Jones, and Ethan Thompson. New York: New York UP, 2009. 104–23. Print.

Morris, Linda. "American Satire: Beginning Through Mark Twain." *A Companion to Satire: Ancient and Modern.* Ed. Ruben Quintero. London: Blackwell, 2006. 377–99. Print.

Moulitsas, Markos. *American Taliban: How War, Sex, Sin, and Power Bind Jihadists and the Radical Right.* Sausalito: Polipoint, 2010. Print.

Moy, Patricia, Michael A. Xenos, and Verena K. Hess. "Priming Effects of Late-Night Comedy." *International Journal of Public Opinion Research* 18.2 (2005): 198–210. *Oxford Journals.* Web.

Nimmo, Dan D., and James E. Combs. *The Political Pundits.* New York: Praeger, 1992. Print.

Nunberg, Geoffrey. *Talking Right: How Conservatives Turned Liberalism into a Tax-Raising, Latte-Drinking, Sushi-Eating, Volvo-Driving, New York Times-Reading, Body-Piercing, Hollywood-Loving, Left-Wing Freak Show.* New York: Public Affairs, 2006. Print.

Palin, Sarah. *Good Tidings of Great Joy: Protecting the Heart of Christmas.* New York: Broadside, 2013. Kindle edition.

Peterson, Russell L. *Strange Bedfellows: How Late-Night Comedy Turns Democracy into a Joke.* New Brunswick: Rutgers UP, 2008. Print.

Reilly, Ian. "Satirical Fake News and the Politics of the Fifth Estate." Diss. University of Guelph, 2010. *Academia.edu.* Web.

Rich, Frank. *The Greatest Story Ever Sold: The Decline and Fall of Truth from 9/11 to Katrina.* New York: Penguin, 2006. Print.

Roberts, Brent W., Grant Edmonds, and Emily Grijalva. "It Is Developmental Me, Not Generation Me: Developmental Changes are More Important than Generational Changes in Narcissism—Commentary on Trzesniewski & Donnellan (2010)." *Perspectives on Psychological Science* 5.1 (2010): 97–102. *SAGE.* Web.

Rosen, Ralph M. "Efficacy and Meaning in Ancient and Modern Political Satire: Aristophanes, Lenny Bruce, and Jon Stewart." *Social Research: An International Quarterly* 79.1 (Spring 2012): 1–32. *ProQuest.* Web.

Said, Edward. *Culture and Imperialism.* New York: Vintage, 1994. Print.

Sarat, Austin. "Terrorism, Dissent, & Repression." *Dissent in Dangerous Times.* Ed. Austin Sarat. Ann Arbor: University of Michigan Press, 2005. 1–19. Print.

Schulzke, Marcus. "Fan Action and Political Participation on *The Colbert Report*." *TWC: Transformative Works and Cultures* 10 (2012). *TWC.* Web.

Sotos, Rachel. "The Fake News as the Fifth Estate." *The Daily Show and Philosophy: Moments of Zen in the Art of Fake News.* Ed. Jason Holt. Malden: Blackwell, 2007. 28–40. Print.

Stark, Craig. "'What, Me Worry?' Teaching Media Literacy through Satire and *Mad* Magazine." *The Clearing House* 76.6 (2003): 305–09. *JSTOR.* Web.

Test, George A., *Satire: Spirit and Art.* Gainesville: UP of Florida, 1991. Print.

Tewksbury, David, and Jason Rittenberg. *News on the Internet: Information and Citizenship in the 21st Century.* Oxford: Oxford UP, 2012. Print.

van Heertum, Richard. "Irony and the News: Speaking through Cool to American Youth." *The Stewart/Colbert Effect: Essays on the Real Impact of Fake News.* Ed. Amarnath Amarasingam. Jefferson: McFarland, 2011. 117–35. Print.

van Zoonen, Liesbet. *Entertaining the Citizen: When Politics and Popular Culture Converge.* Lanham: Rowman and Littlefield, 2005. Print.

van Zoonen, Liesbet, Farida Vis, and Sabina Mihelj. "Performing Citizenship on YouTube: Activism, Satire and Online Debate Around the Anti-Islam Video *Fitna.*" *Critical Discourse Studies* 7.4 (November 2010): 249–62.

Warner, Jamie. "Humor, Terror, and Dissent: *The Onion* After 9/11." *A Decade of Dark Humor: How Comedy, Irony, and Satire Shaped Post-9/11 America.* Eds. Ted Gournelos and Viveca Greene. Jackson: UP of Mississippi, 2011. 57–77. Print.

Wells, Colin. "Satire." *The Encyclopedia of the New American Nation.* Ed. Paul Finkelman. New York: Scribners', 2006. 158. Print.

West, Darrell M. *The Rise and Fall of the Media Establishment.* Boston: Medford/St. Martin's, 2001. Print.

West, Darrell M., and John Orman. *Celebrity Politics: Real Politics in America.* Upper Saddle River: Prentice Hall, 2003. Print.

Winograd, Morley, and Michael D. Hais. *Millennial Momentum: How a New Generation is Remaking America.* New Brunswick: Rutgers UP, 2011. Print.

Xenos, Michael A., and Amy B. Becker. "Moments of Zen: Effects of *The Daily Show* on Information Seeking and Political Learning." *Political Communication* 26.3 (2009): 317–32. *Taylor & Francis Online.* Web.

Xenos, Michael A., Patricia Moy, and Amy B. Becker. "Making Sense of *The Daily Show*: Understanding the Role of Partisan Heuristics in Political Comedy Effects." *The Stewart/Colbert Effect: Essays on the Real Impact of Fake News.* Ed. Amarnath Amarasingam. Jefferson: McFarland, 2011. 47–62. Print.

Young, Dannagal Goldthwaite. "Daily Show Viewers Knowledgeable about Presidential Campaign, National Annenberg Election Survey Shows." *NAES 04: National Annenberg Election Survey.* 21 Sept. 2004. Web.

———. "Late-Night Comedy and the Salience of the Candidates' Caricatured Traits in the 2000 Election." *Mass Communication and Society* 9.3 (2006): 339–66. *Taylor & Francis Online.* Web.

———. "Laughter, Learning, or Enlightenment? Viewing and Avoidance Motivations behind *The Daily Show* and *The Colbert Report.*" *Journal of Broadcasting & Electronic Media* 57.2 (2013): 153–69. *Taylor & Francis Online.* Web.

————. "The Privileged Role of the Late-Night joke: Exploring Humor's Role in Disrupting Argument Scrutiny." *Media Psychology* 11.1 (2008): 119–42. *Taylor & Francis Online*. Web.

Young, Dannagal Goldthwaite, and Russell M. Tisinger. "Dispelling Late-Night Myths: News Consumption among Late-Night Comedy Viewers and the Predictors of Exposure to Various Late-Night Shows." *International Journal of Press/Politics* 11.3 (2006): 113–34. *SAGE*. Web.

Young, Dannagal Goldthwaite, and Sarah Esralew. "Jon Stewart a Heretic? Surely You Jest: Political Participation and Discussion among Viewers of Late-Night Comedy Programming." *The Stewart/Colbert Effect: Essays on the Real Impact of Fake News*. Ed. Amarnath Amarasingam. Jefferson: McFarland, 2011. 99–116. Print.

Index